Leeds Studies in English

New Series XLV

© *Leeds Studies in English* 2014
School of English
University of Leeds
Leeds, England

ISSN 0075-8566
ISBN 978-1-84549-679-1

Copyright
All rights reserved. No part of this publication may be reproduced in any material form (including photocopying or storing it in any medium by electronic means, and whether or not transiently or incidentally to some other use of this publication) without the written permission of the copyright owner, except in accordance with the provisions of the Copyright, Designs and Patents Act 1988, or under terms of a licence issued by the Copyright Licensing Agency Ltd, 33-34, Alfred Place, London WC1E 7DP, UK. Applications for the copyright owner's permission to reproduce part of this publication should be addressed to the Publishers.

Printed in the UK

Publishing Office
Abramis Academic
ASK House
Northgate Avenue
Bury St. Edmunds
Suffolk
IP32 6BB

Tel: +44 (0)1284 700321
Fax: +44 (0)1284 717889
Email: info@abramis.co.uk
Web: www.abramis.co.uk

Leeds Studies in English

New Series XLV

2014

Edited by

Alaric Hall

Reviews editor
N. Kıvılcım Yavuz

Leeds Studies in English

<www.leeds.ac.uk/lse>
School of English
University of Leeds
2014

Leeds Studies in English

<www.leeds.ac.uk/lse>

Leeds Studies in English is an international, refereed journal based in the School of English, University of Leeds. *Leeds Studies in English* publishes articles on Old and Middle English literature, Old Icelandic language and literature, and the historical study of the English language. After a two-year embargo, past copies are made available, free access; they can be accessed via <http://www.leeds.ac.uk/lse>.

Editorial Board:	Catherine Batt, *Chair*
			Marta Cobb
			Alaric Hall, *Editor*
			Paul Hammond
			James Paz
			Oliver Pickering
			Helen Price
			Slavica Ranković
			N. Kıvılcım Yavuz *Reviews Editor*

Notes for Contributors

Contributors are requested to follow the *MHRA Style Guide: A Handbook for Authors, Editors, and Writers of Theses*, 2nd edn (London: Modern Humanities Research Association, 2008), available at <http://www.mhra.org.uk/Publications/Books/StyleGuide/download.shtml>.

Where possible, contributors are encouraged to include the digital object identifiers or, where a complete free access text is available, stable URLs of materials cited (see *Style Guide* §11.2.10.1).

The language of publication is English and translations should normally be supplied for quotations in languages other than English. Each contributor will receive a free copy of the journal, and a PDF of their article for distribution. Please email all contributions to <lse@leeds.ac.uk>.

Reviews

Copies of books for review should be sent to the Editor, *Leeds Studies in English*, School of English, University of Leeds, Leeds LS2 9JT, United Kingdom.

Contents

Ecocriticism and Eyrbyggja saga Carl Phelpstead *Cardiff University*	1
Scyld scyle cempan: The Shield and the Warrior in Old English Poetry Stephen Graham *Trinity College Dublin*	19
Kinsmen Before Christ, Part I: The Latin Transmission P. S. Langeslag *University of Göttingen*	34
John Rykener, Richard II and the Governance of London Jeremy Goldberg *The University of York*	49

Fiction After Felony: Innovation and Transformation in the Eland Outlaw Narratives
    Sharon Hubbs Wright and   *St Thomas More College,*
    Michael Cichon   *University of Saskatchewan*
	71

'The Death of Sir John Ealand of Ealand and his sonne in olde rymthe': Four New Eland Manuscripts and the Transmission of a West Yorkshire Legend
    Sharon Hubbs Wright   *St Thomas More College,*
                                     University of Saskatchewan
	87

Reviews:

Catherine A. M. Clarke, *Writing Power in Anglo-Saxon England: Texts, Hierarchies, Economies*. Cambridge: Brewer, 2012 [Kate Wiles]	131
Donald Scragg, *A Conspectus of Scribal Hands Writing English, 960–1100*. Cambridge: Brewer, 2012 [Thomas Gobbitt]	133

Peter S. Baker, *Honour, Exchange and Violence in 'Beowulf'*.   135
Cambridge: Brewer, 2013
     [Catalin Taranu]

Larissa Tracy, *Castration and Culture in the Middle Ages*. Cambridge: 138
Brewer 2013
     [Paola Scarpini]

Charlotte Brewer and Barry Windeatt, *Traditions and Innovations in*   141
the Study of Medieval English Literature: The Influence of Derek
Brewer. Cambridge: Brewer, 2013
     [Trevor Russell Smith]

Mary C. Flannery and Katie L. Walter, *The Culture of Inquisition in*   143
Medieval England. Cambridge: Brewer, 2013
     [Jan Vandeburie]

Ecocriticism and *Eyrbyggja saga*

Carl Phelpstead[1]

Introduction

According to the early fourteenth-century Hauksbók version of *Landnámabók*, King Haraldr hárfagri of Norway determined that early settlers in Iceland should be allowed to claim no more land than a man could carry fire around in a single day.[2] In chapter 4 of the probably mid-thirteenth-century Icelandic *Eyrbyggja saga* one such early settler from Norway, Þórólfr Mostrarskegg, carries fire in this way around land that he claims as his own on the Snæfellsnes peninsula in western Iceland: 'eptir þat fór Þórólfr eldi um landnám sitt' ('then Thorolf carried fire around his land-claim').[3] Having established the boundaries between his land and the unclaimed country around him, Þórólfr has a farm and a temple built; the construction of boundaries and buildings endows both the cultivated land that he claims and the uncultivated wilderness beyond the new boundaries with meaning: in this way the land enters culture at the same time that it begins to be cultivated. The creation of boundaries is essential to the construction of a nation out of a wilderness: such boundaries are not only physical, but also mental or conceptual — boundaries between nature and culture, animal and human, and nature and the supernatural. In this essay I develop an ecocritical reading of *Eyrbyggja saga* that takes Þórólfr's act of land-taking (*landnám*) as emblematic of the saga's concern with boundaries and its revelation of their permeability.

---

[1] Earlier versions of parts of this essay were presented at: the Anglo-Saxon, Norse, and Celtic Graduate Seminar, University of Cambridge; the 15th International Saga Conference, Aarhus; the Viking Society Student Conference, Leeds; the MEMORI seminar series at Cardiff University; and the Old Norse at Oxford Research Seminar series at the University of Oxford. I am grateful to all those whose contributions to discussion on those occasions enabled me to strengthen and clarify my argument. In addition, Neil Badmington, Tim Bourns, and two anonymous readers for *Leeds Studies in English* commented helpfully on drafts of the completed essay.

[2] *Íslendingabók. Landnámabók*, ed. by Jakob Benediktsson, Íslenzk fornrit, 1 (Reykjavík: Hið íslenzka fornritafélag, 1968), pp. 337 and 339 (H294). The procedure was slightly different for female settlers, who could claim as much land as they could encompass in a day while leading a two-year-old, well-fed heifer (H276).

[3] *Eyrbyggja saga*, ed. by Einar Ól. Sveinsson and Matthías Þórðarson, Íslenzk fornrit, 4 (Reykjavík: Hið íslenzka fornritafélag, 1935), pp. 3–184 (p. 8); English translation from *The Saga of the People of Eyri*, trans. by Judy Quinn, in *Gisli Sursson's Saga and The Saga of the People of Eyri*, ed. by Vésteinn Ólason (London: Penguin Classics, 2003), pp. 71–198 (p. 76). All further references to this edition and translation are given parenthetically in the main text. Whether Haraldr hárfagri's ruling was in place when Þórólfr settled in Iceland is less important for the purposes of this essay than the fact that thirteenth- and fourteenth-century Icelanders thought that such procedures were followed in the settlement period.

Ecocriticism and Eyrbyggja saga

Many of the critical and cultural theories that have influenced literary studies since the 1960s have taken an avowedly political approach to texts from the past, analysing them in ways intended to further emancipatory programmes, whether Marxist, feminist, queer, or postcolonial. Proponents of such approaches maintain that the liberal humanist tradition against which they react was itself political, though it did not often admit — or recognise — this fact. Ecocriticism is a more recent development, emerging prominently only in the late 1990s, and is perhaps most helpfully thought of as a critical orientation, rather than a narrowly defined theoretical position; the most serviceable explanations of the term tend to be very broadly conceived. One workable definition is Cheryll Glotfelty's assertion that 'simply put, ecocriticism is the study of the relationship between literature and the physical environment. [...] ecocriticism takes an earth-centred approach to literary studies'.[4] Greg Garrard offers an even more capacious definition: 'the study of the relationship of the human and non-human'.[5] It can be helpful to distinguish between what might be thought of as traditional thematic studies of aspects of the natural world in literary texts, where the primary aim is to shed light on the text, genre, or period under discussion, and more overtly ecocritical studies in which there is an interest in reading texts in order to inform current environmental debates or action.

With the possible exception of feminist criticism (broadly conceived), explicitly political critical approaches have had a relatively limited and delayed impact on the study of Old Norse-Icelandic literature. Although ecocriticism has recently become a fairly common critical orientation in some other areas of medieval literary studies, it is only just beginning to make an impact on saga studies. Previous work focusing on the relationship between Old Norse-Icelandic literature and the physical environment includes interesting research on landscape, including Gillian Overing and Marijane Osborn's engagingly idiosyncratic book, *Landscape of Desire: Partial Stories of the Medieval Scandinavian World* (1994), articles by Ian Wyatt, and recent work by Eleanor Barraclough.[6] Two contributions that relate more self-consciously to current theoretical developments are Jeffrey Jerome Cohen's brief but stimulating comments on the roles of landscape and objects in *Grettis saga* and an unpublished article by Chris Abram on trees in medieval Iceland and its literature, which in its combination of detailed textual analysis with insights from history and archaeology offers an excellent model for future green readings of Old Norse literature.[7] The saga specialist interested in an

---

[4] *The Ecocriticism Reader: Landmarks in Literary Ecology*, ed. by Cheryll Glotfelty and Harold Fromm (Athens: University of Georgia Press, 1996), p. xix. Good, up-to-date introductions to ecocriticism include Greg Garrard, *Ecocriticism*, New Critical Idiom, 2nd edn (London: Routledge, 2011) and Timothy Clark, *The Cambridge Introduction to Literature and the Environment* (Cambridge: Cambridge University Press, 2011).

[5] Garrard, *Ecocriticism*, p. 5.

[6] Gillian R. Overing and Marijane Osborn, *Landscapes of Desire: Partial Stories of the Medieval Scandinavian World* (Minneapolis: University of Minnesota Press, 1994); Ian Wyatt, 'Narrative Functions of Landscape in the Old Icelandic Family Sagas', in *Land, Sea, Home*, ed. by John Hines, Alan Lane, and Mark Redknap (Leeds: Maney, 2004), pp. 272–82, and, specifically on the use of topography, weather, and geography in an episode in *Eyrbyggja saga*, 'Landscape and Authorial Control in the Battle of Vigrafjǫrðr in *Eyrbyggja saga*', *Leeds Studies in English*, n. s. 35 (2004), 43–56; Eleanor Barraclough, 'Inside Outlawry in *Grettis saga Ásmundarsonar* and *Gísla saga Súrssonar*: Landscape in the Outlaw Sagas', *Scandinavian Studies*, 82 (2010), 365–88, and 'Land-Naming in the Migration Myth of Medieval Iceland: Constructing the Past in the Present and the Present in the Past', *Saga-Book*, 36 (2012), 79–101.

[7] Jeffrey Jerome Cohen, 'Introduction: All Things', in *Animal, Vegetable, Mineral: Ethics and Objects*, ed. by Jeffrey Jerome Cohen (Washington: Oliphaunt, 2012), pp. 1–8; Chris Abram, 'Felling Trees and Feeling Trees in Medieval Iceland', unpublished essay. I am grateful to Dr Abram for kindly sending me his article in advance of publication.

environmentally aware or earth-centred approach can also take inspiration from a very rapidly growing body of ecocritical work on other medieval literatures.[8]

If, as Scott Slovic argues, no text is off-limits to green reading,[9] then this must be as true of an Icelandic saga as of any other text, but one might very justifiably ask what possible use texts from such a remote past as medieval Iceland might be in the environmental debates and interventions of the twenty-first century. Part, at least, of the answer is that the study of such texts can help to bring clarity to the issues. The pioneering British ecocritic Jonathan Bate has written that 'the relationship between nature and culture is the key intellectual problem of the twenty-first century'.[10] If so (and one might justifiably query whether those are precisely the terms in which the problem should be framed), then texts from the past, even such a remote past as the world of the sagas, can contribute to understanding that relationship by revealing ways in which it has been understood and negotiated historically; as Laurence Coupe neatly puts it, 'the writer who challenges modernity needs memory'.[11] Knowledge that things have been different in the past and so need not be the way that they are now offers encouragement to those who seek to ensure that things will be different again in the future.[12]

The Icelandic sagas (and related texts such as Ari Þorgilsson's *Íslendingabók* and the extant versions of *Landnámabók*) offer rich material for ecocritical reading, but this essay focuses primarily on a single text: *Eyrbyggja saga*. The saga was composed around the middle of the thirteenth century, though the earliest surviving manuscript fragment is from the late thirteenth or early fourteenth century.[13] Like other sagas of Icelanders written in the thirteenth and fourteenth centuries, *Eyrbyggja saga* recounts events presented as taking place in the period c. 870–1030, the period during which Iceland was settled, its legal institutions were established, and it converted to Christianity, changing in the process from an island without a human population into a nation of Christendom. The text offers a particularly rich case study for ecocritical saga studies; indeed, a reader new to the saga who turns to the recent Penguin Classics edition of Judy Quinn's translation will find the text introduced by Vésteinn Ólason in terms that immediately resonate with ecocritical concerns: Vésteinn writes that the saga 'draws a memorable picture of a chaotic and half-wild society where either brutal force or a

---

[8] Two pioneering books are: Alfred Siewers's idiosyncratic, occasionally frustrating, but ultimately stimulating *Strange Beauty: Ecocritical Approaches to Early Medieval Literature* (New York: Palgrave Macmillan, 2009), concerned primarily with Welsh and Irish literature, and Gillian Rudd's *Greenery: Ecocritical Readings of Late Medieval Literature* (Manchester: Manchester University Press, 2007), on Middle English texts.

[9] Scott Slovic, 'Ecocriticism: Containing Multitudes, Practising Doctrine', in *The Green Studies Reader: From Romanticism to Ecocriticism*, ed. by Laurence Coupe (London: Routledge, 2000), pp. 160–62 (p. 160).

[10] Jonathan Bate, 'Foreword', in Coupe, *Green Studies Reader*, p. xvii.

[11] Coupe, *Green Studies Reader*, p. 65.

[12] On the value of knowledge of the past for improving the future cf. Terry Eagleton's memorable rhetorical question: 'who is cocksure enough to predict that medieval love poetry might not prove a more precious resource in some political struggle than the writings of Surrealist Trotskyists?' (Terry Eagleton, *The Illusions of Postmodernism* (Oxford: Blackwell, 1996), p. 125).

[13] On manuscripts and editions of the saga see the Íslenzk fornrit edition, pp. xliii–lvii. A brief summary of the arguments for the dating of the saga to the mid-thirteenth century is provided in Bernadine McCreesh, '*Eyrbyggja saga*', in *Medieval Scandinavia: An Encyclopedia*, ed. by Phillip Pulsiano et al. (London: Garland, 1993), pp. 174–75 (p. 174); cf. Klaus Böldl, *Eigi einhamr: Beiträge zum Weltbild der 'Eyrbyggja' und anderer Isländersagas* (Berlin: De Gruyter, 2005), p. 24 on a consensus dating the saga to c. 1250, and Vésteinn Ólason's suggestion of 'around 1270': 'Introduction', in *Gisli Sursson's Saga and The Saga of the People of Eyri*, pp. vii–xlvi (p. vii). In the Íslenzk fornrit edition, Einar Ólafur Sveinsson proposed an earlier date (pp. lvii–lxiv), but his arguments have persuaded few other scholars. Several contributors to *Dating the Sagas: Reviews and Revisions*, ed. by Else Mundal (Copenhagen: Museum Tusculanum Press, 2013) consider the dating of *Eyrbyggja saga*; they discuss a variety of arguments for datings in the period c. 1230–c. 1270.

sly deception seems to decide issues', but also of 'a certain order that is gradually strengthened as the story progresses'.[14]

According to Laurence Coupe, 'the most fundamental question of all for green studies' is 'that of the relationship between the non-human and the human'.[15] In what follows, I explore two different aspects of this question in *Eyrbyggja saga*: the relationship between humans and the non-human physical environment or landscape, and the relationships between humans and non-human forms of life, both plant and animal. My aim is likewise twofold: to demonstrate the difference that taking an environmentally aware approach may make to a reading of the saga and to suggest the difference that ecocritical readings of sagas might make to ecocriticism.

Settling in the landscape

Ecocritics often explore the ways in which humans relate to 'wild' or 'untouched' environments. The encounter with such environments frequently takes the form of attempted mastery, whether physical (for example, by farming) or mental (for example, by naming places, or ascribing meanings to particular features in the physical environment). *Eyrbyggja saga* is, among other things, concerned with the relationship between natural environment and human civilisation — between nature and nation — and specifically with the transition from a physical environment unaffected by humans to a state of 'natureculture' in which human cultivation and culture both bring about changes in the physical environment and also endow it with culturally contingent meanings. To put the matter in these terms is, however, to stage an opposition between two notoriously slippery concepts: 'nature' and 'culture'. Raymond Williams famously described 'nature' as 'perhaps the most complex word in the language' and the word 'culture' is scarcely simpler.[16] In what follows, I make a consciously provisional deployment of the terms 'nature' and 'culture', and 'human' and 'non-human', for heuristic purposes; these oppositions enable an analysis of aspects of the saga text which in turn reveals the inadequacy of the opposition from which that analysis proceeded. Thus, although much of my discussion of *Eyrbyggja saga* will be structured around oppositions between nature and culture, human and non-human, or natural and supernatural, in each case I shall show how these oppositions collapse as the notional boundaries between the two terms of the opposition become blurred. This critical manoeuvre is grounded in Kate Soper's observation that an *a priori* distinction between humanity and nature is assumed in all discussions of the two, even those that see humanity as part of nature.[17] She argues, moreover, that:

> there can be no ecological prescription that does not presuppose a demarcation between humanity and nature. Unless human beings are differentiated from other organic and inorganic forms of being, they can be made no more liable for the effects of their occupancy of the eco-system than any other species, and it would make no more sense to call upon them to desist from destroying 'nature' than to call upon cats to stop killing birds.[18]

[14] Vésteinn Ólason, 'Introduction', p. xxv.
[15] Coupe, *Reader*, p. 119.
[16] Raymond Williams, *Keywords: A Vocabulary of Culture and Society* (London: Fontana, 1983), s.vv. 'Nature', 'Culture'.
[17] Kate Soper, *What Is Nature? Culture, Politics, and the Non-Human* (Oxford: Blackwell, 1995), p. 15.
[18] Soper, *What Is Nature?*, p. 160.

A realist conception of nature (defined in opposition to culture, or the human) can, therefore, be seen as a pragmatic basis for political or social change, of the kind which ecocriticism seeks to facilitate, while one may still affirm, as Soper does, the culturally conditioned and contingent quality of *representations* of nature.

Old Norse-Icelandic literature deserves greater prominence in ecocritical discourse because it is unique (at least within Europe) in offering historically-grounded narratives of human settlement in a land previously completely without human inhabitants. Writing in the early twelfth century in the earliest surviving Icelandic narrative of the nation's past, *Íslendingabók*, Ari Þorgilsson does indeed famously mention Irish monks who had lived as anchorites in Iceland before the Norse settlement, but although they precede the Icelanders, it is precisely in Icelandic narratives such as Ari's that we learn of the Irish monks and their (very limited) impact on the environment. The sagas of Icelanders written in the centuries after Ari are not contemporary with the events they recount, but they offer a unique source for understanding the impact of humans on the physical environment and the nature of the relationship between environment and culture. In these narratives, indebted as they are to earlier oral traditions, we can follow this relationship between humans and their environment from its very beginning in a way that is not possible elsewhere.[19] The settlers come to a wild land and there establish human society, community, law, and culture.

Eyrbyggja saga begins with conflict over land ownership, that anthropocentric engagement with the earth which takes for granted that members of one particular species have a right to dominion over the physical environment. When Ketill flatnefr exceeds his commission from King Haraldr hárfagri of Norway and takes over the Hebrides, his estates in Norway are seized by the king (ch. 1); in the next chapter Ketill's son Bjǫrn is outlawed by the king for trying to seize back the estates. Chapter 3 reports that 'þeir menn, er kómu af Íslandi, sǫgðu þar góða landakosti' (p. 7) ('men who returned from Iceland spoke of the good quality of the land' (p. 75)), and in the next chapter an oracle directs Bjǫrn Ketilsson's friend Þórólfr Mostrarskegg to go to Iceland, where Bjǫrn himself will also eventually settle after visiting the Hebrides. Þórólfr is a priest of Þórr, and earth from under the pedestal on which his statue of Þórr had stood in Norway is taken with the settlers to Iceland: in Norway the land has already been endowed with meaning and value, having become the subject of what the geographer Yi-Fu Tuan calls geopiety, a concept to which I shall return shortly.

Although the soil Þórólfr and his men bring from Norway has been endowed with meaning — brought within culture — they need to do things to the land in Iceland in order to bring it similarly within the cultural sphere: the place where the seat-pillars come ashore is given the name Þórsnes after the god whom Þórólfr serves, beginning its transformation from the (purely) natural to the naturecultural and also associating it with the supernatural. Then, as noted at the start of this essay, Þórólfr carries fire around the area of land he claims as his own and builds his farm and temple. The construction of boundaries, both physical and mental, is the starting-point for the process of establishing a human community in the land.

Timber

Human settlement in Iceland necessarily had consequences for the environment. In chapter 4 of *Eyrbyggja saga* we are told that 'þá var gott matar at afla af eyjum ok ǫðru sæfangi' (p.

---

[19] Hence Overing and Osborn write that 'in the Icelandic sagas, more than in most other European fictions, the presence of the landscape makes a difference in how the story is imagined because the people in these particular "frontier" fictions are interacting with the terrain as well as each other' (*Landscapes of Desire*, p. 105). For a

10) ('there was plenty of food to be had from the islands and the sea', p. 77). Representing the period of earliest settlement as a kind of Golden Age of plenty is a common topos of the *Íslendingasögur*; there is a hint here that the same may no longer be true and that such resources might not be inexhaustible.[20] Natural resources become a source of conflict on occasion later in the saga, suggesting increased pressure on such resources as time goes by: one such conflict is when a large fin whale comes ashore in chapter 57 and Óspakr Kjallaksson and his men steal from the people who have the legal right to flense it.

Probably the most notorious environmental consequence of settlement in Iceland was the island's deforestation. In *Íslendingabók* Ari Þorgilsson famously says of the period of settlement that 'í þann tíma vas Ísland viði vaxit á miðli fjalls ok fjöru'[21] ('at that time Iceland was grown over with trees between the mountains and the shore'), phrasing that draws attention to the fact that this was no longer the case when he wrote in the early twelfth century.[22] The importance of timber as a natural resource becomes very clear in chapter 31 of *Eyrbyggja saga*. Þórólfr bægifótr ('lame-foot') is aware that Snorri goði would like to own Krákunes and its woods, which are said to be 'mest gersemi [. . .] hér í sveit' (p. 85) ('the most precious in this district', p. 128). 'Snorri þóttisk mjǫk þurfa skóginn' (p. 85) ('Snorri considered himself very much in need of the woods', p. 128) and in exchange for them agrees to take on Þórólfr's lawsuit against Þórólfr's own son, Arnkell.

Having acquired the woods, Snorri proceeds to exploit them unsustainably, threatening their destruction:

> Snorri góði lét nú vinna Krákunesskóg ok mikit at gera um skógarhǫggit. Þórólfi bægifót þótti spillask skógrinn; reið Þórólfr þá út til Helgafells ok beiddi Snorra at fá sér aptr skóginn ok kvezk hafa lét honum, en eigi gefit. (p. 90)

> Snorri the Godi started exploiting Krakunes woods with a great deal of tree-felling. Thorolf Lame-foot thought the woods were being destroyed, so he rode over to Helgafell and asked Snorri to give him back the woods, claiming that he had only lent them and not given them to him. (p. 132)

Þórólfr seems surprised by the way in which Snorri is felling an excessive amount of timber, suggesting perhaps that his own use of the woods had been managed more sustainably and that his attempt to wrest back the woods may be (partly) motivated by a concern for their future (if only as a continuing resource) as much as by mere greed. Snorri opposes Þórólfr's environmental activism with the law, according to which he is now the owner of the woods: one could not hope for a clearer example of the way in which human community depends upon the control of physical environment and organises such control culturally through the law.

Þórólfr's green credentials are still more impressive, however. He asks his son Arnkell to recover the woods from Snorri because 'mér þykkir þat verst, er hann skal sitja yfir hlut okkrum, en hann vill nú eigi lausan láta skóginn fyrir mér' (p. 91) ('it's the worst thing in the world that he oppresses us and won't give me back the woods', p. 132). Arnkell refuses to help, even though he believes that Snorri lacks the legal right to the woods. Faced with this

---

reading of the settlement narrative in *Eyrbyggja saga* alongside other medieval sources from a different perspective from that adopted here, see Böldl, *Eigi einhamr*, ch. 4.

[20] Cf. Abram, 'Trees'.
[21] *Íslendingabók*, p. 5.
[22] Further discussion of Icelandic deforestation is provided in Chris Abram's unpublished article on trees in medieval Iceland and its literature.

indifference to environmental destruction Þórólfr goes home, refuses to eat, and dies during the night. Tempting though it may be to read this death as self-sacrifice on behalf of the environment, there is probably more to Þórólfr's desire to recover the woods than a love of trees. His behaviour reminds us that environmental activism may be motivated either by a sense of the independent value of the non-human environment or by self-interest, the need to preserve natural resources because humans are dependent on them.

Þórólfr's death is not the end of the matter. Having opposed the destruction of woodland while alive, Þórólfr wreaks environmental havoc as a revenant after death. Chapter 34 of the saga records that the oxen that had transported his corpse are ridden to death; all livestock that comes near his cairn goes wild and dies; a shepherd and his flock are killed; birds landing on his cairn die; Þórólfr's own wife is frightened to death. The undead Þórólfr is said to devastate all the nearby farms: the balance of the relationship between humans and their environment has been upset by Snorri's deforestation and then by the undead Þórólfr. Eventually this catalogue of environmental catastrophe is curtailed by reburying Þórólfr in a more remote location and behind a high wall. But even that does not bring the hauntings to an end, and we shall return to Þórólfr bægifótr towards the end of this essay.[23]

After Þórólfr's death Snorri goði continues to exploit the Krákunes wood and is involved in a legal dispute with Arnkell over his ownership of this precious natural resource. A slave whom he sends to cut down a lot of timber is killed in the course of the dispute and Arnkell is in turn killed by Snorri's men during a fight in a haystack: the mound in which Arnkell is subsequently buried is said, with grim irony, itself to be as big as a haystack ('sem stakkgarðr mikill', p. 103). It seems fitting that this dispute over natural resources and their exploitation comes to an end in a haystack and is memorialised in a haystack-like burial mound.

Outlawry, the wild, and geopiety

The transformation of nature into nation through settlement, cultivation, and community building is reflected in the Icelandic concept of outlawry and its association with uninhabited environments. Kirsten Hastrup, among others, has commented on the implications of the term used for full outlawry in medieval Iceland: *skóggangr*, literally, 'forest going'.[24] The word associates the outlaw, the one beyond human community, with wilderness. Eleanor Barraclough has similarly noted that terms such as *skógarmaðr* (forest-man) and *vargr* (wolf, used of outlaws in the *Grágás* lawcode) 'connect social outcasts with the physicality of wilderness or with the creatures that live in it'.[25] In *Eyrbyggja saga* the most telling example of the correlation between being outside the law and inhabiting an environment outside the settled human community is provided by Eiríkr rauði ('the Red'), who is outlawed in chapter 24 and so obliged to leave Iceland; he goes on to discover a new wilderness, Greenland, and begin a new Norse settlement there.

The most famous correlation of outlawry with environment in the sagas of Icelanders occurs not in *Eyrbyggja saga*, but in the roughly contemporary *Njáls saga*. When the outlawed

---

[23] On Þórólfr's career as a revenant see also Böldl, *Eigi einhamr*, pp. 117–24.

[24] Kirsten Hastrup, *Culture and History in Medieval Iceland: An Anthropological Analysis of Structure and Change* (Oxford: Clarendon, 1985), p. 139. Full outlawry required that the offender leave Iceland forever; if he failed to do so he could be killed with impunity and it was forbidden to assist such an outlaw: the sentence was therefore in effect a death sentence for anyone who refused to go abroad within the allotted time.

[25] Barraclough, 'Inside Outlawry', p. 367.

Gunnarr Hámundarson falls from his horse, he looks up at his farm at Hlíðarendi and fatally declares that 'fǫgr er hlíðin, svá at mér hefir hon aldri jafnfǫgr synzk, bleikir akrar ok slegin tún, ok mun ek ríða heim aptr ok fara hvergi'[26] ('fair is the slope, so that it has never seemed as fair to me, the pale fields and the mown home-field; I shall ride back and go nowhere'; my trans.). This passage justifies a digression from *Eyrbyggja saga* because it so memorably expresses an aesthetic appreciation of landscape; Gwyn Jones describes Gunnarr as 'the archetypal land-lover'.[27] The development of ecocriticism has been closely associated with the study of literature of the Romantic period, and at first glance Gunnarr's love of the landscape might seem ahead of its time.[28] It is certainly highly unusual, if not unique, in the sagas: Overing and Osborn refer to it as 'one of the few places in the sagas where landscape is identified as aesthetically beautiful'.[29] It is, however, not always recognised that the landscape that Gunnarr loves is not a natural, wild one, but a thoroughly tamed one of fruitful fields and mown meadows.[30] Gunnarr's words are an expression of geopiety, but his affection is for a naturalcultural, rather than purely natural, landscape, one that has been shaped by and has meaning because of human activity.

Yi-Fu Tuan adopts and adapts the term 'geopiety' from the work of John K. Wright; he writes that the term reminds us today of a loss: 'by now nature is largely secularized; gods no longer inhabit the mountains', but also notes that 'geopious feelings are still with us as attachment to place, love of country, and patriotism'.[31] The key to the concept is its recognition that affection for particular places is grounded in the meanings attributed to those places within culture: 'human territoriality, in the sense of attachment to place, differs in important ways from the territoriality of animals unburdened by symbolic thought'.[32]

The primary example of geopiety in *Eyrbyggja saga* is the veneration accorded to the headland and mountain of Helgafell, which the early settler Þórólfr Mostrarskegg sets apart as sacred to his god Þórr, so that it becomes a naturalcultural object of devotion:

[26] *Brennu-Njáls saga*, ed. by Einar Ól. Sveinsson, Íslenzk fornrit, 12 (Reykjavík: Hið íslenzka fornritafélag, 1954), p. 182.

[27] Gwyn Jones, *A History of the Vikings*, 2nd edn (Oxford: Oxford University Press, 1984), p. 464; the phrase appears in the index and I owe this reference to Overing and Osborn, *Landscapes of Desire*, p. 64.

[28] It indeed inspired the Romantic poet Jónas Hallgrímsson's poem 'Gunnarshólmi', written in 1837 and available with translation and commentary by Dick Ringler at <http://www.library.wisc.edu/etext/jonas/Gunnar/Gunnar.html> [accessed 12 May 2014].

[29] Overing and Osborn, *Landscapes of Desire*, p. 65, cf. pp. 57–59, 64–66. M. I. Steblin-Kamenskij emphasises that this episode is atypical and argues that the fact that landscape is elsewhere completely absent in sagas is of much greater significance, indicating an absence of aesthetic appreciation of 'nature' in the world of the sagas: *The Saga Mind*, trans. by Kenneth H. Ober (Odense: Odense University Press, 1973), pp. 76–77). Lars Lönnroth's argument that the scene may be influenced by *Alexanders saga* (*Njáls saga: A Critical Introduction* (Berkeley: University of California Press, 1976), p. 154), has been rebutted by David Ashurst in his 'Bleikir akrar — Snares of the Devil? The Significance of the Pale Cornfields in *Alexanders saga*', *Saga-Book* 25 (2000), 272–91; for further discussion of the episode in the context of metaphors of growth and productivity in the saga see Andrew Joseph Hamer, '*Njáls saga* and its Christian Background: A Study of Narrative Method' (Ph.D. dissertation, Rijksuniversiteit Groningen, 2008), available at <http://dissertations.ub.rug.nl/FILES/faculties/arts/2008/a.j.hamer/thesis.pdf>, ch. 4 [accessed 12 May 2014].

[30] One critic who does recognise this is Heather O'Donoghue in her *Old-Norse Icelandic Literature: A Short Introduction* (Oxford: Blackwell, 2004), p. 60.

[31] Yi-Fu Tuan, 'Geopiety: A Theme in Man's Attachment to Nature and to Place', in *Geographies of the Mind: Essays in Historical Geosophy in Honor of John Kirtland Wright*, ed. David Lowenthal and Martyn J. Bowden (New York: Oxford University Press, 1976), pp. 11–39 (pp. 12, 13). The term has been employed in relation to Old Norse literature by Osborn and Overing, *Landscapes of Desire*, pp. 8, 52.

[32] Tuan, 'Geopiety', p. 13. It may be worth noting that at least some animals may be capable of symbolic thought.

> í því nesi stendr eitt fjall; á því fjalli hafði Þórólfr svá mikinn átrúnað, at þangat skyldi enginn maðr óþveginn líta ok engu skyldi tortíma í fjallinu, hvárki fé né mǫnnum, nema sjálft gengi í brott. Þat fjall kallaði hann Helgafell [...] þar var ok svá mikill helgistaðr, at hann vildi með engu móti láta saurga vǫllinn, hvarki í heiptarblóði, ok eigi skyldi þar álfrek ganga, ok var haft til þess sker eitt, er Dritsker var kallat. (pp. 9–10)
>
> the headland is in the form of a mountain, and Thorolf invested so much reverence in it that no one was allowed to look towards it without having washed and nothing was allowed to be killed on the mountain, neither man nor animal unless it died of natural causes. He named this mountain Helgafell [...] He considered the ground so sacred that he would not allow it to be defiled in any way, either by blood spilt in rage, or by anybody doing their elf-frighteners there — there was a skerry named Dritsker (Shit-Skerry) for that purpose. (p. 77)

This passage employs the language of pollution: human waste (though in this case an entirely natural product) will desecrate and defile (*saurga*) the mountain — as well as scare the elves.[33] The episode also illustrates a point to which I shall return towards the end of this essay: for medieval Icelanders, the non-human environment extended beyond what we would refer to as nature to encompass also the supernatural — here, both elves and the god Þórr.

Þórólfr Mostrarskegg is spared the experience of Helgafell's pollution, but his son Þorsteinn þorskabítr (cod-biter) faces the possibility of its desecration by the Kjallekling family, who think of themselves as above others in the area (ch. 9). The saga describes Þorsteinn as determined to defend the land rather than see it defiled: 'vildi hann eigi þola, at þeir saurgaði þann vǫll, er Þórólfr, faðir hans, hafði tignat umfram aðra staði í sinni landeign' (p. 15) ('he was in no mind to allow them to defile the ground that his father Þórólfr had worshipped above all other parts of his estate', p. 80). Unfortunately, in the attempt to prevent desecration by defecation blood is shed which itself pollutes the mountain. Þórðr gellir (bellower) brokers a truce: 'en vǫllinn kallar hann spilltan af heiptarblóði, er niðr hafði komit, ok kallar þá jǫrð nú eigi helgari en aðra' (p. 17) ('he argued that since the ground had been defiled by blood spilt in rage, the earth could no longer be considered more sacred there than anywhere else', p. 82). As a consequence, legal assemblies are no longer to be held there, a revealing indication of the close connection between community building and cultural meanings of landscape: sacred earth is where social and legal structures attain validity. This remains the case when the *þing* is moved to a new site, described as 'inn mesti helgistaðr, en eigi var mǫnnum þar bannat at ganga ørna sinna' (p. 18) ('the holiest of places, but it was not forbidden to relieve oneself there', p. 82).[34]

Helgafell, like Hlíðarendi in *Njáls saga*, is a part of the landscape that is endowed with meaning in a way that blurs the distinction between human life and the physical environment, between nature and culture. The mountain is both a geological feature and a meaning-bearing

---

[33] In a learned and stimulating reading of this episode Kevin Wanner suggests that the elves referred to here probably correspond to land-spirits or *landvættir*: see Kevin J. Wanner, 'Purity and Danger in Earliest Iceland: Excrement, Blood, Sacred Space, and Society in Eyrbyggja saga', *Viking and Medieval Scandinavia*, 5 (2009), 213–50 (p. 216).

[34] For discussion of the immunity of the new *þing* site from the conditions attached to the old one, see Wanner, 'Purity and Danger', pp. 225–26. Helgafell stimulated renewed geopiety when it became the site of a Christian (Augustinian) monastery from 1184 onwards. It has often been suggested that *Eyrbyggja saga* may have been written at the monastery (see the extensive list of references in Wanner, 'Purity and Danger', p. 232 n. 9) and Wanner explores the ways in which that milieu may be reflected in the saga, including possible biblical sources for the saga's interest in pollution ('Purity and Danger', pp. 234–46).

Ecocriticism and Eyrbyggja saga

part of human culture: a naturecultural, rather than purely natural or cultural, phenomenon. In a similar manner, the distinction between human and animal life in the saga also turns out to be less than clear-cut.

Humans and animals

Recent years have seen the development of several related and overlapping academic fields which may be regarded as broadly ecocritical in their concern with aspects of the relationship between humans and the non-human, but which focus specifically on animals, their interactions with human beings, and their cultural roles and meanings. Within the broader discipline of animal studies, critical animal theory has an explicitly emancipatory agenda (comparable in some ways to that of feminist, queer, or postcolonial scholarship) and is directed to the abolition of animal exploitation, subjugation, and cruelty.[35] Such critical work has blurred or even erased the conventional sharp distinction made between humans and (other) animals. Influential texts include Jacques Derrida's delightful *The Animal That Therefore I Am* and Giorgio Agamben's *The Open: Man and Animal*, both of which interrogate limits and boundaries in ways that resonate with the present reading of *Eyrbyggja saga*.[36] Erica Fudge and Donna Haraway have also focused attention on the difficulties of defining human/animal difference and on the variety of ways in which humans relate to animals as wild or domestic.[37] The work of these and other theorists has shown how animals, the concept of 'animal', and the opposition between humans and (other) animals are socially constructed and so historically contingent, so that Greg Garrard writes that 'the most startling and significant insight of ecocriticism and animal studies is that the supposedly distinct realms of culture and nature are naturalcultural throughout'.[38] While animal studies have in recent years become increasingly prominent in the study of medieval English literature, they have as yet made little impact on the study of Old Norse-Icelandic texts. Lena Rohrbach's *Der tierische Blick: Mensch-Tier Relationen in der Sagaliteratur* (2009) is a rich and pioneering study of animals in the Icelandic sagas, but although she is aware of the development of critical animal studies in the English-speaking world she distances herself somewhat from that discipline and adopts a different, less explicitly theorised approach.[39]

---

[35] Margo DeMello, *Animals and Society: An Introduction to Human-Animal Studies* (New York: Columbia University Press, 2012) is an eye-opening textbook covering the whole range of human-animal studies, historically informed but with a focus on the contemporary USA.

[36] Jacques Derrida, *The Animal That Therefore I Am*, trans. David Wills, ed. by Marie-Louise Mallet (New York: Fordham University Press, 2008), pp. 2–3, 29–31; Giorgio Agamben, *The Open: Man and Animal*, trans. by Kevin Attell (Stanford: Stanford University Press, 2004), esp. pp. 13–16.

[37] See, for example, Erica Fudge, *Perceiving Animals: Humans and Beasts in Early Modern Culture* (Houndmills: Macmillan, 2000); *Animal* (London: Reaktion, 2002); *Pets* (Stocksfield: Acumen Press, 2008); Donna J. Haraway, *The Companion Species Manifesto: Dogs, People, and Significant Otherness* (Chicago: Prickly Paradigm Press, 2003); *When Species Meet* (Minnesota: University of Minnesota Press, 2008).

[38] Garrard, *Ecocriticism*, p. 205.

[39] Lena Rohrbach, *Der tierische Blick: Mensch-Tier Relationen in der Sagaliteratur* (Tübingen and Basel: Francke, 2009), p. 14. For a recent survey of animals in Norse religion and archaeology see Kristina Jennbert, *Animals and Humans: Recurrent Symbiosis in Archaeology and Old Norse Religion* (Lund: Nordic Academic Press, 2011); studies of animals in medieval Europe more generally include Joyce E. Salisbury, *The Beast Within: Animals in the Middle Ages*, 2nd edn (London: Routledge, 2011); Susan Crane, *Animal Encounters: Contacts and Concepts in Medieval Britain* (Philadelphia: University of Pennsylvania Press, 2013) provides an erudite and theoretically aware study of human-animal relations in medieval texts from Britain and Ireland.

Most of the animals we encounter in *Eyrbyggja saga* are used by humans in some way, and most are domesticated farm animals. Some are unlucky enough to be sacrificed in Þórr's temple, as we are told in chapter 4: 'þat var þess konar blóð, er svœfð váru þau kvikendi, er goðunum var fórnat' (p. 9) ('this blood, which was called sacrificial blood, was the blood of live animals offered to the gods', p. 76).

Several incidents in the saga illustrate the importance of owning livestock. In chapter 14 Snorri goði surprises Bǫrkr by being able to afford to buy his land. Bǫrkr offers to stay on since Snorri has so little livestock, but Snorri refuses and tells him to enjoy his livestock away from Helgafell. In the next chapter Snorri's uncle Már Hallvarðsson comes to live with Snorri at the farm and brings lots of livestock with him (ch. 15). Livestock later becomes a source of conflict when people gather to sort the sheep at Tunga between the Lax rivers in ch. 23.

The farmer Úlfarr is introduced in chapter 30 with a relatively rare recognition of the extreme climatic conditions in which Icelandic society was established and, perhaps, of the perils associated with the introduction of non-native species into an alien physical environment: 'hann var ok svá fésæll, at fé hans dó aldri af megri eða drephríðum' (p. 81) ('he was so lucky with his livestock that none of his animals ever died from starvation or in blizzards', p. 125).[40]

Horses are particularly prominent animals in the saga. There is a reference in chapter 13 to characters riding horses. In chapter 18 we are told that Þórarinn svarti of Mávahlíð has a 'víghest góðan á fjalli' (p. 33) ('good fighting stallion which he grazed up on the mountain', p. 92).[41] Þorbjǫrn inn digri also grazes many horses on the mountain pastures, killing a few each autumn (for meat, presumably).[42] The disappearance of Þorbjǫrn's horses and suspicions of the people of Mávahlíð leads to a violent encounter, in the confusion of which Oddr Kǫtluson cuts off the hand of Þórarinn's wife Auðr. Oddr seeks magical assistance from his mother Katla to prevent Þórarinn's men catching him, and the witch chooses to disguise Oddr by transforming him into farm animals: a goat which she plays with and grooms, and then a domestic boar that lies under a pile of waste or refuse.[43] It turns out later that Þorbjǫrn's horses have died in the mountains; they had been unable to hold the pasture against Þórarinn's fighting stallion (ch. 23).

This episode of conflict centred around horses depends upon various kinds of blurring of the distinction between human and animal: Þórarinn's stallion is trained to fight; the verses commemorating the human fight figure human violence in terms of animals; Katla transforms the fugitive Oddr into a goat and a boar; the conflict between human groups siding with Þorbjǫrn or Þórarinn, is paralleled by the death of Þorbjǫrn's horses caused by Þórarinn's stallion.

There are, then, numerous domesticated animals in the saga: sheep, horses, and other livestock. On the one hand, these farm animals are treated as non-human: they are sacrificed alive to the gods, trained to take part in horse fights, and used as beasts of burden. But this apparently straightforward distinction between humans and animals is somewhat undermined by the way in which both inhabit the same spaces (as occasionally happened quite literally in

---

[40] Elsewhere the saga makes another brief allusion to the hazards of the Icelandic climate when it states in ch. 37 that 'there was a big freeze and all the fjords iced over' (p. 138) and there is a further allusion to icing over in ch. 45.

[41] On horse-fighting as a 'sport' in the sagas see Rohrbach, *Der tierische Blick*, pp. 54, 73–76, 184–88.

[42] Ari Þorgilsson famously records that the eating of horse meat was allowed to continue after Iceland's conversion, but was banned a few years later (*Íslendingabók*, p. 19).

[43] The remedy for Katla's magic is to put her head in a seal-skin bag.

early Iceland, where farm animals sometimes lived in the family home).[44] Together humans and animals form humananimal communities, not purely human communities separated from non-human nature. Though the relation is a very unequal one, humans and animals are dependent on each other.

This point is underlined by the clear contrast in *Eyrbyggja saga* between farm animals who feature in the prose narrative of the humananimal communities of which they are part, and wild animals, most of which appear not in the prose, but in skaldic verses quoted in the saga. Whereas we meet sheep, horses, and cows in the prose, it is in the verse that we encounter swallows, ravens, adders, a she-wolf, geese, hawks, gulls, and eagles (sea creatures form the major exception to this division, with fish, a mysterious seal, and a whale all appearing in the saga prose).[45] Table 1 lists the animal references that occur in the skaldic verses in *Eyrbyggja saga*. It is striking that many of these wild animals figure *human* violence: the animal/human boundary is disturbed when animals appear in kennings for blood, sword, and hand, and as beasts of battle who will feed on the human dead in a reversal of the relationship between farmers and their livestock.[46]

Berserks and revenants: the physical supernatural

In *The Natural and the Supernatural in the Middle Ages* Robert Bartlett shows that the thirteenth century was a period during which scholastic theologians and philosophers began to draw a sharper distinction between the natural and the miraculous than patristic tradition had done; it is the period when the word supernatural (*supernaturalis*) first becomes an important tool for organising thought.[47] As Bartlett notes,

> marking off the natural from other things had always been a major concern of Western thinkers, for if nature is not to be regarded, somewhat vacuously, as a synonym for 'everything', it obviously has things it is defined against.[48]

In the thirteenth century the supernatural emerges more prominently as a category against which to define the natural. The thirteenth-century *Eyrbyggja saga* is similarly (though independently) concerned with boundaries, not only between the human and the natural, but also between the natural and the supernatural. For the medieval scholastic tradition, rationality constituted what Bartlett calls the 'indispensable conceptual boundary between human and

---

[44] Although animal sheds were normally separate from the farmhouse (though within the farm enclosure), a Viking-period house excavated near the beginning of this century at Aðalstræti 14–16 in Reykjavík had stalls for animals (goats or sheep) inside the house, as was more commonly the case in early Norwegian longhouses: see William R. Short, *Icelanders in the Viking Age: The People of the Sagas* (Jefferson, NC: McFarland, 2010), p. 89. The archaeological report *Excavations at Aðalstræti, 2003*, ed. H. M. Roberts, with contributions by Mjöll Snæsdóttir, Natascha Mehler, Oscar Aldred, Garðar Guðmundsson, Árný E. Sveinbjörnsdóttir, Jan Heinemeier, Karen Milek and Alex Chepstow Lusty (Fornleifastofnun Íslands: Reykjavík, 2004) is available at <http://www.nabohome.org/uploads/fsi/FS243-00162_Adalstraeti_2003.pdf> [accessed 12 May 2014]: see p. 97 for a plan of the house.

[45] In addition, an eagle appears in the prose to carry off Egill sterki's fox hound to Þórólfr bægifótr's cairn in chapter 43. On the place of fish and other sea creatures in Icelandic culture see Gísli Pálsson, 'The Idea of Fish: Land and Sea in the Icelandic World-View', in *Signifying Animals: Human Meaning in the Natural World*, ed. by Roy Willis (London: Routledge, 1994), pp. 119–33.

[46] The field of skaldic diction is a potentially rich one for future ecocritical analysis, as Abram shows in his unpublished discussion of tree kennings in skaldic verse.

[47] Robert Bartlett, *The Natural and the Supernatural in the Middle Ages* (Cambridge: Cambridge University Press, 2008), pp. 12–13.

[48] Bartlett, *Natural and Supernatural*, p. 17.

ch. 17, st. 1	dolg-svǫlu	battle-swallows (= ravens)
ch. 18, st. 3	ǫrn	eagle
	valnaðrs	slay-adders (= swords)
ch. 18 st. 5	Hugins nið	raven
ch. 18 st. 8	hrein	raven
ch. 18 st. 10	kunnfáka [...] borða	horse of planks (= ship)
	síks [...] sælingr	fish of armour (= sword)
	hrafn	raven
ch. 18 st. 11	ylgteiti	she-wolf's joy (= battle)
ch. 18 st. 12	Nágǫglum	corpse-geese (= ravens)
ch. 18 st. 15	hrafn–víns	ravens' wine (= blood)
ch. 18 st. 16	haukaness	hawk's spur (= hand)
ch. 18 st. 17	hrafn	raven
	haukr [...] hræva	hawk of corpses
ch. 26 st. 20	benskárar	wound-mews (= ravens)
ch. 37 st. 26	sár-orra	bird (heathcock) of wounds (= raven)
	Leifa máreifir	Leifi's gull (= raven)
ch. 40 st. 27	fenris brunni	wolf's well (= pool of blood)
	hesta [...] rastar [...] hlunns	current's horse (= ship)
ch. 40 st. 29	hafviggs	sea's steed (= ship)
ch. 40 st. 30	svanna fold	earth of swans (= sea)
ch. 44 st. 33	svangreddir [...] sára dynbǫru	feeder of the swan of blood (= raven > warrior)
	ǫrn	eagle
	ulfs	wolf

Table 1: Animal references in the skaldic verse of *Eyrbyggja saga*.

animal'.⁴⁹ The writer and audience of *Eyrbyggja saga* are likely to have made a similarly clear-cut conscious distinction between humans and animals, but as we have seen, the narrative inadvertently blurs that boundary, or perhaps suggests that the significant distinction is not between humans and animals but between humans and domesticated animals on the one side and wild animals on the other.

The boundary between human and animal in the saga is further blurred in an episode involving two Swedish berserks (chapters 25 to 28). As the shape-changing implications of the likely etymology 'bear-shirt' imply, berserks inhabit a liminal space on the porous borders between human and animal, but they also inhabit the border between natural and supernatural.⁵⁰ The Swedish berserks in *Eyrbyggja saga* are bigger and stronger than other men, and 'váru þá eigi í mannligu eðli, er þeir váru reiðir, ok fóru galnir sem hundar' (p. 61) ('once they had worked themselves up into a frenzy they were not like human beings. They went mad like dogs', pp. 110–11). The way in which the Swedish berserks are passed as possessions from Earl Hákon to Vermundr inn mjóvi ('the slender') Þorgrímsson, and then to his brother Styrr as if they were livestock perhaps underlines this bestial aspect (they complain that Vermundr had no right to give them away to his brother like slaves, a further category of living being that blurs the simple human/animal distinction). When Vermundr delays finding a wife for the berserk Halli, another animal comparison is made: 'en er Halli fann þat, sló hann á sik úlfúð ok illsku' (p. 63) ('when Halli realized this, his wolf mind took over and he became ill-tempered', p. 112).

In their new home Halli falls in love with Styrr's daughter Ásdís and this threat to an ontological boundary cannot be tolerated; Styrr seeks the advice of Snorri goði on how to get rid of the berserks: ambiguously human berserks have to be purged from the human community for society to be secure. As part of Snorri's plan, the berserks are set to making a path across a lava field between pastures. The situation here is a paradoxical one in which the wild landscape is to be mastered and brought under human control by ambiguously human beings, wild or animal-men, one might say. This task exhausts the berserks 'sem háttr er þeira manna, sem eigi eru einhama' (p. 74) ('as is the way with those men who are not always in human shape', p. 120). In this exhausted state the berserks can be killed when they try to escape from the excessive heat of Styrr's bathhouse; Snorri goði then gets the girl and becomes a safely human son-in-law for Styrr.

There is further evidence later in the saga for the contingent nature of the dividing line between human and animal. In chapter 61 it is said of Þrándr Ingjaldsson that '[hann] var kallaðr eigi einhamr, meðan hann var heiðinn, en þá tók af flestum trollskap, er skírðir váru' (p. 165) ('when he was a heathen he was known as a shape-shifter, but most people gave up magic when they were baptized', p. 186). As with the berserks, the boundary between human and animal here becomes associated with that between nature and the supernatural. Baptism brings an end to such boundary crossing as the conversion to Christianity is an essential stage on the way to the establishment of a stable Icelandic nation.⁵¹

The conversion does not, however, bring about an immediate end to hauntings. In chapter 51 a portentous shower of blood foretells the death of Þórgunna, the Hebridean guest of

---

⁴⁹ Bartlett, *Natural and Supernatural*, p. 91.

⁵⁰ For an up-to-date account of research on the etymology of *berserkr* see Vincent Samson, *Les berserkir: Les guerriers-fauves dans la Scandinavie ancienne, de l'Âge de Vendel aux Vikings (VIe–XIe siècle)* (Villeneuve d'Ascq: Presses Universitaires du Septentrion, 2011), ch. 2.

⁵¹ The brief account of the conversion in chapter 49 notes that Snorri goði built a church at Helgafell.

Þuríðr and Þóroddr at Fróðá. Þuríðr prevents her husband carrying out his promise to burn Þórgunna's bed and bedclothes after her death, as Þuríðr has had her covetous eye on them since Þórgunna first unpacked them. En route to Þórgunna's requested burial at Skálholt (a focus for Christian geopiety mirroring that of pagans towards Helgafell earlier in the saga), the party of corpse bearers is refused food at a farm where they lodge and the undead Þuríðr arises in the night to cook a meal naked. It takes a (naturally) naked (supernatural) revenant to enforce the cultural norms of hospitality.

The shower of blood that presaged Þórgunna's death is just one of several examples in the saga of the non-human environment correlating with human fate. Another is the 'weird-moon' (*urðar máni*, p. 146) that appears each evening for a week in chapter 52, portending further hauntings at the farm of Þóroddr and Þuríðr. In the following chapter a shepherd is bewitched, dies, and walks as undead, killing Þórir viðleggr (woodleg), who then joins him in revenant evening rambles. A mysterious seal's head also appears in the fireplace until hammered into the ground by Kjartan (ch. 53).

We saw above that Þórólfr bægifótr's return as a revenant was a kind of supernatural revenge for deforestation. Þóroddr and his men are drowned while depleting another natural resource, fish (ch. 54), and their deaths are prefigured by the tearing and mysterious consumption of dried fish at the farm.

The hauntings at Fróðá are eventually ended, on Snorri goði's advice to Kjartan, when the twin forms of human social regulation, the law and the Christian religion, are deployed against the non-human (or no longer human) supernatural: Þórgunna's bedding is finally burned, the undead Þóroddr and his men are prosecuted, and a priest says mass and hears confessions. Order is re-established through a combination of law and Christianity.

The distinctive quality of Norse revenants is what William Sayers calls their 'intense corporality'.[52] This physicality troubles and problematizes a simple opposition between the natural and the supernatural: in the sagas the supernatural can be manifested in very solidly physical form. Nor is this the only distinction undermined by the revenants of the sagas: Sayers writes of their 'crossing of the boundary back into life':

> Ignoring the boundary between death and life as set in natural law, *draugr* predation on the community also ignores the laws of property and social hierarchy and violates the norms of reciprocity by being one-sided and wholly destructive.[53]

Nevertheless, Sayers argues that the ghosts at Fróðá are open to legal arguments because of 'their nostalgia for communal life'.[54] The supernatural and the naturecultural do not exist in isolation from one another.

After the hauntings at Fróðá, the undead Þórólfr bægifótr makes a reappearance in the saga. We are told in chapter 63 that Þórólfr's renewed hauntings have caused the farm of Bólstaðr to be deserted because people and livestock were killed there. Þórólfr's body is removed from his cairn, taken to the liminal foreshore and burned. The ashes are mostly deposited in the sea, but some blow about. Þóroddr returns to his farm and meets a cow that takes fright, breaks her leg, and is later often seen licking the stones on which Þórólfr's ashes had blown. The cow goes missing when Þóroddr intends to have it killed, but returns to her

---

[52] William Sayers, 'The Alien and Alienated as Unquiet Dead in the Sagas of Icelanders' in *Monster Theory: Reading Culture*, ed. Jeffrey Jerome Cohen (Minneapolis: University of Minnesota Press, 1996), pp. 242–63 (at p. 244).
[53] Sayers, 'Alien and Alienated', pp. 243, 258.
[54] Sayers, 'Alien and Alienated', p. 249. On this see also John D. Martin, 'Law and the (Un)dead: Medieval Models for Understanding the Hauntings in *Eyrbyggja saga*', *Saga-Book* 29 (2005), 67–82.

cowshed just before Yule, pregnant. The cow gives birth to a heifer and then a bull calf; the latter is so big that giving birth kills the cow. A blind old woman on the farm, Þóroddr's foster-mother, takes fright at the noise the bull makes and advises that it be killed: 'þetta eru trolls læti, en eigi annars kvikendis' (p. 171) ('that's the sound of a troll, not the sound of a natural beast', p. 191).[55] Þóroddr ignores her advice. When the bull is four years old and has acquired a name, Glæsir, that is indicative of his incorporation in a humananimal community, Þóroddr decides to kill it; the bull seems to understand his speech.[56] The bull is referred to in a verse (p. 192) as 'king of the herd' (*hjarðar vísi*; p. 173), a humanising metaphor, and seems to be a kind of reincarnation of Þórólfr bægifótr engendered by the mother cow's consumption of the revenant's ashes, further blurring the human/animal distinction. When Þóroddr goes to kill the bull it tosses him in the air and impales him on one of its horns: this ultimate vengeance of the natural world over the human farmer is followed by the bull rushing into a bog and sinking.

If ecocriticism is concerned with the relationship between the human and the non-human, then in a saga like *Eyrbyggja saga* this must include not only the relationships between humans and the physical environment or humans and animals: it must also embrace the relationship between humans and the *super*natural non-human. In his introduction to Quinn's translation of *Eyrbyggja saga*, Vésteinn Ólason writes that 'there is no clear line between the natural and supernatural' in the text.[57] With its ready acceptance of the supernatural, medieval literature, including the sagas of Icelanders, may have something to teach ecocritics. When it takes for granted that the non-human is limited to the natural, ecocriticism is an unreflective child of its time. Medieval literature, including a text such as *Eyrbyggja saga*, reminds us that such an assumption is characteristic of a tiny minority of the human beings who have so far existed on earth. The environmentally aware reader might be moved to reflect that it is only in the last couple of hundred years, precisely the period during which the natural environment has come under gravest threat from human beings, that belief in the supernatural has disappeared among sizable parts of the human population. Without necessarily arguing that the answer to our current environmental woes is simply to retreat from Enlightenment rationalism back to belief in the supernatural, one might at least maintain that there may be advantages to fostering a greater awareness of what has been lost as the world has become disenchanted. In his *Cambridge Introduction to Literature and the Environment*, Timothy Clark argues that it is a requirement of ecocriticism to take a religious stance, though I take it that this does not mean that an ecocritic is obliged to espouse any particular historical religion.[58] Yi-Fu Tuan similarly maintains that although 'piety' is becoming an obsolete term, 'it can be argued that people would live more in harmony with nature could the sentiment be restored', a restoration which perhaps need not require renewal of actual belief in the supernatural.[59]

---

[55] Quinn's translation, like that of Hermann Pálsson and Paul Edwards ('that isn't a natural creature's voice, it's a monster's'; *Eyrbyggja Saga* (London: Penguin, 1989), p. 157) exaggerates the distinction between nature and the supernatural; *kvikendi* is more literally simply a 'living creature'.

[56] While it is true that inanimate objects (such as weapons) are also occasionally given names in the sagas, the naming of animals blurs the distinction between human and animal, exposing their common membership of a humananimal community, because such names are used when speaking to the animal, whereas named objects are very rarely so addressed. The responsiveness of animals to human address is a thread running through both Derrida's *The Animal That Therefore I Am* and Haraway's *When Species Meet*.

[57] Vésteinn Ólason, 'Introduction', p. vii.

[58] Clark, *Cambridge Introduction*, p. 5.

[59] Tuan 'Geopiety', p. 33.

Indeed, my use of the term 'supernatural' above, though in accord with today's idiom, may be looser than that of scholastic theologians of the thirteenth century. Bartlett notes that a writer such as Gervase of Tilbury, writing in 1215, was careful to distinguish the miraculous, which was supernatural and caused by God, from the marvellous, which was beyond human understanding but nevertheless natural.[60] To understand fully the way in which berserks, shape-shifters, and revenants in *Eyrbyggja saga* call into question the distinction between nature and the supernatural it may be necessary to adopt this scholastic distinction between the marvellous and the miraculous or, perhaps, to invoke the category of the preternatural, that which is outside or beyond nature, but not necessarily 'above' it.[61]

A medieval text such as *Eyrbyggja saga* challenges ecocritics to account or allow for the supernatural (or whatever is or might be beyond what we habitually think of as natural) and to consider its relationship to nature and to culture — or at least to recognise the prevalence and potential value of human belief in the supernatural. The realist presentation of the supernatural in medieval literature, and especially the unusually physical manifestation of the undead in the sagas, is one of the most significant ways in which such literature challenges twenty-first century understandings of the relationship between nature and culture, between humans and the non-human. This exposure of assumptions underlying the distinctions as they are currently made may be one of the most valuable contributions an ecocritical approach to medieval literature, including the sagas, can make to contemporary green studies.

Conclusion

Eyrbyggja saga is, among other things, about establishing a stable human community in a previously uninhabited land. This involves the construction of boundaries, both physical and conceptual. Wild nature must be divided from cultivated farmland, Icelandic society from the realm of the outlaw, human from animal, nature from the supernatural.

Particular features of the landscape are named, endowed with meaning, and sometimes become the objects of geopiety, taking on a sacred significance that is at least as much given them by humans as recognised. The society that is established is not, however, a purely human one. It is a humananimal community in which farm animals and humans depend upon one another, wild animals figure human violence in skaldic verse, and bestial berserks blur the boundaries between human and animal and between natural and supernatural. To create this community the land must be brought under control so that the nation may thrive. It is not only a case of cultivating the wilderness and domesticating animals: it is also about expelling the undesirable supernatural. Þrándr gives up shape-shifting after the conversion; the revenants at Fróðá are evicted by the law and exorcised by a priest.

Insofar as this process is successful, an ordered and stable community is established, as extensive genealogies tracing characters' descendants in the final chapter of the saga bear

---

[60] Bartlett, *Natural and Supernatural*, pp. 18–19. Bartlett further notes (pp. 20, 23) that for many thirteenth-century writers demons and magic were natural, not supernatural, marvels, and that the canonisation process in this period took pains to distinguish the magical (natural) from the miraculous (supernatural).

[61] Ármann Jakobsson has recently expressed dissatisfaction with the term 'supernatural' and prefers instead to write of the 'paranormal' in Old Icelandic literature since that term 'has its roots in human experience rather than in nature': 'The Taxonomy of the Non-Existent: Some Medieval Icelandic Concepts of the Paranormal', *Fabula*, 54 (2013), 199–213 (p. 199 n. 2). Ármann's use of this term is, however, predicated on the assumption (articulated in the title of his essay) that the phenomena it encompasses are 'Non-Existent'; I am here, however, concerned precisely to allow for the possibility that there may be more to reality than the natural.

witness. The narrative preceding that final chapter shows, nevertheless, on what precarious foundations and by what contingent means this nation is established. The opposition between nature and nation is continually called into question, blurred, or shown to be inadequate. Dividing lines between human and animal, between natural and humanised landscape, and between the natural and the supernatural are continually crossed. Þórólfr Mostrarskegg's carrying of fire across the land to establish the boundaries of his settlement in chapter 4 of the saga is characteristically both an essential and also an ultimately futile attempt to separate the human from the non-human.

Scyld sceal cempan

The Shield and the Warrior in Old English Poetry

Stephen Graham[1]

Introduction

Two Exeter Book poems illustrate the importance of the shield in the life of the Anglo-Saxon warrior.[2] *Maxims I* contains the assertion 'scyld sceal cempan' ('the shield must go with the warrior', l. 129)[3] suggesting that possession of a shield was fundamental to the concept of what a warrior was.[4] In Exeter Riddle 5, usually solved as 'shield', the close connection between the object and its bearer forms the basis of the poem's controlling metaphor. An old shield is personified as an ageing warrior, worn out from years of fighting:

>   Ic eom anhaga   iserne wund,
>   bille gebennad,   beadoweorca sæd,
>   ecgum werig.   Oft ic wig seo,
>   frecne feohtan.   Frofre ne wene,
>   þæt me geoc cyme   guðgewinnes,
>   ær ic mid ældum   eal forwurðe,
>   ac mec hnossiað   homera lafe,
>   heardecg heoroscearp, hondweorc smiþa,
>   bitað in burgum;   ic abidan sceal
>   laþran gemotes.   Næfre læcecynn
>   on folcstede   findan meahte,

---

[1] I am grateful to Alice Jorgensen, Helen Conrad O'Briain, Gerald Morgan and the two anonymous reviewers for their helpful comments and suggestions on earlier versions of this essay.

[2] The only book-length study of the shield is by Ian P. Stephenson, *The Anglo-Saxon Shield* (Stroud: Tempus, 2002). The authoritative guide to the archaeology of shields from the early Anglo-Saxon period is by Tania Dickinson and Heinrich Härke, *Early Anglo-Saxon Shields* (London: Society of Antiquaries of London, 1992). General studies of Anglo-Saxon weapons that feature a section on the shield include Richard Underwood, *Anglo-Saxon Weapons and Warfare* (Stroud: Tempus, 1999), pp. 77–91; Stephen Pollington, *The English Warrior from Earliest Times Till 1066*, rev. edn (Hockwold-cum-Wilton: Anglo-Saxon Press, 2002), pp. 150–61.

[3] All line numbers to Old English poems refer to *The Anglo-Saxon Poetic Records: A Collective Edition*, ed. by George Philip Krapp and Elliott Van Kirk Dobbie, 6 vols. (New York: Columbia University Press, 1931–53), apart from *Beowulf*, which refers to *Klaeber's Beowulf and the Fight at Finnsburg*, ed. by R. D. Fulk, Robert E. Bjork and John D. Niles (Toronto: University of Toronto Press, 2008). All translations are my own.

[4] Several synonyms for 'warrior' in *Beowulf* are compounds that literally mean 'the one having a shield': *lindhæbbend(e)*, ll. 245, 1402; *rondhæbbend(e)*, l. 861; *bordhæbbend(e)*, l. 2895.

> þara þe mid wyrtum   wunde gehælde,
> ac me ecga dolg   eacen weorðað
> þurh deaðslege   dagum ond nihtum.
>
> I am solitary, wounded by iron, injured by swords, sated with battle, weary of (sword-) edges. Often I see battle, fierce conflict. I do not expect comfort, that I might get help in battle, before I perish completely among men, but the remnant of hammers strikes me, the hard-edge, battle-sharp, handiwork of smiths bites in the strongholds; I must await a more hateful encounter. I never found in the people's dwellings one of the race of physicians who could heal my wounds with herbs, but for me the wounds of swords increase day and night through death-stroke.

The numerous correspondences that allow the life of the shield to be presented here as the life of the warrior eloquently reinforces the point contained in the maxim: the shield does indeed 'go with' the warrior. However, while the object and the person inhabit the same harsh environment, other literary and cultural evidence from the Anglo-Saxon period suggests that in poetry the shield only goes with a certain kind of warrior. This riddle begins with the claim that the warrior and shield are solitary. Yet, even when used conspicuously by heroic figures such as Byrhtnoth in *The Battle of Maldon* or Beowulf, the shield is not usually associated with the warrior as an individual, as a solitary figure; instead it typically denotes the warrior who exists in a social relationship with others, the warrior who is part of the group. This association arises not only because of the shield's unique physical properties, which denied it certain associations available to other weapons and armour, but also because of the way it was used in combat. To be a 'shield-bearer' in Anglo-Saxon society entailed more than simply carrying a means of personal protection; it was also a social position, one in which an individual bore responsibility for the welfare of the community.

Her byð scyld læne: the history of Anglo-Saxon weapons and armour

In the Exeter riddle, the metaphor of the tired warrior recalling the effects of earlier battles introduces a property normally absent from poetic depictions of the Anglo-Saxon shield: history. Unlike other types of weapons and armour such as swords, mail-coats, and helmets, poets do not generally call attention to a shield's past. Swords, for example, are regularly described and celebrated for having a history of some sort. The honorific 'old sword' is used in several poems ('ealdsweord', *Beowulf*, l. 1663; 'ealde swurd', *The Battle of Maldon*, l. 46; 'alde mece', *Exodus*, l. 495; 'gomel sweord', *Beowulf*, ll. 2620, 2681–2). Past owners and past generations are alluded to through references to a sword being an 'old heirloom' ('ealde lafe', *Beowulf*, ll. 795, 1488, 1688, *Exodus*, l. 408; 'gomele lafe', *Beowulf*, l. 2563); these owners are sometimes specified ('Hreðles lafe', *Beowulf*, l. 2191; 'Eanmundes laf', *Beowulf*, l. 2611). Mention is sometimes made of a sword's makers, whether that is a mythical race of giants ('ealdsweord e(o)tonisc', *Beowulf* ll. 1558, 2616, 2979; 'enta ærgeweorc', *Beowulf* l. 1679) or a legendary smith ('Welandes worc', *Waldere I*, l. 2). Mail-coats are also discussed in *Beowulf* in terms of their past, on one occasion as an 'heirloom of ancestors' ('gomelra lafe', l. 2036) or again as the work of Weland ('Welandes geweorc', l.455); likewise, in *Waldere* a mail-coat is referred to as 'Ælfhere's legacy' ('Ælfheres laf', *Waldere II*, l. 18). Finally, in *Beowulf* a helmet is also mentioned by reference to its makers ('entiscne helm', l. 2979). Outside of the imaginative conventions of the riddle-genre, it is difficult to find any shield depicted in terms of its history. The only shield whose origins are of poetic interest poet seems to be the 'eall irenne [...] wigbord wrætlic' ('all-iron [...] wondrous war-board', ll. 2338–9) Beowulf orders made to face the dragon. In a poem where weapons and armour so often lead the audience from the narrative present into the distant past this shield is notable for having no history at all.

No explanation is given why some objects are celebrated for having a history while others are not, but two possible reasons why shields are not considered in this way concern the materials from which they were made and their role in combat. Another irony about the shield Beowulf uses against the dragon is that it is constructed from the type of material that seems necessary for a weapon or piece of armour to be considered in terms of its history. The Anglo-Saxon sword, mail-coat, and helmet were all primarily metal objects and are depicted that way in poetry.[5] Even when uncared for, objects constructed from this material could potentially last a very long time. In *Beowulf*, for example, the dragon's hoard contains swords so old they are 'thoroughly eaten through with rust as though they had remained a thousand years [...] in the earth's embrace' ('omige þurhetone, wið eorðan fæðm | þusend wintra [...] eardodon', ll. 3049–50). Although these swords have corroded, the analogy used here recognises the longevity of metal as a construction material. The maintenance of metal weapons and armour was carried out by *feormynd* (*Beowulf*, l. 2256, *-leas* l. 2761) — these were 'polishers' or 'cleaners' whose task it was to keep metal weapons and armour in a state of good repair.

The Anglo-Saxon shield, by contrast, was constructed from far more perishable materials. The use of *-wudu* in 'bordwudu' ('board-wood', *Beowulf*, l.1243) and 'campwudu' ('battle-wood', *Elene*, l.51) confirms archaeological evidence recovered from early weapon burials[6] and suggests that, unlike Beowulf's iron shield, the main part of the Anglo-Saxon shield — the shield board — was made from wood.[7] Like the swords in the dragon's hoard, a shield's metal fittings (the boss, grip, rim, and decorative appliques where they were used) are often recovered from archaeological sites in a heavily corroded state;[8] however, apart from traces of wood around these fittings the board itself does not survive.[9] In the real world, then, the materials from which shields were made meant that as intact objects they were far less likely to survive over the long term. That the spear, another predominantly wooden weapon, is similarly

---

[5] On the construction of Anglo-Saxons swords see Hilda Ellis Davidson, *The Sword in Anglo-Saxon England: Its Archaeology and Literature* (Woodbridge: Boydell, 1998), pp. 15–103; Underwood, pp. 47–67. On mail-coats and helmets, see Underwood, pp. 91–106.

[6] 'The vast majority of Anglo-Saxon inhumation cemeteries of the fifth to seventh/eighth centuries have burials with shields' (Dickinson and Härke, p. 63); the main period of deposition was the fifth and sixth centuries (p. 1)

[7] Evidence for shield boards is discussed by Dickinson and Härke, pp. 43–55; see also Stephenson, pp. 26–45. The widespread use of *lind* as a poetic term for shield (*Genesis*, l. 244; *Exodus*, ll. 228, 239, 251, 301; *Andreas*, l. 46; *Beowulf*, ll. 2341, 2365, 2610; *Judith*, ll. 191, 214, 303; *The Battle of Finnsburh*, l. 11; *The Battle of Maldon*, ll. 99, 244; *The Metrical Charms 4: For a Sudden Stitch*, l. 7) might further suggest that shields were made specifically from 'linden-wood' or the wood of the lime tree. However, where it has been possible to identify the type of wood used, the majority of shields recovered appear to have been constructed from other species such as alder, poplar, and willow: Dickinson and Härke, p. 48; Stephenson, pp. 39–40. The discrepancy between poetic convention and archaeological data has been explained as owing to the prevalence of lime trees in the pre-migration heartlands of central and north-western Europe: Pfannkuche, cited in Dickinson and Härke, p. 48.

[8] On the different kinds of shield fittings see Dickinson and Härke, pp. 31–42, 61–62; Stephenson, pp. 17–26, 46–54. Shields were sometimes decorated with metal lozenges or discs; this might provide an archaeological explanation for a reference in *Beowulf* to shields bearing metal 'plates' ('fætte scyldas', *Beowulf*, l. 333) although this could also be the result of poetic embellishment.

[9] Stephenson, p. 34; Dickinson and Härke, p. 56.

not depicted in terms of its history seems to suggest that the kind of material from which an object is made has a bearing on its representation in poetry.[10]

Another, related explanation why the shield is not considered in historical terms is its role in combat. In the violent world depicted in heroic poetry, all objects, irrespective of the materials from which they were made, had the potential to be destroyed. Helmets could be shorn (*Beowulf*, ll. 1526, 2973, 2979–80; *The Battle of Finnsburh*, l. 45), mail-coats could be cut (*The Battle of Maldon*, l. 144; *The Battle of Finnsburh*, l. 44) and in the hands of someone like Beowulf swords could be broken (l. 2680). Nevertheless, as the shield's narrative in the Exeter riddle suggests, there seems to have been an acceptance that the shield in particular would eventually be destroyed in day-to-day use, and its destruction would be unremarkable. The language of battle in Old English poetry, both in the Exeter Riddle and elsewhere, is the language of shields being broken (*gebrec/-bræc*, *Elene*, l. 114; *The Battle of Maldon*, l. 295; *Beowulf*, l. 2259) and hewn ((*ge*)*heawan*, *Judith*, l. 303; *Beowulf*, l. 682; *The Battle of Brunanburh*, l. 6).[11] This imagery gives battle scenes much of their dynamism and energy, but it also means that there could be little expectation that objects used this way would survive for very long. Outside poetry there is some evidence of shields being passed from one generation to the next, although it is not clear if such objects had been used in battle or if they had undergone repair.[12]

In poetry, the capacity of an object to have a long history is significant because it provides the basis of other poetic associations. A weapon or piece of armour with such a history also has the potential to acquire an 'identity'[13] based on that history. The references in *Beowulf* to the dragon's hoard recognise that metal weapons and armour[14] have the capacity to retain their general form over time, to keep their basic physical identity, and to be recognizable as a sword or helmet even after hundreds of years. This constancy of form permits a level of individuation by which, in some cases, the identity of an inanimate object can almost approach that of an animate being. Weapons and armour referred to as heirlooms, or the work of a famous smith, derive their identity as unique objects both from their great age and their connection to celebrated figures from the past. Named objects such as swords (e.g. Hrunting, *Beowulf*,

---

[10] The spear is also identified in Old English poetry using terms that highlight the use of wood in its construction (e.g. *æsc*, *Beowulf*, l. 1772, *The Battle of Maldon*, ll. 43, 310, Riddle 22, l. 11; *æscholt*, *Beowulf*, l. 330, *The Battle of Maldon*, l. 230; *garwudu*, *Exodus*, l. 325; *þrecwudu*, *Beowulf*, l. 1246; *mægenwudu*, *Beowulf*, l. 326; *guðwudu*, *The Battle of Finnsburh*, l. 6); on Anglo-Saxon spears see Underwood, pp. 39–46.

[11] In poetry, the destruction of metal weapons and armour are perhaps to be taken as signalling that a particular encounter was exceptionally violent. George Clark, 'Beowulf's Armor', *ELH*, 32 (1965), 409–41 (p. 412) argues, for instance, that 'in *Beowulf* the "sword versus helmet" theme epitomizes the ferocious savagery of heroic warfare'.

[12] Ætheling Æthelstan, son of King Æthelred and his first wife Ælgifu, leaves two shields (*mines targan* and *mines bohscyldes*) in his early eleventh-century will to a retainer and another individual. Shields often appear in Anglo-Saxon wills, usually as part of weapon heriots, which are discussed in more detail below. Æthelstan's bequest is different because the shields in question are clearly his own. Dorothy Whitelock, *Anglo-Saxon Wills* (Cambridge: Cambridge University Press, 1930), p. 60.

[13] Identity is understood here as 'the sameness of a [...] thing at all times or in all circumstances', *OED*, s.v. 'identity', 2.a. Anglo-Saxon weapons and armour, including shields, were often highly decorated. While this is another way of approaching the issue of identity my concern here is with the general characteristics of weapon and armour types. On the decoration and symbolism of shields see Dickinson and Härke, pp. 50–4, 61–2; Stephenson, pp. 50–2, 103–24; Underwood, pp. 86–89; Pollington, p. 160. The possible social significance of different kinds of shield-decoration is discussed in Tania Dickinson, 'Symbols of Protection: The Significance of Animal-ornamented Shields in Early Anglo-Saxon England', *Medieval Archaeology*, 49 (2005), 109–64.

[14] The hoard also contains many 'old and rusted' ('eald ond omig', l. 2763) helmets.

ll. 1457, 1490, 1659, 1807, Nægling, l. 2680; Mimming, *Waldere I*, l. 3) also derive their identity partly from their history, although they do so in a different way. As Isaacs notes, the personification of a sword can be so complete it 'is not only given human attributes but it is also given a distinct personality all its own.'[15] In the case of Hrunting, for example, this is achieved by referring to it in human terms (e.g. 'guðwine', 'battle-friend', l. 1810), by implying that it can act independently ('næs þæt forma sið | þæt hit ellenweorc æfnan scolde', 'that wasn't the first time it had to perform a courageous deed', ll. 1463–64), and by alluding to the many earlier conflicts in which it was involved (ll. 1460–64).[16] Like the shield in the Exeter riddle, Hrunting is thus presented as a warrior with his own unique history; significantly however, unlike the shield it is Hrunting's longevity as an object that provides the basis for its personification, rather than the use of personification providing the impression that it has had a long history.

As a potentially short-lived object the shield did not support this kind of individuation. Due to the way it was used in combat the wooden shield board was 'likely to have been damaged in most serious encounters'.[17] Indirect evidence for repair indicates that when the slats that made up the board became damaged they were removed and replaced.[18] If the entire board was destroyed there was also the option of remounting the fittings onto a new board, in much the same way that modern archaeologists have remounted the fittings recovered from sites like Sutton Hoo.[19] Stephenson suggests thinking of the shield as an object that could have various 'incarnation[s]',[20] with boards being refitted regularly, not necessarily with the same type of wood, and with the possibility of warriors using entirely new boards each time they went into battle.[21] In this sense, the shield differed from metal weapons and armour insofar as the main part of it could be changed repeatedly and was in effect 'disposable'.[22] The shield thus lacked that stable physical core that forms the basis for the strong sense of identity we find among objects made from more durable materials.

Weapons and armour with long histories of their own were also important for what they offered societies depicted in heroic poetry. These objects provided individuals and groups with a sense of history they could literally grasp with their hands, a tangible connection to ancestors and legendary figures, a means by which a people could attire itself in a glorious and mythical past. This was not simply a convention within literature. The early eleventh-century will of Ætheling Æthelstan, for example, includes a bequest of several swords. The name of one sword's former owner indicates that Æthelstan was bequeathing one sword he believed to be over two hundred years old: 'ic geann Eadmunde minon breðer þæs swurdes þe Offa cyng ahte' ('I grant to Edmund my brother the sword which belonged to King Offa').[23] Presumably this sword belonged to a number of people since it belonged to the Mercian king, but Æthelstan still regards it as Offa's weapon either because he is the most famous of the sword's previous

---

[15] Neil D. Isaacs, 'The Convention of Personification in *Beowulf*', in *Old English Poetry: Fifteen Essays*, ed. by Robert P. Creed (Providence, RI: Brown University Press, 1967), pp. 215–48 (p. 220).
[16] For a more detailed discussion of the personification of Hrunting see Isaacs, pp. 220–2.
[17] Dickinson and Härke, p. 56.
[18] On the evidence for shield repair see Dickinson and Härke, pp. 55–60.
[19] For a discussion of the Sutton Hoo shield see Rupert Bruce-Mitford, *The Sutton Hoo Ship-Burial*, 3 vols (London: British Museum, 1975–83), II (1978), 1–137.
[20] Stephenson, p. 40.
[21] pp. 54, 126.
[22] p. 40.
[23] Whitelock, p. 58.

owners or he is the one who had it made. Either way, it is evidence that the desire for physical connection with the past found in poetry is an expression of a broader cultural phenomenon.

War-gear, Commonality, and Community: Byrhtnoth at Maldon

Celebrating an object for its age is a celebration of its material value. A relatively consistent value-hierarchy existed throughout the Anglo-Saxon period, and it is perhaps unsurprising to discover that metal weapons and armour requiring great skill and labour to produce were considered more valuable than predominately wooden objects like the shield and spear. In the weapon burials of the early Anglo-Saxon period, the shield was the second most common piece of war-gear deposited in Anglo-Saxon graves. Evidence of shields is present in four out of ten weapon burials, less than the most common of all Anglo-Saxon weapons, the spear, which occurs in nine out of ten, but more than the sword, which appears in one out of ten.[24] Much less common was the deposition of helmets and mail-coats, which appear in only a 'handful of very rich burials'.[25] At the other end of the Anglo-Saxon period, in the half-century prior to the Norman Conquest, Cnut II produced a law-code stipulating the number and type of weapons and armour to be rendered as heriot. For the different ranks of English society the code effectively calls for a payment of two shields and two spears for every sword.[26] Depending on the rank, the code further calls for the number of helmets and mail-coats to be given at a rate either equivalent to or half that of swords. This ratio is reflected in a number of late Anglo-Saxon wills where there are generally fewer swords bequeathed in comparison to shields and spears, and where, in many cases, the number of shields and spears is exactly double that of swords.[27]

Shields and spears are more common in weapon heriots because, as Brooks notes, this combination was the basic battlefield equipment of all warriors.[28] The free man was armed with just a shield and spear; warriors of higher rank would additionally have had swords, helmets, and mail-coats.[29] The possession of metal weapons and armour was thus a symbol of wealth. Indeed, among the weapon sets found in early weapon burials, the combination of sword, shield, and spear is relatively rare, and found in only one in twenty-five burials, whereas the combination of shield and spear is found in one in four.[30] In poetry, emphasising specific kinds of weapons and armour creates a particular impression about the world of the poem and its characters. In *Beowulf*, celebrating the history of swords, helmets, and mail-coats evokes a rarefied world of affluence and privilege. In a poem like *The Battle of Maldon*, calling attention to different weapons at different times can have a narrower function, and can say something about a character's relationship to those around him:

---

[24] Heinrich Härke, ' "Warrior Graves?" The Background of the Anglo-Saxon Burial Rite', *Past and Present*, 126 (1990), 22–43 (p. 34); Dickinson and Härke, p. 67.

[25] Härke, pp. 25–26.

[26] Felix Liebermann, *Die Gesetze Der Angelsachsen*, 3 vols (Halle: Max Niemeyer, 1903-16), I (1903), 356–60; Ryan Lavelle, *Alfred's Wars: Sources and Interpretations of Anglo-Saxon Warfare in the Viking Age* (Woodbridge: Boydell, 2010), pp. 115–6; see also Rosemary J. Cramp, '*Beowulf* and Archaeology', *Medieval Archaeology*, 1 (1957), 57–77 (p. 60).

[27] See, for example, Whitelock, pp. 2, 26, 30, 42, 54, 80.

[28] Nicholas Brooks, 'Arms, Status, and Warfare in Late-Saxon England', in *Communities and Warfare 700-1400*, ed. by Nicholas Brooks (London and Rio Grande: Hambledon, 2000), pp. 138–61 (p. 141).

[29] The heriot of a wealthy man would include the basic equipment for fully-armed warriors and their attendants; the latter would carry just a shield and spear (Brooks, pp. 144–47).

[30] Härke, p. 34.

Byrhtnoð maþelode,   bord hafenode,
wand wacne æsc,   wordum mælde,
yrre and anræd   ageaf him andsware:
'Gehyrst þu, sælida,   hwæt þis folc segeð?
Hi willað eow to gafole   garas syllan,
ættrynne ord   and ealde swurd,
þa heregeatu   þe eow æt hilde ne deah.'
(ll. 42–8)

Byrhtnoth spoke, raised his shield, waved his slender ash spear, declared with words, angry and resolute, answered him: 'Do you hear, seafarer, what this people says? They will give you spears as tribute, the deadly point, and old swords, that war-gear which will be of no use to you at battle.'

Eode þa gesyrwed   secg to þam eorle;
he wolde þæs beornes   beagas gefecgan,
reaf and hringas   and gerenod swurd.
þa Byrhtnoð bræd   bill of sceðe,
brad and bruneccg,   and on þa byrnan sloh.
To raþe hine gelette   lidmanna sum,
þa he þæs eorles   earm amyrde.
Feoll þa to foldan   fealohilte swurd;
ne mihte he gehealdan   heardne mece,
wæpnes wealdan.
(ll. 159–68)

Then an armed warrior went to that nobleman; he wanted to carry off the man's rings, treasures, armour, and decorated sword. Byrhtnoth then drew his sword, broad and bright-edged and struck at the mail-coat. Too soon a Viking hindered him when he wounded the nobleman's arm. The gold-hilted sword then fell to the earth; he could not hold the hard blade, wield the weapon.

In general, *The Battle of Maldon* reflects the hierarchy of weapons discussed above. In a literary analogue to the early archaeological evidence, references to spears in this poem occur most often, followed by references to shields, then swords.[31] The above passages in particular, taken together, identify Byrhtnoth as belonging to the elite of English society by depicting him as someone who could afford to carry a sword, shield, and spear. In the two speeches given by Byrhtnoth in this poem, the first to the Viking messenger (ll. 45–61) and the second to God (ll. 173–80), the choice of weapon takes on a further thematic significance in reinforcing the way Byrhtnoth chooses to identify himself on both occasions. In the first passage, Byrhtnoth's brandishing of the most common pairing of Anglo-Saxon weapons and armour underlines his complete identification with the rest of the Essex *fyrd*, who are likely to have been carrying a similar combination, and to whom he refers on a number of occasions in terms that make no distinction between ranks (l. 45, 'þis folc'; l. 56, 'urum sceattum'; l. 57, 'urne eard'; l. 61, 'we'). Similarly, while Byrhtnoth's later use of a sword is to be expected of a wealthy Anglo-Saxon warrior, it takes place after the narrative focus has shifted onto him and immediately prior to his short final speech in which he offers what is uniquely his (i.e.

---

[31] Spear: 28 references (*æsc*, *æscholt*, *daroð*, *franca*, *gar*, *ord* (as spear), *spere*, *wælspere*); shield: 17 references (*bord*, *lind*, *rand*, *scyld*); sword: 12 references (*bill*, *ecg*, *iren*, *mece*, *swurd*). Other weapons and armour mentioned are mail-coat: 4 references (*byrne*, *hringloca*); arrow: 2 references (*flan*).

his soul) to God. Here he is alone, giving an account of his behaviour as a Christian leader. He refers to himself (*ic/min(um)*) six times in the space of eight lines,[32] something he does only three times in his seventeen-line speech to the Viking messenger.[33] This second passage is concerned with Byrhtnoth alone, apart from the group, and associates material exclusivity with spiritual exclusivity; it represents a change from the inclusiveness of his first speech where the use of shield and spear emphasise Byrhtnoth's connection to those around him.

The shield and social relationships

In Old English poetry metal weapons and armour were very much associated with the unique, the individual, the exclusive in Anglo-Saxon culture. As potentially long-lived objects with their own unique histories these items could both acquire names of their own and provide a link to famous names from earlier times. The example of Byrhtnoth demonstrates that the shield not only lacked these associations, but it was also much more likely to be associated with the opposite of this — that which is common, undifferentiated, unnamed. While the perishability of the shield meant that it was not used to discuss the relationship between present and past, in depictions of shield-use the shield did offer poets a means of discussing existing social relationships, both their importance and how they can be compromised. Indeed, even in the one instance from Old English poetry where the shield in question is not the common wooden shield, the importance of social relationships is a key theme.

Beowulf's iron shield is in one sense all about Beowulf. He orders it made because against the dragon

>   wisse he gearwe
> þæt him holtwudu   helpan ne meahte,
> lind wið lige
> (ll. 2339–41)
>
> he knew well that wood couldn't help him, linden-wood against flame.

Beowulf's decision to arm himself with equipment suited to the task is a product of a wisdom born out of a long history fighting monsters that is as peculiar to Beowulf as the object itself. He demonstrates a foresight here which will, with his death, be lost to the Geats, and which can be contrasted with the impetuousness of the young retainer Wiglaf, who, moved by the thought of Beowulf suffering, is unable to restrain himself ('ne mihte ða forhabban', l. 2609); he snatches up his own wooden shield and rushes into the dragon's barrow only to meet the fate that Beowulf has been careful to avoid:

>   Lig yðum for;
> born bord wið rond.   Byrne ne meahte
> geongum garwigan   geoce gefremman,
> ac se maga geonga   under his mæges scyld
> elne geeode,   þa his agen wæs
> gledum forgrunden
> (ll. 2672–77)
>
> Fire advanced in waves; the shield was burned up to the boss. The mail-coat could not help the young warrior, provide aid, but the young kinsman went with courage under his kinsman's shield when his own was consumed by flames.

[32] ll. 173, 174, 175, 176, 177, 179.
[33] ll. 51, 53, 55.

Although Beowulf uses a shield against the dragon specifically to meet the threat it poses, it is worth noting that of all Beowulf's fights, this is the only one in which he both uses a shield and fights with a companion.[34] While the shield itself is materially unique, the enduring images of the final part of the dragon fight do not emphasise what is distinctive about Beowulf or his shield, but rather what he shares with that companion. After his sword Nægling breaks (l. 2680) and he becomes pinned by the dragon, Wiglaf, ignoring the threat to himself, strikes the dragon so that the flames abate, allowing Beowulf time to cut into the underside of the creature and kill it. The passage concludes with an explanation of what it was that killed the creature:

> Feond gefyldan — ferh ellen wræc —
> ond hi hyne þa begen   abroten hæfdon,
> sibæðelingas.
> (ll. 2706–8)
>
> They killed the enemy — courage drove out life — and they both had killed it, the related nobles.

Wiglaf may not possess Beowulf's practical knowledge in dealing with monsters but he does possess his courage and sense of duty. The recognition here that it was a shared virtue that killed the dragon leads Irving to argue that the credit for the dragon's death should not go to either or even to both men, but rather to the relationship that exists between them:

> What kills the dragon? Neither one of the two heroes as individuals, but the relationship between these two *sibæðelingas* almost as a hypostatized entity in itself, the reality of heroic comradeship, affectionate loyalty, and self-sacrificing courage.[35]

If the dragon's death is achieved through the relationship that exists between the lord and his retainer, then Beowulf's shield protects that relationship, and provides the safe physical space from which both men strike out at the creature.

The use of the shield as a form of shared protection, while it arises due to Wiglaf's lack of experience and occurs in a fantastic context, resonates with more general imagery of shields in Old English poetry, in particular the depictions of shield-use on the Anglo-Saxon battlefield. In accounts of large scale encounters the shield is perhaps the only weapon or piece of armour that is described being used cooperatively. Poets often note the use of the 'shield-wall', a close-order battle formation employed by the English and their enemies during the period. As the name suggests, the shield-wall was a continuous barrier created by the front rank of warriors arranging their shields into a line.[36] The metaphors for the shield-wall

---

[34] It might perhaps be expected that Beowulf would not use a shield in the fights that begin or take place entirely in water (Grendel's mother; the sea-monsters during the swimming contest against Breca), although in both he does use sword and mail-coat. In the two fights that take place on dry land (Grendel, Dæghrefn) he dispatches his enemies using no weapons at all; he scorns the use of sword and shield before combat with Grendel (ll. 677–87) and boasts about using only his hands to kill Dæghrefn (ll. 2497–509).

[35] Edward B. Irving Jr., *A Reading of Beowulf* (New Haven: Yale University Press, 1968), p. 163.

[36] As Pollington notes (p. 215), there is no consensus on the precise structure of the shield-wall, whether it was a relatively loose arrangement with warriors simply raising their shields to a similar position, or whether it was a much tighter formation, with shields held edge to edge or even overlapped. There appears to be no evidence in Old English poetry to support either view. Bosworth and Toller note references to shields being held edge to edge (lit. 'shield against shield', 'skjǫldr við skjǫld') in an account of the Battle of Stamford Bridge in the Old Norse *Haralds saga harðráða*: Joseph Bosworth, and T. Northcote Toller, *An Anglo-Saxon Dictionary* (Oxford: Clarendon, 1898) s.v. *scildburh* (hereafter BT). Another suggestion is that the shield-wall began as a tight structure but loosened as the sides came together to allow room for weapons to be used more freely: Underwood, p. 90; Pollington, pp. 215–16).

in Old English poetry find various ways of describing the structure; it is not only a wall of shields (*bordweall*, *Beowulf*, l. 2980; *The Battle of Brunanburh*, l. 5; *The Battle of Maldon*, l. 277; *scildweall*, *Beowulf*, l. 3118), but also an enclosing hedge[37] (*wihaga*, *The Battle of Maldon*, l. 102; *bordhaga*, *Elene*, l. 652), and a fortress (*scildburh*, *Judith*, l. 304; *The Battle of Maldon*, l. 242). In Old Norse kennings, the ground-words suggested by Snorri Sturluson in *Skáldskaparmál* for the shield-wall offer more developed images of a three-dimensional protective space: 'skjaldborgin er kǫlluð hǫll ok ræfr, veggr ok golf' ('the shield-wall is called hall and roof, wall and floor').[38] Taken literally, these Old Norse terms more appropriately describe the kind of protection afforded by the Roman *testudo*, the protective 'box' created by the wall of legionaries shields held to the front, sides, and the 'roof of overlapping shields'[39] held above the head. While Old English poetry contains nothing comparable to the language of *Skáldskaparmál*, the sense of enclosure implied in both -*haga* and -*burh* suggests that the Anglo-Saxons did consider the shield-wall as something more than a simple barrier. Indeed, in a metaphorical sense, the shield-wall was a kind of hall; on the battlefield it served a number of the same functions as the hall and was often presented in similar terms.

Heall on wælstowe: the shield-wall in *The Battle of Maldon*

As a protected social space, the hall in Old English poetry represents the positive element in a binary opposition between two very different environments. Hume, for example, describes the hall as a 'circle of light and peace enclosed by darkness, discomfort and danger'.[40] Using similar language, Neville calls it an 'enclosure within which light, order, value and safety prevail', to be distinguished from the natural world where 'darkness, chaos and danger rage'.[41] The hall was the centre of communal life 'where the vital and affectionate interchanges of social solidarity, the giving and taking of rewards and service, responsibility and gratitude' were carried on.[42] To the extent that the physical structure could be identified with the society that built and inhabited it, the hall was, as Magennis notes, an image of the community itself.[43]

In a poem like *Beowulf*, the narrative is driven by external threats to the poem's two great halls, to Heorot and Beowulf's hall in Geatland. However, in both cases the more insidious threat to what the hall represents does not come from outside, but from within. In Denmark, for example, Grendel's attacks against Heorot have over time led not only to the diminishment of Hrothgar's warrior-band ('wigheap gewanod', l. 477), but also to a gradual collapse of Danish morale, as eventually warriors start to abandon the hall and choose their own personal safety over the safety of the symbolic centre of their society:

---

[37] Although -*haga* in the compounds *bordhaga* and *wihaga* can be translated simply as 'hedge' (BT, s.v. *bordhaga*; Scragg, p. 75) the noun *haga* carries a sense of 'enclosure'. BT translate it as 'a place fenced in, an enclosure, a haw, a dwelling in a town.' 'Haw' is a now-obsolete term meaning 'a hedge or encompassing fence' and, by extension, 'a piece of ground enclosed or fenced in' (*OED*).

[38] Snorri Sturluson, *Edda: Skáldskaparmál*, ed. by Anthony Faulkes, 2 vols (London: Viking Society For Northern Research, 1998), I 49.

[39] Adrian Goldsworthy, *The Complete Roman Army* (London: Thames and Hudson, 2003), p. 194.

[40] Kathryn Hume, 'The Concept of the Hall in Old English Poetry', *Anglo-Saxon England*, 3 (1974), pp. 63–74 (p. 64).

[41] Jennifer Neville, *Representations of the Natural World in Old English Poetry* (Cambridge: Cambridge University Press, 1999), p. 57.

[42] Edward B. Irving Jr., *Rereading Beowulf* (Philadelphia: University of Pennsylvania Press, 1989), p. 137.

[43] Hugh Magennis, *Images of Community in Old English Poetry*, Cambridge Studies in Anglo-Saxon England, 18 (Cambridge: Cambridge University Press, 1996), pp. 35–40.

> þa wæs eaðfynde   þe him elles hwær
> gerumlicor   ræste sohte,
> bed æfter burum
> (ll. 138–40)
>
> then it was easy to find the one who sought a resting-place, a bed elsewhere, further away among the dwellings

This process continues until finally Heorot 'idel stod' ('stood idle', l. 138). This abandonment of the communal centre of Danish life is also the abandonment of the idea of community itself. A similar fate befalls the Geats following the dragon's attack on Beowulf's hall. When Beowulf goes to avenge the attack, it is made clear that he does not have a 'group of close companions' ('heape handgesteallan', l. 2596) to protect him; these have 'fled to the forest to protect their lives' ('hy on holt bugon, | ealdre burgan', ll. 2598–99), leaving only Wiglaf to help him. In both cases the external threats to the hall have led to what are arguably greater threats to the communities concerned as members of the group cease to behave according to the shared system of values that hold their society together. By placing these communities under psychological pressure the attacks have revealed points of weakness within them and discovered their potential for disintegration.

The symbolism of the shield-wall in Old English poetry is not as rich as that of the hall but the structure is depicted in a similar way. It too is a barrier that protects those inside from external danger, and in that sense it is also part of a binary opposition between two very different environments. In his examination of how the structure partitions physical space on the battlefield, Pollington notes an analogous, if less dramatic, contrast between both sides of the shield-wall:[44]

us	:	them
behind the shieldwall	:	beyond the shieldwall
defensive behaviour	:	threatening behaviour
solidarity	:	hostility

To be effective the shield-wall relied on warriors being conscious that they were fighting as part of a group, and that their welfare relied on the welfare of those around them. Abels, for instance, notes that the strength of a shield-wall lay in 'unit cohesion, and this in turn depended upon the morale of the troops. Once morale was broken the battle was lost'.[45] In Old English poetry the maintenance of the shield-wall represents the collective will to fight; its destruction often signifies the decision point of a battle. In *Elene*, the breach of the Huns' 'shield barrier' ('bræcon bordhreðan', l. 122) also marks the end of their resistance to the Romans; in *Judith* the sheering of the shield-wall ('scildburh scæron', l. 304) leads to the rout of the Assyrians at the hands of the Hebrew army; in *The Battle of Brunanburh*, the celebration of King Æthelstan's victory begins with the claim that he and Eadmund Ætheling clove the shield-wall ('bordweal clufan', l. 5).

In some poems the shield-wall represents the same image of community that the hall represents in *Beowulf*. In *The Battle of Maldon*, for example, the shield-wall is central to the poem's thematic concerns, and its destruction is presented in terms of individuals abandoning

---

[44] Pollington, p. 202 n. 8.
[45] Richard Abels, 'English Tactics, Strategy and Military Organization in the Late Tenth Century', in *The Battle of*

both the community and the sense of community that the structure symbolises. Immediately after he decides to cede the river crossing, Byrhtnoth

>   mid bordum het
> wyrcan þone wihagan   and þæt werod healdan
> fæste wið feondum
> (ll. 101–3)
>
> ordered the construction of a shield-wall with shields and that the company hold fast against the enemy

Once the shield-wall is established, the risk to the welfare of the group comes less from the external threat posed by the Vikings than the handful of warriors who put their own interests over those of the community. The turning point of the battle in this poem is the flight of Godric and his brothers, who are mistaken for Byrhtnoth leaving the field on horseback. When Offa complains about their cowardice, he makes a direct connection between the unity of the group and the integrity of the shield-wall:

>   Us Godric hæfð,
> earh Oddan bearn,   ealle beswicene.
> Wende þæs formoni man,   þa he on meare rad,
> on wlancan þam wicge,   þæt wære hit ure hlaford;
> forþan wearð her on felda   folc totwæmed,
> scyldburh tobrocen.
> (ll. 237–42)
>
> Godric, wretched Odda's son, has betrayed us all. Many men believed when he rode off on the horse proud from war, that it was our lord. Therefore the people became divided here in the field, the shield-wall broken.

The destruction of the shield-wall is presented here as a fracturing of social bonds, with the collective unity of the *fyrd* being destroyed by the selfishness of Godric and his brothers. It is a violation of two statements that stand adjacent in *Maxims II* and which this incident suggests are related: 'fyrd sceal ætsomne, | tirfæstra getrum. Treow sceal on eorle' ('the army must be together, the troop of men set on glory. There must be loyalty in the man', ll. 31–32).

 In *The Battle of Maldon* the collapse of the shield-wall does not signal the end of English resistance. Those who are left find themselves in the same position as Wiglaf, conscious that they are no longer acting as part of a group, but as individuals struggling with an external enemy out of a sense of duty to their lord. In these circumstances, the hall becomes a point of reference for the ideal of social unity. Ælfwine, for example, in a speech intended to rally those around him, explicitly recalls the hall and what was said there:

> Gemunan þa mæla   þe we oft æt meodo spræcon,
> þonne we on bence   beot ahofon,
> hæleð on healle,   ymbe heard gewinn;
> nu mæg cunnian   hwa cene sy.
> (ll. 212–15)
>
> Let us remember the times that we often spoke at mead, when we on the bench raised boasts, heroes in the hall, about hard struggle; now we might know who is brave.

Here the image of the hall appears to take the place of the shield-wall that has been broken. However, these remarks actually seem to question whether the hall is really an authentic and

Maldon, AD 991, ed. by Donald Scragg (Oxford: Blackwell, 1991), pp. 143–55 (p. 149).

truthful image of community, and whether what is said there has any validity in the real world. Ælfwine's remarks should perhaps be read in conjunction with the scepticism of Offa who warns that earlier 'on þam meþelstede' ('in the meeting place', l. 199), 'manega spræcon | þe eft æt þearfe þolian noldon' ('many spoke boldly who afterward would not endure at a time of need', ll. 198–201). This concern about the relevance of words uttered in the hall is reflective of a deeper cultural concern evident in several other poems. In *Beowulf*, Wiglaf tries unsuccessfully to encourage his companions to help Beowulf by reminding them of promises made in the 'biorsele' ('beer-hall', l. 2635), while *Vainglory* condemns outright the making of proud boast-speeches in the hall, saying that there are too many ('sindan to monige', l. 25) who engage in it. In a sense, therefore, because the shield-wall is established on the battlefield, it arguably represents a truer test of a warrior's commitment to the welfare of the group. The danger that threatens it is more immediate than that which faces the hall and the warriors who stand in the front rank literally have the security of the community in their hands.

Red Sea shield-walls: the Old English *Exodus*

One other poem from the corpus that depicts the shield-wall as a hall-like structure is the Old English *Exodus*. This poem appears to contain two references to metaphorical shield-walls. The first occurs when Moses addresses the Israelites gathered upon the shore of the Red Sea. He describes his own actions as he strikes the waters and they part; he then urges the Israelites to hurry across and take the opportunity God has given them to escape the pursuing Egyptians:

> Ofest is selost
> þæt ge of feonda   fæðme weorðen,
> nu se agend   up arærde
> reade streamas   in randgebeorh.
> Syndon þa foreweallas   fægre gestepte,
> wrætlicu wægfaru,   oð wolcna hrof.
> (ll. 293–98)

> Haste is best so that you escape the grasp of enemies, now the Creator has raised up the Red Sea into a rampart/shield-wall. The walls are fairly erected up to the roof of the heavens, a wondrous track through the waves.

Later in the poem, with the Israelites safely on the far shore, the poet describes the coming together of the seas and the drowning of the Egyptians:

> Randbyrig wæron rofene,   rodor swipode
> meredeaða mæst,   modige swulton,
> cyningas on corðre,   cyre swiðrode
> sæs æt ende.   Wigbord scinon
> heah ofer hæleðum,   holmweall astah,
> merestream modig.
> (ll. 464–67)

> The ramparts/shield-walls of water were broken, the greatest of sea-deaths lashed the sky, the proud ones died, kings in a troop, their choice diminished, at the seas end. The war-shields shone, high over the warriors, the wall of sea-water rose up, the raging sea waters.

The translations of 'randgebeorh' and 'randbyrig' (sing. *randburh*; cf. *scildburh*) given here are those suggested by Lucas and Irving respectively.[46] As is evident, there is no consistent interpretation of either term, with editors and critics split on whether the poet is referring specifically to the Red Sea being raised up into a metaphorical shield-wall, or whether the terms refers more generally to the form of the structural boundary of water. Tolkien, like Lucas, does not read *randgebeorh* as a reference to shields, preferring 'marginal protection'; he translates 'randbyrig wæron rofene' in a similar way: 'the ramparts on either margin were broken'.[47] Clark Hall, by contrast, offers 'shield-wall of waves' for *randbyrig* and 'protecting shield of waves' for *randgebeorh*.[48] Roberta Frank suggests 'shield-walls' for *randbyrig* and 'shield-enclosure' for *randgebeorh*.[49] Finally, Bosworth and Toller offer 'a protection such as that afforded by a shield' for *randgebeorh* but are uncertain of *randbyrig*, asking: 'are the walls formed by the water compared to the arrangement of the line of battle when the shields overlapped?'[50]

The above discussion suggests that the answer to Bosworth and Toller's question is 'yes' and that Irving is correct in reading both *randgebeorh* and *randbyrig* as references to a metaphorical shield-wall of water erected by God to aid the fleeing Israelites. Frank rightly notes the semantic distinction between -*gebeorh* ('a defence, protection, safety, refuge') and -*burh* ('a fortified place, fortress, castle, walled town, dwelling surrounded by a wall or rampart of earth),[51] but the broader associations that the shield-wall had in Old English poetry provide a good basis for believing that a conection is being made here between the structure God uses to protect the faithful and the structure Anglo-Saxons used to defend themselves on the battlefield. Like the hall and the literal shield-wall, two hugely different environments are kept apart by this metaphorical shield-wall — the community of Israelites is protected and safe on one side, danger and destruction await on the other. Such a reading seems to be complemented by the references to war-shields shining above the heads of the warriors as the ramparts of water collapse, which, developing the shield-wall metaphor could be a reference to the reflections from the wave-tips as they crest and come down. These passages are perhaps an example of what Tolkien himself describes as the 'adaptation of English/Germanic atmosphere to biblical narrative',[52] in which an indigenous idiom is used to convey an exotic image; in this case a shield-wall holds back the waters of the Red Sea to create a defensive space for the Israelites to pass through, in the same way that the shield-wall in *The Battle of Maldon* resists the Viking tide.

The imagery of *Exodus*, perhaps more forcefully than *The Battle of Maldon*, highlights the temporariness of the shield-wall. In *Exodus*, its existence depends upon the will of God and when that changes the structure collapses; in *The Battle of Maldon* the integrity of

---

[46] *Exodus*, ed. by Peter J. Lucas (Exeter: University of Exeter Press, 1994); *The Old English Exodus*, ed. by Edward B. Irving Jr. (New Haven: Yale University Press, 1953).

[47] *The Old English Exodus: Text, Translation, and Commentary by J.R.R. Tolkien*, ed. by Joan Turville-Petre (Oxford: Clarendon, 1981), pp. 61, 71.

[48] J.R. Clark Hall, *A Concise Anglo-Saxon Dictionary*, 4th edn (Toronto: University of Toronto Press, 1960), s.v. *randburg, randgebeorh*.

[49] Roberta Frank, 'What Kind of Poetry Is *Exodus*?', in *Germania: Comparative Studies in the Old Germanic Languages and Literatures*, ed. by Daniel G. Calder and T. Craig Christy (Woodbridge: Brewer, 1988), pp. 191–205 (p. 199).

[50] BT, s.v. *randgebeorh, randburg*.

[51] BT, s.v. *gebeorh, burh*.

[52] Turville-Petre, p. 39.

the shield-wall relies upon the will of individuals which, as the actions of Godric and his brothers demonstrate, is also subject to change. For warriors this change was a product of human weakness, a moral fragility that mirrored the material fragility of the shield itself. The sense in the Exeter riddle that a shield will eventually collapse under the blows of swords is echoed in the imagery of the shield-wall by the fear that the shield-bearer might undergo an equally disastrous moral collapse, a failure that would have dire consequences for the entire community.

Conclusion: *bitað in burgum*

In a literary culture that valued weapons and armour for their longevity, the Anglo-Saxon shield was not an object celebrated by poets. It was constructed largely from cheap, perishable materials and used with an expectation that it would be damaged or destroyed. Unlike metal weapons and armour, the shield lacked the constancy of form that provided the basis for some objects to develop an identity of their own. Not only was it rarely of interest itself, in societies where physical objects provided a means for the past to live on in the present, the shield offered little by way of connection to what had gone before.

Yet precisely because of its commonness and fragility the shield did offer a means for poets to talk about other kinds of connections. The shield was the piece of Anglo-Saxon war-gear that best captured the importance of the reciprocal relationship between the community and the individual warrior. Depictions of the shield provide a counterweight to the focus on heroic individualism that marks so much Old English poetry and which is embodied by objects like swords, helmets, and mail-coats that are celebrated for their uniqueness. While the community needed the courage of individuals to protect and sustain it, there were also occasions when it was necessary for the community to act together to protect the individual. Whether in struggles against legendary creatures or in mass engagements on the battlefield, using an object that could be used cooperatively entailed a moral choice about the value of cooperation, and whether the survival of the group was more important than the survival of the individual. Beowulf and Wiglaf offer one answer, Godric and his brothers offer another.

In *Beowulf*, the name of the Danish patriarch Scyld Scefing alludes to his role as protector of his people.[53] In a sense, though, every Anglo-Saxon who carried a shield into combat bore a responsibility for the welfare of others. The shield in the Exeter riddle says that in battle the weapons of his enemies 'bite in the strongholds' ('bitað in burgum)'; the use of *burh* here suggests that this particular shield was actually one that was used in the shield-wall (*scyld-/rand-burh*). In battle it protected the individual warrior as the warrior worked with those around him to maintain the structure of the shield-wall, the symbol of the community on the battlefield. The Exeter shield thus not only embodied the warrior's fragility, it also embodied the fragility of the social group to which the warrior belonged.

---

[53] Fulk, Bjork and Niles, p. 111.

Kinsmen Before Christ, Part I

The Latin Transmission

P. S. Langeslag[1]

Introduction

In some of the more widely read genres of early medieval literature, source studies are commonly approached from a text-static perspective in which one editorially codified text is compared to another. While this approach has led to many perfectly valid intertextual connections, it tends to yield deceptively direct lines of transmission. It sidesteps such complexities as a plurality of redactions on the part of the source text or a multi-stage, multi-author development of the target text. This situation is not helped by the fact that much of the early vernacular poetry, for instance, survives in single manuscript witnesses, leaving critics with no positive data on which to base a more nuanced account of a work's composition and development.

This classical literary model of direct derivation contrasts with the stemmatic reconstruction carried out by the text-critical editor faced with the task of uncovering a single work's transmission history in the face of many witnesses. Investigations of this kind, though often aimed at finding a single best text, award transmission the focal primacy and treat at least the *form* of a text as fluid: each new transcript is likely to introduce small corruptions or innovations in spelling, diction, and syntax. On the basis of such variation, the stemmatic method produces a treelike overview of influences and divergences, yielding a great deal of insight into the development of the text and differences between sibling branches.

A limitation of the text-critical model of stemmatics is its inability to account for intertextual dissemination. Since the basic unit of this approach is the whole text, the analysis cannot incorporate cognate passages appearing in other texts. Editors will note such connections in their commentary if they are sufficiently striking, but a systematic consideration of motifs and arguments appearing in other works is beyond the scope of the text's stemmatic analysis.

---

[1] This article and its sequel, P. S. Langeslag, 'Kinsmen Before Christ. Part II: The Anglo-Saxon Transmission', *Leeds Studies in English*, 46 (forthcoming), have profited tremendously from the insights of Rob Getz and Stephen

P. S. Langeslag

To do justice to the intertextual spread of shorter passages, one has to abandon the text as a basic unit and acknowledge that motifs, arguments, and sections within a work may travel horizontally between texts and redactions — that the structural *content* of a text, too, is fluid, and that these elements may be added, shed, or changed as the compiler sees fit. In a process of intertextual exchange, each able scribe in the chain of transmission is at liberty not only to compare redactions of a passage and choose the better one, but indeed to supply a more satisfying formulation of the same idea found in a different work or in his approximate recollection of such a work, as well as to interpolate new material from a preexisting source or from his own imagination.

The intertextual recombination of passages was common practice in the scriptoria that produced the many Latin and vernacular homilies extant from the early Middle Ages. In a genre of this sort, characterised by works that are composite in nature and whose structures are punctuated by numerous recognisable topoi, the stemmatic method may usefully be applied at the local level of the individual motif in order to uncover routes of intertextual influence and attain greater horizontal insight into a motif's dissemination. An investigation of this nature will be demonstrated below with reference to a homiletic topos described elsewhere as 'no aid to kin'.[2] This article seeks to uncover how this motif reached the Old English homiletic tradition, where it is especially prevalent. Its dissemination within the Anglo-Saxon tradition will be taken up in the next volume of this journal.

The Old English form of the theme may be exemplified by its attestation in the so-called Macarius homily (hereafter *HomU 55*):[3]

> Ne mæg þær þonne gefultmian se fæder þæm suna, ne se suna þæm fæder, ac sceal þonne anra gehwilc æfter his agenum gewyrhtum beon demed. (ll. 27–9)
>
> ('A father will then not be able to help his son there, nor a son his father, but each will then be judged according to his own works.')

Generic though it may sound, this sentence represents a specific motif with a limited dissemination, whose core consists of (1) one kinsman being unable or unwilling to help another in (2) an eschatological setting referenced by way of (3) a deictic word or phrase (in *HomU 55* the locative adverb *þær*).[4] Apart from this passage in Cambridge, Corpus Christi College MS 201, these specifics are repeated in a range of further homiletic texts and redactions. At least eight distinct Old English texts contain the full motif, while more than a dozen answer to a looser definition, including a late text whose language is more appropriately classified as early Middle English.[5] Meanwhile, the High German tradition turns up a small

---

Pelle. I am grateful also to the staff of the e-codices project, who gave me advance access to their facsimile of Einsiedeln, Stiftsbibliothek MS 199 (638).

[2] Patrizia Lendinara, '"frater non redimit, redimet homo...": A Homiletic Motif and its Variants in Old English', in *Early Medieval English Texts and Interpretations: Studies Presented to Donald G. Scragg*, ed. by Elaine Treharne and Susan Rosser, Medieval and Renaissance Texts and Studies, 252 (Tempe, AZ: ACMRS, 2002), pp. 67–80.

[3] *Dictionary of Old English* short titles will be employed throughout this paper to refer to Old English texts. For *HomU 55* I follow *Theodulfi Capitula in England: Die altenglischen Übersetzungen, zusammen mit dem lateinischen Text*, ed. by Hans Sauer, Münchener Universitäts-Schriften: Texte und Untersuchungen zur englischen Philologie, 8 (Munich: Fink, 1978), pp. 411–16.

[4] The eschatological use of *þær* is otherwise especially common in descriptions of heaven, as described in Hildegard L. C. Tristram, 'Stock Descriptions of Heaven and Hell in Old English Prose and Poetry', *Neuphilologische Mitteilungen*, 79 (1978), 102–13 (pp. 102–05).

[5] The motif's presence in Anglo-Saxon homiletics was first noted in Gustav Grau, *Quellen und Verwandtschaften der älteren germanischen Darstellungen des jüngsten Gerichtes*, Studien zur englischen Philologie, 31 (Halle:

number of attestations with varying degrees of divergence from the classical pattern. The closest match of this group is concisely contained in the Old High German *Muspilli* (c. 830):[6]

> 57   Dar ni mac denne mak andremo   helfan uora demo muspille.[7]

('There one kinsman will not then be able to help another before the *muspilli*.')

A less exact Old High German parallel has been identified in Otfrid's *Evangelienbuch* (863×71),[8] and a further echo may be found in a Middle High German homily. All these Germanic occurrences of the motif will be printed and discussed in part two of this series. This first part seeks to document how the motif reached Germanic authors in the first place.

Nodes and Transmission

The motif has a biblical-prophetic ring to it, but no exact biblical parallel exists. Ziolkowski in his discussion of another, Latin attestation of the pattern[9] attributes it to Ezekiel 18:20:

> Anima quae peccaverit ipsa morietur. Filius non portabit iniquitatem patris et pater non portabit iniquitatem filii.[10]

> ('The soul that sins will itself die. A son will not bear the iniquity of his father and a father will not bear the iniquity of his son.')

This is arguably the closest biblical analogue to the motif as defined above, but it is no exact match. *Iniquitatem portare* ('to bear [someone else's] iniquity') could certainly be semantically relaxed into *helfan/gefultumian* ('help') in transmission, but since there are multiple vernacular instances that bear witness to this development, a closer, shared Latin model should be presumed in the first instance. Moreover, the setting here is legal-theocratic rather than eschatological. The verse furthermore lacks a deictic specification *ibi/ubi*, and finally there is an inversion of the order in which father and son are mentioned.

Other Bible passages that may be considered include the following:

> Non occidentur patres pro filiis, nec filii pro patribus, sed unusquisque pro suo peccato morietur. (Dt 24:16)

Niemeyer, 1908), pp. 240–42. Many individual instances not discussed by Grau have been independently identified by Lendinara. For a full list of attestations, see Langeslag, 'Kinsmen Before Christ II' and its Appendix 1.

[6] For the dating of *Muspilli* see Wolfgang Golther, *Die deutsche Dichtung im Mittelalter: 800 bis 1500*, rev. edn (Wiesbaden: Marix, 2005), p. 37; Herbert Penzl, *Althochdeutsch: Eine Einführung in Dialekte und Vorgeschichte*, Germanistische Lehrbuchsammlung, 7 (Bern: Lang, 1986), §162.2. The *Muspilli* connection too was first noted in Grau, pp. 240–42.

[7] 'Muspilli', ed. by Wilhelm Braune, in *Althochdeutsches Lesebuch*, 17th edn rev. by Karl Helm and Ernst A. Ebbinghaus (Tübingen: Niemeyer, 1994), pp. 86–89.

[8] Otfrid's participation in the motif is mentioned in Lendinara (p. 75); the correspondence between Otfrid and *Muspilli* was recognised by such early scholars as Piper (*Otfrids 'Evangelienbuch'*, ed. by Paul Piper, 2nd edn, 2 vols (Freiburg and Tübingen: Mohr, 1882–87), I, notes to V. 19, ll. 47–50). For the dating, see Linda Archibald, 'Otfrid of Weissenburg', in *German Literature of the Early Middle Ages*, ed. by Brian Murdoch (Rochester, NY: Camden House, 2004), pp. 139–56 (p. 139).

[9] *The Cambridge Songs (Carmina Cantabrigiensa)*, ed. and trans. by Jan M. Ziolkowski, Garland Library of Medieval Literature, A66 (New York and London: Garland, 1994), p. 227, note to stanza 20, ll. 3–4. The text in question is discussed below, pp. 43–45.

[10] All biblical citations are from *Biblia Sacra iuxta vulgatam versionem*, ed. by Robert Weber, 5th edn rev. by Roger

('Fathers will not perish on behalf of their sons, nor sons on behalf of their fathers, but each will die on account of his own sin.')

Qui confidunt in virtute sua, et in multitudine divitiarum suarum gloriantur, frater non redimit. Redimet homo? Non dabit Deo placationem suam et pretium redemptionis animae suae. (Ps 48:7–9 *iuxta* LXX)

('Those who rely on their strength, and glory in the abundance of their riches, a brother does not redeem. Will man redeem? He will not appease God and pay him the price of the redemption of his soul.')[11]

The first passage concerns punishment on account of sin, but here too the context is legal-theocratic rather than eschatological. The Psalm does reference death and hell in its theme of the transience of worldly riches, and it uses a verb with a beneficial sense approximating 'help'. Accordingly, Lendinara considers it 'likely' that several of the Old English attestations derive the motif directly from this verse.[12] This is surely a hasty conclusion: the Psalm in any translation is rather a remote approximation of the motif, lacking as it does even the elements of father and son, the most persistent two agents in the Old English subset of the tradition. Moreover, the deictic specification is absent from all three biblical passages. Of course, biblical matter may well have inspired the first inception of the motif; the verses from Deuteronomy and Ezekiel are especially likely to have informed it, along with turns of phrase from further scriptural passages.[13] However, the form of the motif as here defined is not found in Scripture, which must therefore be left out of the chain of transmission at this stage.[14]

The name that has most persistently been associated with the kinsmen motif is that of Ephraem the Syrian, though the work of interest here is suspected merely to have circulated

---

Gryson (Stuttgart: Deutsche Bibelgesellschaft, 2007), with punctuation and capitalisation added according to context.

[11] One of the central difficulties in the Vulgate reading follows from a corruption proper to the text of the Septuagint. The above punctuation and translation serves grammaticality but fails to convey the intent of the ultimate Hebrew source, and it is questionable whether the Greek translator had this reading in mind. McClellan explains that the first finite verb in the sequence 'redimit redimet' in fact renders a Hebrew infinitive absolute like that translated by the ablative in *morte mori*, whose sense is not so much 'die (by means of) death' but rather 'surely die': W. H. McClellan, 'Obscurities in the Latin Psalter [VI]', *The Catholic Biblical Quarterly* 2.2 (April 1940), pp. 173–78 (pp. 176–77). Jerome had access to the Hebrew text or a grammatical intermediary: he rendered it more accurately in his translation from the Hebrew, which reads 'qui fiduciam habent in fortitudine sua, et in multitudine divitiarum suarum superbiunt; fratrem redimens non redimet vir, nec dabit Deo propitiationem pro eo, neque pretium redemptionis animae eorum' ('those who have confidence in their strength, and take pride in the abundance of their riches; a man will certainly not redeem his brother, nor will he appease God on his behalf, nor pay him the price of redemption of their souls.' The relative clause at the beginning of the quotation originally had an antecedent in verse 6, but the antecedent does not survive in the Latin versions.) The Vetus Latina tradition as represented by Sabatier's edition is a close match to Jerome's translation from the Septuagint: *Bibliorum sacrorum latinæ versiones antiquæ, seu vetus italica*, ed. by P[ierre] Sabatier, 3 vols (Rheims: Reginaldum Florentain, 1743–49). There are several further difficulties in the Psalm, which deserves a textual and reception study of its own. Lendinara, who considers the passage of influence on the English branch of the kinsmen motif, does not discuss the textual problems contained in the biblical sequence, nor does she offer a translation (Lendinara, pp. 77–78).

[12] Lendinara, pp. 73, 76–78.

[13] e.g. Is 9:19; Mt 10:21; Mc 13:12; Lc 21:16.

[14] The same is true of a series of extrabiblical texts pointed out to me by Stephen Pelle. Rather than pursue their relationship to the kinsman motif here, I will merely provide a few references: Pseudo-Ephraem, *Sermo de fine mundi*, ll. 55–59, ed. in Daniel Verhelst, 'Scarpsum de dictis Sancti Efrem prope fine mundi', in *Pascua mediaevalia: Studies voor Prof. Dr. J.M. de Smet*, ed. by R. Lievens, E. van Mingroot, and W. Verbeke (Leuven: Universitaire Pers Leuven, 1983), pp. 518–28 (ll. 55–59); Paulinus of Aquileia, *Liber exhortationis*, ch. 49,

under that name. Charles Wright has pointed out the close indebtedness of the opening section of *HomU 55* to the Ephraemic Latin homily *De paenitentia*,[15] itself a translation of a metrical Greek original that may not have had a Syriac model.[16] The Latin text contains the following sentence:

> Ibi non liberabit frater proprium fratrem, nec iterum pater filium suum, sed unusquisque stabit in ordine suo, tam in vita quam in incendio. (p. 108)[17]

> ('A brother will not free his own brother there, nor indeed a father his son, but everyone will stand in his own place, both in life and in the fire.')

The equivalent sentence in *HomU 55* occurs a little beyond the midway mark of a 468-word opening section based on *De paenitentia*. The text up to the kinsmen motif is a fairly faithful rendering of the Ephraemic text, though there are omissions.[18] Immediately following the motif, however, the correspondences become more sporadic. All the same, given the sheer volume of closely analogous material, Wright cannot be faulted for concluding that the entire opening section derives from Pseudo-Ephraem: he was looking at two texts, one of which is unmistakably a translation of the other. The advantage of local stemmatics over a text-centric approach, however, is that the wording of a short motif may be compared across a large number of attestations to find the closest match. Although the Old English attestation of the kinsmen motif may be judged to be a faithful translation of Pseudo-Ephraem on the whole, *gefultumian* ('help') is nowhere else in the *Dictionary of Old English Web Corpus*[19] used to translate *liberare* ('free'), and there is no reason why it should be. Instead, we expect *alysan*, *(ge)freogan*, *(ge)freolsian*, or *(ge)friþian*, the typical glosses for this verb. Taking Pseudo-Ephraem as a direct source, one is forced to conclude that the translator here altered the sense of his material, whether intentionally or otherwise. However, this conclusion leaves the problematic question of how the *Muspilli* poet was led to adopt the same imprecise translation when he chose the verb *helfan* ('help'). This parallel development is a first indication that not all witnesses in the motif's Germanic tradition represent a straightforward translation of the passage in *De paenitentia*.

Fortunately, a rudimentary Latin dissemination history for the motif had already been established when Wright discovered the Ephraemic roots of *HomU 55*. The sources in question have been associated especially with an Old English homily in Cambridge, University Library

---

Patrologia cursus completus: Patrologia latina, ed. by J.P. Migne (Paris: Migne, 1844–64), 99, col. 253B (hereafter *PL*); St. Gall, Stiftsbibliothek Cod. Sang. 193, pp. 230–65 (p. 262).

[15] Charles D. Wright, 'The Old English "Macarius" Homily, Vercelli Homily IV, and Ephrem Latinus, *De paenitentia*', in *Via Crucis: Essays on Early Medieval Sources and Ideas in Memory of J. E. Cross*, ed. by Thomas N. Hall, Thomas D. Hill, and Charles D. Wright (Morgantown, WV: West Virginia University Press, 2002), pp. 210–34.

[16] T. S. Pattie, 'Ephraem the Syrian and the Latin Manuscripts of *De paenitentia*', *British Library Journal*, 13 (1987), 1–27 (p. 2); Sebastian P. Brock, 'The Syriac Background', in *Archbishop Theodore: Commemorative Studies on His Life and Influence*, ed. by Michael Lapidge, Cambridge Studies in Anglo-Saxon England, 11 (Cambridge: Cambridge University Press, 1995), pp. 30–53 (p. 40).

[17] St Gall, Stiftsbibliothek Cod. Sang. 93, pp. 99–111. The manuscript is here cited as a ninth-century witness to a text not yet available in a critical edition. For the dating see Gustav Scherrer, *Verzeichnis der Handschriften der Stiftsbibliothek St. Gallen* (Halle: Niemeyer, 1875; repr. Hildesheim: Olms, 1975), item 93.

[18] See Wright, 'Macarius'.

[19] Ed. by Antonette diPaolo Healey, John Price Wilkin, and Xin Xiang (2009) <http://tapor.library.utoronto.ca/doecorpus/> [accessed 2 April 2014].

MS Ii. I.33 designated *HomM 8*.[20] This text contains one of the more heterogeneous Old English attestations of the kinsmen motif, which is formulated as follows:

> Eala, man þe þis gehyrst þæt ic ðe secge, þæt on þære stowe þe fæder ne gehelpð his suna, ne him to nane gode beon ne mæg, ne suna þam fæder, ne moder þæra dohter, ne nan oðer freond ne mæg to nane helpe.[21] (ll. 58–61)

> ('O you man who hears this that I am telling you, that in that place a father does not help his son, nor may he be of any use to him, nor a son to his father, nor a mother to her daughter, nor may any other friend [be] of any help.')

A sixteenth- or seventeenth-century hand in the manuscript identifies this text as 'Augustini sermo',[22] an identification Fadda attributes to its overlap with multiple Pseudo-Augustinian homilies.[23] For our passage, the relevant text circulates as number 68 among an extended collection of the spurious *Sermones ad fratres in eremo*.[24] As printed by Migne, its version of the motif runs as follows:

> Pensemus, charissimi, quomodo […] de tam inani hujus mundi pompa, dira gehennalis provenit poena: de qua non liberabit pater filium, nec pro patre filius fidejubebit; ubi non reperitur amicus qui redimat, nec frater qui succurrat. (col. 1355)

> ('Let us consider, dearest men, how […] the horrendous punishment of hell proceeds from such ostentation in this vain world, from which a father will not free his son, nor will a son offer surety for his father; where a friend is not found who may redeem one, nor a brother who may come to one's aid.')

As Willard, Cross, and Murfin point out, however, the correspondences are insufficiently exact to warrant direct borrowing. Cross and Murfin adduce a further text that combines a reworked excerpt from *Sermo ad fratres LXVIII* with parts from *Sermones LXVI* and *LXIX* of that series[25] and circulated under Isidore's name as *Sermo III*.[26] Following Migne's printing, Pseudo-Isidore's text contains the following version of the kinsmen motif, here reproduced in context:

> O fratres, intelligite: dicit psalmista, 'Non mortui laudabunt te, Domine, neque omnes qui descendunt in infernum.' Fratres, quomodo possunt nominare Deum, qui semper

---

[20] 'Sermone di Agostino', in *Nuove omelie anglosassoni della rinascenza benedettina*, ed. and trans. by A. M. Luiselli Fadda (Florence: Felice le Monnier, 1977), pp. 139–57; see also Kathleen Much Murfin, 'An Unedited Old English Homily in MS. Cambridge, U.L. Ii. I33' (unpublished MA thesis, Rice University, 1971).

[21] A main verb *beon* is lacking (see translation).

[22] Fol. 207ʳ, top margin.

[23] Fadda, p. 139.

[24] Ed. by Migne, *PL* 40, cols 1354–55. The seventeenth-century Maurist edition on which Migne based his text provides an early index of medieval authors who rejected Augustine's authorship of virtually all of the *Sermones ad fratres in eremo*: *Sancti Aurelii Augustini hipponensis episcopi opera omnia*, [ed. by Thomas D. Blampin], 2nd edn, 11 vols (Paris: Gaume fratres, 1835–38), edition at vi, cols 1977D–79D; introduction at cols 1800–1. The text here relevant is a late addition to that group, considered spurious even within the collection of falsely attributed homilies. The core group of the *Sermones ad fratres* is commonly defined as either the 23 texts so labelled in Jordan of Quedlinburg's autograph, or the 35 in the containing section of that document. These are of diverse origins, though many seem to have been written in the fourteenth century: see E. L. Saak, *The Sermones ad fratres in eremo*, in *Creating Augustine: Interpreting Augustine and Augustinianism in the Later Middle Ages* (Oxford: Oxford University Press, 2012). Clearly, number 68 has a longer history.

[25] Rudolph Willard, 'The Address of the Soul to the Body', *PMLA*, 50 (1935), 957–83 (p. 960); J. E. Cross, '*Ubi sunt* Passages in Old English: Sources and Relationships', *Vetenskaps-Societetens i Lund Årbok* (1956), 25–44 (pp. 33–36); Murfin, pp. 11–14; cf. Fadda, pp. 139–40.

[26] Ed. by Migne, *PL* 83, cols 1223–25.

sunt in tenebris, et in loco tenebroso, et semper clamant, 'Vae tam tenebrosum locum, tam tenebrosam foveam, tam obscuram cavernam, tam amarum locum, tam miserrimam vitam, tam dolorosam mansionem!'? O miseri, de tam parva vita tam longam mortem, de tam parva consolatione tam longam captivitatem, de tam parva laetitia tam longam tristitiam, de tam parvo lucro tam grave damnum, de tam parvo honore tam longos dolores, de tam parva jucunditate tam amaras lacrymas, tam immensa suspiria, tam luctuosos gemitus, tam magnam iram et tristitiam. Ibi non adjuvat pater ad filium, nec filius ad patrem; ibi non invenitur amicus qui redimat amicum, neque frater qui succurrat fratri. Ibi amatur poenitentia, sed tarde agitur. Vae! duram mansionem, tam cruciabilem flammam, tam immensa tormenta. (col. 1224B)

('O brethren, understand: the Psalmist says, "The dead will not praise you, O Lord, nor will all those who go down into hell." Brethren, how can they call God by name, those who are always in the dark, and in a dark place, and continually call out, "Alas! such a dark place, such a dark pit, such a dim cave, such a bitter place, such a most wretched life, such a painful dwelling!"? O wretches! Such a long death following from such a brief life; such long captivity from such brief comfort; such long sadness from such brief joy; such grave harm from such brief gain; such long sufferings from such brief honour; such bitter tears from such brief delight; such boundless sighings, such mournful groans, such great anger and sadness. A father does not help his son there, nor a son his father; a friend is not there found who may redeem a friend, nor a brother who may come to a brother's aid. There penitence is loved, but slow to be accomplished. Alas! the harsh dwelling, such excruciating flame, such boundless torments.')

Murfin points out that *HomM 8* as a whole shares a considerable number of details with Pseudo-Augustine, while others agree with Pseudo-Isidore. She concludes that the Old English homily is a close translation of an intermediary, which she identifies as an earlier version of Pseudo-Isidore that would have constituted a more faithful but expanded reworking of the three Pseudo-Augustinian excerpts.[27]

Based on the witnesses in *PL*, it may be observed that Pseudo-Augustine, like Pseudo-Ephraem, uses the verb *liberare*, whereas Pseudo-Isidore's revision uses *adiuvare*, a more than plausible model for *gehelpan* in *HomM 8* but also for *helfan* in *Muspilli* and *gefultumian* in *HomU 55*. This innovation may certainly have been inspired directly by Pseudo-Augustine, who uses *adiuvare* a few lines down, in the passive construction 'nec ob hoc sic poenitens adjuvatur' ('nor is the penitent thereby helped against this', col. 1355), part of a sentence omitted in Migne's text of Pseudo-Isidore. The substitution of *adiuvare* for *liberare* should thus be expected to have been present in Murfin's intermediary.

Since neither Pseudo-Augustine's nor Pseudo-Isidore's homily has been critically edited or subjected to extensive text-critical investigation, scholars of the kinsmen motif have cited *Patrologia latina* without investigating either Migne's sources or independent variants, a practice that has been demonstrated to hinder source analysis in similar cases.[28] For Pseudo-Augustine's homily, Migne relied on the seventeenth-century Maurist edition of Augustine's works, whose editor refers loosely to a manuscript then in the Abbey of Saint-Germain-des-Prés in present-day Paris,[29] and thus presumably transferred to the Bibliothèque nationale

---

[27] Murfin, pp. 11–12.
[28] Wright, 'A Doomsday Passage in an Old English Sermon for Lent, Revisited', *Anglia*, 128 (2010), 28–47.
[29] Blampin, vi, part 2, cols 1803–4.

during the French Revolution.[30] The Maurist edition notes that the compiler of that exemplar took a rather liberal approach to his material.[31] Migne's source for Pseudo-Isidore's text was probably Faustino Arévalo's 1797–1813 edition of Isidore's works,[32] which presumably builds on one or more Roman manuscripts.[33] However, even a perfunctory query yields more than a dozen manuscript items in almost as many libraries with corresponding incipits to those of the homilies attributed to Augustine and Isidore (since these differ in word order only), and more can surely be found given a systematic consultation of the catalogues. Although an account of the texts' transmission history will have to wait until all manuscripts have been consulted, the evidence of even just a few variants sheds a good deal of light on the transmission of both the homily and the kinsmen motif, and they suggest that the *PL* text is a condensed and isolated variant rather than a representative recension.[34]

The redaction on pages 452–59 of Einsiedeln, Stiftsbibliothek MS 199 (638) is instructive for present purposes. This text generally follows the argument and wording of Pseudo-Isidore's *Sermo III* according to Migne but occasionally agrees with Pseudo-Augustine's *Sermo LXVIII* against it. Its version of the kinsmen motif is worth citing in context:

> Dic ubi su*nt* regis, ubi principis, ubi imperatores? Ubi su*nt* diuites, ubi aur*um* & ornamenta eor*um*? Ipsi uelud umbra transierunt & ut somniu*m* euanuerunt. Aur*um* & argentu*m* eor*um* & orname*n*ta eor*um* remanserunt in hunc mundo et ille sine fine cruciantur in infernum ubi uermis eor*um* non moriuntur & ignis eor*um* non extinguuntur, quia sicut scriptu*m* es*t*, 'Potentes potenter torme*n*ta patiuntur'. Uę tam tenibrosa mansione, tam obscura cauerna; de tam breue uita tam lo\n/ga morte; de ta*m* parua consulatione ta*m* longa captiuitate; de tam breue l*ae*titia ta*m* longa tristitia; de tam breue luce ta*m* longas tenibras; de tam breue lucr*um* ta*m* grande damnu, & ta*m* forte periculu*m* de tam breue temporis potentia; ta*m* longa sine fine torme*n*ta; de ta*m* parua iocunditate ta*m* longas & ta*m* amaras lacrimas; ubi non adiuuat pater filiu*m* nec filius patre*m*; ubi amicus non inuenitur qui redimat neque frat*er* qui succurrere debeat; ubi multi querunt finem mortis & mori non possunt; ubi amara penitentia tarde agitur sed [paenitens][35] non adiuuat*ur*. (pp. 455–56)

> ('Tell me: where are the kings, where the princes, where the emperors? Where are their riches, where their gold and trappings? They have passed like a shadow, and they have dissolved like a dream. Their gold and silver and trappings have remained in this world, and they are tormented without end in hell where their worms do not die and their fires are not extinguished, as it is written, "The powerful suffer torments powerfully." Alas! such a dark dwelling, such a dim cave; such a long death following from such a brief life; such long captivity from such brief comfort; such long sadness from such brief joy; such long darkness from such brief light; such great harm from such brief gain, and such severe destruction from power so brief of duration; such long torments without end; such long

---

[30] Cf. Léopold Delisle, *Le cabinet des manuscrits de la Bibliothèque nationale*, 3 vols (Paris: Imprimerie nationale, 1868–81), II, 40–103, with an index of lost Latin manuscripts at pp. 54–56. I have been unable to identify the manuscript used by the Maurists with the help of the BnF catalogue and digital reproductions.

[31] Cols 1803–4.

[32] *S. Isidori hispalensis episcopi hispaniarum doctoris opera omnia*, ed. by Faustino Arévalo, 7 vols (Rome: Antonius Fulgonius, 1797–1803), VII, 313–16. Arévalo does not reference a base manuscript.

[33] The editor gives an account of his methods in I, 3–5.

[34] Most readily available at the time of writing are St Gall, Stiftsbibliothek Cod. Sang. 614, motif at p. 44; St Gall, Stiftsbibliothek Cod. Sang. 682, at p. 182; Munich, Bayerische Staatsbibliothek Clm 6342, at fol. 160ʳ; Munich, Bayerische Staatsbibliothek Clm 17059, at fol. 46ᵛ; and Einsiedeln, Stiftsbibliothek MS 199 (638), at p. 456. The Munich manuscripts are accessible at <http://www.digitale-sammlungen.de> [accessed 2 April 2014]; the others at <http://www.e-codices.unifr.ch> [accessed 2 April 2014].

[35] 'paenitens' not in MS; cf. the text in Migne cited above.

and bitter tears from such brief delight; where a father does not help his son, nor a son his father; where a friend is not found who may redeem one, nor a brother who would be under obligation to help; where many seek an end through death, and they cannot die; where bitter penitence is slow to be accomplished, but [the penitent] is not helped.')

The first thing to note is that, like Migne's text of Pseudo-Isidore, this redaction uses *adiuvare* for *liberare*. However, it also retains the presumed model for this transformation, the passive form 'adiuuatur' shortly after, suggesting that this redaction is closer to the Pseudo-Augustinian source than that in Migne.[36] Equally important is the form of the *ubi sunt* formula and the subsequent *vae tam* sequence. Although the rhetorical questions of Pseudo-Isidore's *ubi sunt* contain roughly the same elements across Migne and the Einsiedeln, St Gall, and Munich manuscripts consulted, the Latin quotation in *HomM 8* is closer in word order to all five manuscripts than to Migne; it matches most closely Cod. Sang. 682,[37] which lacks only the familiar relative clause 'qui ante fuerunt', present in *HomM 8* but absent from all Latin manuscripts consulted. The *vae tam* lamentation that follows in the Latin text does not recur in full in *HomU 55*, but nine of the ten elements (five pairs) of the rhetorical sequence in the Old English text have counterparts in the Einsiedeln, Munich 17059, and Cod. Sang. 614 manuscripts. Migne's copies of Pseudo-Augustine and Pseudo-Isidore match seven of these elements each, as does Munich 6342; Cod. Sang. 682 matches eight but also shares with *HomU 55* the omission of three elements retained in the other Latin versions. By this metric, then, four of the manuscripts consulted approximate more closely than either *PL* text the source of the motif in *HomU 55*, and all five manuscript witnesses are closer to *HomM 8* than the *PL* texts. Accordingly, Migne had best be abandoned in this connection and representative manuscript redactions cited instead until a critical edition of *Sermo III* materialises.

While Pseudo-Isidore's *Sermo III* may thus be identified as a source of the core Anglo-Saxon kinsmen motif, none of the Pseudo-Isidorian manuscripts consulted offers a model for the second half of the *HomU 55* attestation, 'ac sceal þonne anra gehwilc æfter his agenum gewyrhtum beon demed' ('but each will then be judged according to his own works'). Given that the *HomU 55* compiler was working with a text of *De paenitentia* for much of the surrounding passage, this clause was likely inspired by Pseudo-Ephraem's 'sed unusquisque stabit in ordine suo' ('but everyone will stand in his own place'), and perhaps contaminated by a recollection of the relevant scriptural analogues.[38] How should these mixed correspondences be explained?

This is where the longer structure of each text may offer clarification. It has been observed already that the section in *HomU 55* preceding the kinsmen motif is unquestionably derived from Pseudo-Ephraem; it may here be added that there is nothing in the Pseudo-Augustinian group of texts to match it. The final clause of the kinsmen motif in the Old English homily likewise agrees with *De paenitentia* against the other pseudo-Church Fathers. However, the core element of the Germanic motif as here defined must in the majority of cases derive from Pseudo-Isidore's homily if we are to explain why it consistently seems to translate *adiuvare*

---

[36] The same reading is found in the Munich manuscripts. Cod. Gall. 682 has the active construction 'sed non adiuuat eis' (p. 183), while the incomplete variant on pp. 42–44 of St Gall, Stiftsbibliothek Cod. Sang. 614 breaks off due to a missing leaf immediately after the verb of the kinsmen motif, here 'adiuuatur', suggesting that its scribe omitted the text between 'adiuuat' and 'adiuuatur' through eyeskip, so that this witness too postdates the change of verb. Interestingly, Migne's text (cited above) may have retained a more authentic reading for this clause, as the manuscript versions lack a subject.

[37] pp. 180–81.

[38] e.g. Iob 34:11; Ps 61:13; Prv 24:12; Mt 16:27; Rm 2:6; 2 Cor 5:10; Apc 2:23.

rather than *liberare*, while the same derivation is favoured by the Anglo-Saxon primacy of father and son rather than a fraternal pair.[39] The solution must therefore be that the translator or compiler behind *HomU 55* on encountering the kinsmen motif in his Ephraemic source was reminded of Pseudo-Isidore's phrasing of the same motif. He adopted this not from memory, but from a copy physically available to him, since he adapted also parts of Pseudo-Isidore's *vae tam* sequence along with the *ubi sunt*.[40] Preferring the phrasing in Pseudo-Isidore's text, which in his model must have contained *adiuvare* for *liberare* as well as the chiasmatic combination of father and son, the compiler chose to substitute it for the Ephraemic wording. He then returned to Pseudo-Ephraem for the conclusion of the motif but took a freer approach to his model for the remainder of the section, and possibly modified the Ephraemic conclusion of the motif to reflect a handful of biblical passages.

Even with the reading *adiuvare* for *liberare*, the Latin sources consulted thus far differ from the Germanic texts in two noteworthy details. The first of these is the setting, which in Pseudo-Augustine and Pseudo-Isidore is hell, whereas in *Muspilli* and *HomU 55* (though not in *HomM 8*) it is Judgement Day. Pseudo-Ephraem actually references both locales. His central aim is to call his audience to repentance before it is too late; the distinction between judgement and punishment is of no great value to this proposition. However, the imagery he uses is mostly infernal both in the immediate vicinity of the motif and in the work as a whole. Pseudo-Augustine's focus on hell is accordingly true to its source, but it would hardly be surprising if a text building directly on Pseudo-Ephraem were to concentrate on Judgement Day instead. An author working from Pseudo-Augustine or Pseudo-Isidore could do the same, of course: the *HomU 55* translator saw fit to use both *De paenitentia* and *Sermo III* and adapt them to a Judgement Day setting. All the same, an identifiable setting can serve as a clue when deciding between possible routes of transmission, and for this purpose it is worth noting that the majority of Germanic witnesses contrast with at least Pseudo-Augustine and Pseudo-Isidore.

The second point of contrast is that the Latin sources contain no auxiliary verb *posse* to match Germanic *magan* ('be able', lacking only in the initial clause of *HomM 8*): the Latin homilists observe simply that one kinsmen will (or rather 'does', a present indicative) not help another, inability being understood. These differences form no major objection to the Germanic occurrences deriving directly from Pseudo-Isidore's homily, as the innovations are minor and could conceivably have taken the same form independently between *HomU 55* and *Muspilli*. For the setting, however, it may be worth considering the role played by a further Latin text, one that does share with the majority of Germanic attestations a Judgement Day context.

The Pseudo-Bedan acrostic poem on the fleeting nature of life on earth sometimes entitled *Versus de contemptu mundi* has received limited attention in the context of the kinsmen motif.[41] Dating to the Merovingian era,[42] it contains the following stanza and refrain:

> 20   Veniet dies iudicii
>   et erit fortis districtio,

---

[39] Cf. Appendix 1 in part two of this series.
[40] *HomU 55*, ll. 61–69.
[41] Its participation in the kinsmen motif is briefly noted in Lendinara, n. 29 on p. 76.
[42] Ziolkowski, p. 226.

> ubi non adiuvat⁴³ pater filium
> nec filius defendit⁴⁴ patrem.
>   Adtende homo, quia de terra factus es
>   et in terra ponendus eris.⁴⁵

('The day of judgement will come, and there will be great severity, in which a father does not help his son, nor does a son defend his father. Give heed, man, because you were made of soil and you will be deposited in the soil.')

The poem uses Pseudo-Isidore's verb *adiuvare* rather than Pseudo-Ephraem's *liberare*, and the parties involved are limited to father and son in the same chiasmatic configuration found in Pseudo-Isidore. Moreover, the two lines in question are identical with the motif in Pseudo-Isidore excepting the verb *defendit*, which two editors have proposed to omit because it renders the line metrically deficient.⁴⁶ Pseudo-Isidore also decries the sentiment 'juuinis sum & tempus habeo mundo fruere' ('I am young and have time to enjoy the world', Einsiedeln, p. 455), whose refutal is the object of *De contemptu*. The relevant stanza of the poem may thus confidently be derived from Pseudo-Isidore. Compared to that text, the setting is the only innovation. Although *districtio* ('severity') could be read as a reference to the punishments reserved for the wicked,⁴⁷ the term is just as commonly used with reference to a court pronouncement as with the imposed penalty.⁴⁸ Since Judgement Day is announced in the preceding line, this instance of the motif may safely be understood to share with the majority of the vernacular attestations a Judgement Day setting, against the infernal locale of the other Latin witnesses and that in *HomM 8*. A shift in setting thus takes place when Pseudo-Isidore's text is adapted by the *HomU 55* homilist, but also when it is adapted by Pseudo-Bede.

It should be emphasised that this twofold parallel shift in setting is an all but unavoidable conclusion. Although a single chain of transmission with a one-time shift in locale would normally be more likely, the circumstances in this case preclude it. *HomU 55* contains too many details from Pseudo-Isidore to have derived from Pseudo-Bede instead. The only alternative that cannot be ruled out is that its compiler may have known both. The reverse transmission, from *HomU 55* to Pseudo-Bede, would require *HomU 55* to have been composed no later than the very early ninth century, a hundred years earlier than hitherto assumed.⁴⁹ Moreover, such a reading would require positive evidence of the poem's English origins. Although the earliest two manuscripts containing *De contemptu* do indeed have substantial Insular connections (Cologne 106, for instance, contains three Anglo-Saxon hands,

---

[43] A variant 'ut' is found for 'ubi'. This, however, requires the subjunctive form 'adiuvet', so emended by Ziolkowski, who translates 'such that a father may not help his son'.

[44] Var. *liberat*; Mone and Meyer have proposed omitting the verb altogether on metrical grounds and changing the word order, not the sense, of the remainder of the couplet: Franz Joseph Mone, 'Versus de contemptu mundi', in *Lateinische Hymnen des Mittelalters*, 3 vols (Freiburg: Herder'sche Verlagshandlung, 1853–55), item 288 (I, 396, apparatus for ll. 79–80); Meyer, 'Versus de contemptu mundi', ed. by Karl Strecker, in *Rhythmi aevi Merovingici et Carolini*, Monumenta Germaniae historica, Poetae Latini Medii Aevi, 4 part 2 (Berlin: Weidmann, 1923), pp. 495–500 (apparatus for stanza 20, p. 499).

[45] Ed. by Strecker.

[46] See note 44 above.

[47] Such is its usage, for instance, in *PL* 17, col. 977D, and *PL* 52, col. 693C.

[48] See, e.g., *PL* 23, col. 1425B; *PL* 52, cols 717C, 731D; *PL* 99, col. 883A; *PL* 119, col. 963C. The term does not occur in the Vulgate, but was in common use in medieval Latin: *Dictionary of Medieval Latin from British Sources*, 17 vols, ed. by R.A. Latham and others (London: Oxford University Press, 1975–2013), s.v. *districtio* (III (1986), 700–1).

[49] Sauer, p. 94 and the literature there cited; Wright, 'Macarius', pp. 213–14.

diverse works by Alcuin and Bede, and is bound in the Insular manner),[50] in each case there is nothing connecting the poem itself with England, even if attempts to associate it with Ireland and Mozarabic Spain have been unconvincing.[51] Surely a conceptual association between the last judgement and hell is easier to demonstrate than a textual one between Pseudo-Bede and England. *De contemptu* and *HomU* 55 thus independently come to share a judicial setting.

It is time now to investigate the High German attestations, in order that their relationship to the Latin and Old English traditions may be understood. The longest of the German matches is found in Otfrid's *Evangelienbuch*:

> Ni mag thar manahoubit   helfan hereren uuiht,
>   kind noh quena, in uuare,   — sie sorgent iro thare —
>   Odo iauuiht helphan thanne   themo filu richen manne:
> 50 sie sint al ebanreiti   in theru selbun arabeiti. (V. 19, ll. 47–50)[52]

('A serf cannot help his lord there at all, nor his child or wife in truth — they will worry for themselves there — or anything help the very rich man then: they will all be equal in the same misery.')

Otfrid's use of the motif diverges from the precise definition here employed by giving serfdom sequential priority over blood relation; the setting, on the other hand, is again clearly the last day, this being the stated subject of this section of the poem. The verb also is *helfan*, mirroring the majority of Germanic attestations. However, the couplet immediately preceding the motif as quoted makes clear that it was not taken from the Pseudo-Augustinian tradition:

> 45 Ni losent thar in noti   gold noh diuro wati,
>   ni hilfit gotowebbi thar,   noh thaz silabar in war. (V. 19, ll. 45–46)

('Neither gold nor precious vestments will set one free there in one's need, nor will silk or silver help there in truth.')

The sentiment that gold, silver, and clothing cannot set one free derives directly from the sentence preceding the kinsmen motif in Pseudo-Ephraem's *De paenitentia*:

> Aurum & argentum non liberabit nos ab illo igne terribili. Vestes et deliciae in condemnationem nostram erunt. (p. 108)

('Gold and silver will not free us from that terrible fire. Clothes and luxuries will be counted towards our damnation.')

Moreover, the verb *losen* ('free') is an accurate translation of *liberare*, not *adiuvare*. The two instances of *helfan* in the lines that follow, including the kinsmen motif proper, must have been

---

[50] Leslie Webber Jones, 'Cologne MS. 106: A Book of Hildebald', *Speculum*, 4 (1929), 27–61 (p. 29); Bernhard Bischoff, *Katalog der festländischen Handschriften des neunten Jahrhunderts (mit Ausnahme der wisigotischen)* (Wiesbaden: Harrassowitz, 1998–), item 1919. The contents of the volume also correspond roughly to those of a handbook Alcuin sent to Arno of Salzburg in 802, as described in *Epistolae Karolini aevi*, II, ed. by Ernst Dümmler, Monumenta Germaniae historica, Epistolae, 4 (Berlin: Weidmann, 1895), item 259 (p. 417).

[51] Philipp August Becker, *Zur romanischen Literaturgeschichte: Ausgewählte Studien und Aufsätze* (Bern: Francke, 1967), pp. 107–8; Hans Spanke, 'Ein lateinisches Liederbuch des 11. Jahrhunderts', *Studi medievali*, n. s. 15 (1942), 111–42 (pp. 116, 128). The other manuscript with an English connection is St Gall, Stiftsbibliothek Cod. Sang. 1395; see Scherrer, item 1395 (*De contemptu* is found incomplete on the verso of leaf 468, identified in Scherrer as the first of two leaves under unit XIV).

[52] Ed. Piper, whose text is here reproduced without diacritics.

chosen by Otfrid as a way of varying his diction around the base word *losen*. That these choices brought his text more in line with the parallel Pseudo-Isidorian and Old English tradition must be a consequence of the semantic relationship between verbs for liberate and help. Otfrid's text thus depends directly on Pseudo-Ephraem, despite its similarities to the Pseudo-Isidorian family of texts. As noted above, it is not especially surprising that it adopts a Judgement Day setting, as this context has a minority presence in *De paenitentia*.

Since the *Muspilli* attestation is especially concise ('dar ni mac denne mak andremo helfan uora demo muspille', l. 57), its exact derivation cannot be established beyond doubt. Ruled out at the outset is a dependence on Otfrid's *Evangelienbuch*, which not only postdates *Muspilli* but also aims the motif in the first instance at an obligation from serfdom, not blood relation. Beyond that, it comes down to a calculation of probabilities. Between Otfrid and Pseudo-Isidore, as was seen, *liberare* is twice independently altered to a verb with the more general sense of 'help'; between Otfrid, Pseudo-Bede, and *HomU 55*, the setting is three times independently moved from hell to Judgement Day, the last two attestations of this set deriving from a model with a purely infernal setting. This demonstrates that there is a shared conceptual logic to these innovations, and makes clear that a further instance of each in *Muspilli* is certainly possible. However, it remains more likely that the poet had knowledge of a text with *adiuvare* and a Judgement Day setting already in place. *De contemptu* is such a text, and it had a German presence by the early ninth century,[53] early enough to influence the *Muspilli* poet. Accordingly, although an immediate reliance of *Muspilli* on Pseudo-Ephraem is not out of the question, the likelier derivation is from Pseudo-Bede.

A more confident genealogy may be posited for the Middle High German attestation of the motif. This text, a homily of the twelfth century[54] entitled *De virginibus*, holds to a tight focus, identifying in simple terms the various metaphors employed in the parable of the ten virgins. In the context of the husband's coming and the good virgins' refusal to share their oil with the bad virgins, this text reads,

> An der stete mac niemen dem anderen niht gehelfen, da moz ein iegilch mennesce uur sich selben antwrten. (129.3–4)[55]

---

[53] Among the poem's earliest witnesses is Cologne, Dombibliothek MS 106, a product of extensive collaboration from diverse schools, but thought to have been compiled in early ninth-century Werden: Bernhard Bischoff, *Mitteralterliche Studien: Ausgewählte Aufsätze zur Schriftkunde und Literaturgeschichte*, 3 vols (Stuttgart: Hiersemann, 1966–81), n. 8 on p. 7; *Katalog*, item 1919; B. C. Barker-Benfield, 'The Werden "Heptateuch"', *ASE*, 20 (1991), 43–64 (p. 58); Michael Lapidge, *Anglo-Latin Literature: 600–899* (London: Hambledon, 1996), p. 242; contrast Wilhelm Arndt, *Schrifttafeln zur Erlernung der lateinischen Palaeographie*, 3d edn, rev. by Michael Tangl (Hildesheim: Olms, 1976), Plates 44–47; W. M. Lindsay, *Palaeographia Latina*, 6 vols (London: Oxford University Press, 1923–29), III, 7; Edward Kennard Rand, 'On the Symbols of Abbreviations for -*tur*', *Speculum*, 2.1 (January 1927), 52–65 (pp. 57–58); Jones, 'Cologne MS. 106' *passim*; *The Script of Cologne: From Hildebald to Hermann* (Cambridge, MA: Mediaeval Academy of America, 1932), p. 42. It also appears in the Cambridge Songs manuscript: Cambridge, University Library, Gg. 5.35, fol. 437ʳ; see further Karl Breul, *The Cambridge Songs: A Goliard's Song Book of the 11th Century* (Cambridge: Cambridge University Press, 1915); Ziolkowski. While this manuscript was produced in eleventh-century England, the Cambridge Songs are overwhelmingly German in origin, though several have been shown to be French (Ziolkowski, pp. xxxii–xxxvii). At any rate they are all texts that had currency in Germany. For a full list of *De contemptu* manuscripts see Strecker, p. 495, textual apparatus, alongside pp. 448–54, or Francesco Lo Monaco, *Carmina cantabrigiensia: Il canzoniere di Cambridge* (Ospedaletto (Pisa): Pacini, 2009), p. 45, alongside pp. 13–14.

[54] For the dating see *Speculum ecclesiae: Eine frühmittelhochdeutsche Predigtsammlung (Cgm. 39)*, ed. by Gert Mellbourn, Lunder germanistische Forschungen, 12 (Lund: Gleerup, 1944), pp. vii–xvi, xxii.

[55] Ed. by Mellbourn, pp. 127–29

('In that place, no-one will be able to help the others; everyone will have to answer for himself there.')

The use of the motif is highly appropriate: the homilist explicitly connects the parable with Judgement Day, using stock eschatological rhetoric such as the call to reflect on the horrors of latter-day events, here the separation of the righteous and wicked souls (129.4–7). The motif's reference to kinship is omitted, a simplification that is congruent with the elementary nature of the exegesis here practised, and sensible because it avoids confusing the image of the ten virgins with references to blood relations. Nevertheless, the unprompted locative specifications 'an der stete' ('in that place') and 'da' ('there') suggest the passage's indebtedness to the Ephraemic tradition, while the remainder of the second clause is reminiscent of Pseudo-Ephraem's own conclusion 'unusquisque stabit in ordine suo'. Indeed, a direct reliance on Pseudo-Ephraem's *De paenitentia* explains what brought the motif to the homilist's mind, as this is the only other text in this tradition that makes reference to the parable of the ten virgins (pp. 109–10). It may thus be assumed that the borrowing bypassed both known Old High German attestations and goes back directly to Pseudo-Ephraem. However, this makes it yet another instance of the shift from *liberare* to *adiuvare*. It is also another instance of a new focus on Judgement Day, but this is the less striking of the two innovations, as Pseudo-Ephraem also makes some use of judgement imagery. Although the lexical transformation may seem more significant, the fact that several such shifts have now been identified demonstrates that this innovation is hardly a unique derivational fingerprint. In the present case, it does not outweigh the evidence connecting *De virginibus* directly with *De paenitentia*.

The above considerations yield the stemma in Figure 1.

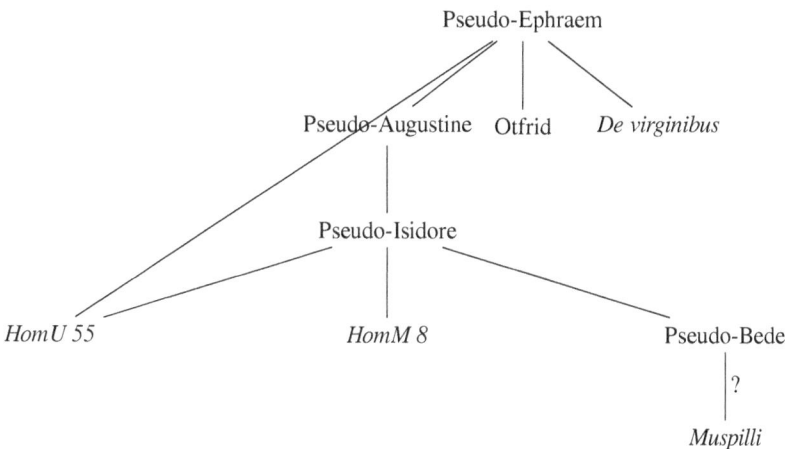

Figure 1: The Latin derivation of the motif's Germanic branches.

Conclusions

The greatest degree of insight into a culture of textual transmission is to be had if palaeographical and material clues are combined with two dimensions of textual investigation. The default textual axis runs along the length of the text under study and permits the researcher to investigate variants across a longer stretch of text. This is the most reliable tool by which to determine the stages of a work's development and the relationships between the surviving witnesses, but it assumes these witnesses are all versions of one text. In a genre characterised by the practice of borrowing short motifs in isolation, a valuable secondary tool is the depth-axis, a means of textual comparison on a local level. By comparing the implementation of a short passage between multiple nodes, it is possible to cover a large number of texts and copies and come to an approximation of the relationships between them. The greatest accuracy may be attained only where longer passages are shared between texts, or multiple shorter passages are transmitted along the same route, so that the depth analysis benefits from comparison along the length-axis. Nevertheless, it is local depth analysis that provides the greatest insight into the synthesis of short passages from multiple sources, even if conclusions reached by this route are often conjectural.

The application of local stemmatics to the kinsmen motif has yielded a plausible network of routes by which this formula reached Germanic authors. In addition, the results here obtained may guide our understanding of Pseudo-Ephraem's influence on early medieval literary culture and shed light on the mechanics of motif transmission more generally.

Noteworthy in this regard is the parallel independent development taking place across different branches of the dissemination. As mentioned, Otfrid and Pseudo-Isidore independently replace *liberare* with a word for 'help', while Pseudo-Bede and the Macarius homilist independently shift the motif's setting from hell to Judgement Day, with less pronounced examples of the same pattern visible in Otfrid and *De virginibus*. Both these binaries are useful metrics by which to judge a text's origins, but preferably as elements in a weighed consideration, as they have proved to be remarkably commonplace by themselves. A specific lesson that may be drawn from the lexical shift is that semantic relaxing, or the translation of a specific by a general word, is considerably more likely than the reverse process and accordingly less valuable as a tool of stemmatic analysis. If we saw *adiuvare* ('help') translated as *freolsian* ('free') in multiple texts, we would not hesitate to posit a shared intermediary. The translation of *liberare* ('free') into *gehelpan* ('help') and cognates, by contrast, has been shown to be a common tendency. Accordingly, when multiple texts show evidence of semantic relaxing within the same motif, this increases the likelihood of their close kinship, but it also imposes limits on the ability of one textual relation to help another.

John Rykener, Richard II and the Governance of London

Jeremy Goldberg

On the first Sunday of December 1394 between the hours of eight and nine at night, John Rykener was solicited for sex in Cheapside. In the darkness of the winter evening John Britby, a Yorkshireman and innocent abroad, supposedly mistook Rykner by his dress for a woman.[1] The two men adjourned to a side street to do the deed. There they were immediately detected 'by certain officers of the city' lying together 'over [*super*] a stall in a lane called Soper Lane' doing 'illud vitium detestabile nephandum et ignominiosum', a knowingly opaque circumlocution that here perhaps signals anal sex.[2] Caught *flagrante delicto*, they were arrested, imprisoned, and subsequently brought before the mayor's court. Questioned before the mayor, Rykener told how he first dressed as a woman to sell sex and took the working name Eleanor. He then proceeded to confess to a litany of homosexual encounters with friars and secular clergy whilst masquerading variously as an embroideress and as a barmaid, but also heterosexual couplings with both nuns and a laywoman. All allegedly occurred during the course of a prolonged trip to Burford, via Oxford and returning to London by way of Beaconsfield and lastly the lanes by St Katherine's Hospital just beyond the walls to the east of the city. It is a remarkable narrative.

The unusually full account contained in the London Plea and Memoranda Rolls of John Rykener's appearance before the mayor's court is both vivid and dramatic. Its narrative of cross-dressing, male prostitution, gay sex, clerical promiscuity and the like seems to offer a rare window onto late medieval sexuality and sexual mores. The discussion of the case offered by David Boyd and Ruth Karras in 1995 helped firmly to locate Rykener in the

---

[1] Rykener has lately achieved a posthumous fame as a cross–dressing male prostitute: R. M. Karras and D. L. Boyd, ' "Ut cum muliere": A Male Transvestite Prostitute in Fourteenth Century London', in *Premodern Sexualities*, ed. by L. Fradenburg and C. Freccero (London: Routledge, 1996), pp. 99–116.

[2] The Rykener case is recorded in London Metropolitan Archives, *Plea and Memoranda Roll A34, m.2*. All transcriptions of the Latin text and translations into modern English are my own. *Stall* here is a term for a table on which merchandise is displayed: *MED* under *Stal(le (n.)*, 2. The meaning of *super* is ambiguous since it could also be translated as 'by' or 'on'. 'By' implies the two men lay on the ground, which seems unlikely given the filthy state of the lane. 'On' is more likely, but 'over' would make the most sense of the city's officers' supposed conviction of the nature of the sexual act being performed. Soper Lane is one of a number of narrow streets that open off Cheapside. Historically associated with the pepperers, by the late fourteenth century it was occupied by mercers, drapers, and fishmongers. Some shops appear to have been run down by this date. The narrow lanes opening off the south side of Cheapside had a long association with prostitution, suggested by the names of the nearby Gropecunt and Popkirtle Lanes: *ibid*., pp. 203, 241; D. J. Keene and V. Harding, *Historical Gazetteer of London before the Great Fire, vol. 1: Cheapside* (Cambridge: Chadwyck-Healey, 1987), pp. 645–810.

history of gender and sexuality.[3] The focus, therefore, has been on the person of John/Eleanor Rykener and what he and the narrative about him can tell us about late medieval constructions of sexuality.[4] Subsequently the case has stimulated some excellent scholarship. Karras and Boyd themselves argued that Rykener's cross dressing and his 'passive' role when engaged in anal sex with other men points to a medieval understanding of gender as performative.[5] Their view that the mayor's court was more anxious about Rykener's gender transgression than prostitution or sodomy has become something of an orthodoxy.[6] Carolyn Dinshaw and Ruth Evans consider the cultural climate of late fourteenth-century London, which Evans comments was 'a nodal point for the production and dissemination of numerous texts that are beginning to create a public discourse about political events'.[7] Dinshaw suggests resonances between the 1395 'Twelve Conclusions of the Lollards', Chaucer's *Canterbury Tales*, and the Rykener text.[8] Evans, who is interested in the idea of the cross-dressing, multi-tasking Rykener as 'imitator', sees resonances between the Rykener text and Thomas Favent's slightly earlier *Historia Mirabilis Parliamenti*.[9]

My own initial reading echoes the cultural concerns of Dinshaw and Evans by drawing attention to the magisterial agenda with (dis)honest trading that runs through the text. Rykener is here represented as a tradesperson who purports to be an embroideress and a barmaid, but actually sells sex. His labour is thus in allowing his body to be used for the sexual gratification of others rather than honest work. Even as a prostitute he is a dishonest trader: he poses as a woman selling straight sex to male clients, whereas he is in fact a man masquerading as a woman.[10] The sex he sells to his unwitting, and hence cheated customers is in fact anal sex. This is the purpose of John Britby's reported testimony that he believed Rykener to be a woman. Britby here colludes with the magistrates' agenda to highlight Rykener's dishonesty. Rykener is no less complicit in his testimony. In offering a salacious history of cross-dressing and sexual transgression, Rykener allows the mayor and his fellow magistrates ammunition against a variety of targets.

[3] D. L. Boyd and R. M. Karras, 'The Interrogation of a Male Transvestite Prostitute in Fourteenth Century London', *GLQ*, 1 (1995), 459–65, expanded the following year as Karras and Boyd, ' "Ut cum muliere" ', pp. 99–116. The underlying text was brought to their attention by Sheila Lindenbaum.

[4] For subsequent Rykener scholarship see C. Dinshaw, *Getting Medieval: Sexualities and Communities, Pre- and Postmodern* (Durham, NC: Duke University Press, 1999), pp. 100–12, 138–39; F. Rexroth, *Deviance and Power in Late Medieval London*, trans. by P. E. Selwyn (Cambridge: Cambridge University Press, 2007), pp. 269–71; J. M. Bennett, 'England: Women and Gender', in *A Companion to Britain in the Later Middle Ages*, ed. by S. H. Rigby (Oxford: Blackwell, 2003), pp. 87–106 (pp. 87–8 and 100–1); T. Linkinen, 'Sukupuolinen vieras John "Eleanor" Rykener: Naisena esiintynyt miesprostituoitu 1300-luvun Lontoossa', *Historiallinen aikakauskirja*, 3 (2004), 326–34; C. Beattie, 'Gender and Femininity in Medieval England', in *Writing Medieval History*, ed. by Nancy Partner (London: Arnold, 2005), pp. 153–70; R. Evans, 'The Production of Space in Chaucer's London', in *Chaucer and the City*, ed. by A. Butterfield (Cambridge: Brewer, 2006), pp. 41–56: J. M. Bennett and S. McSheffrey, 'Early, Erotic and Alien: Women Dressed as Men in Late Medieval London', *History Workshop Journal*, 77 (2014), 1–25. Rexroth's book was first published in German in 1999. I have only listed some more important items. I have not read Tom Linkinen's article.

[5] Karras and Boyd, ' "Ut cum muliere" ', pp. 109–10. Cf. Beattie, 'Gender and femininity', pp. 155–58.

[6] E.g. 'gender transgression, rather than sodomy or prostitution, is at issue in the legal proceedings against ... John Rykener': R. S. Sturges, *Chaucer's Pardoner and Gender Theory: Bodies of Discourse* (New York: Macmillan, 2000), p. 183, n. 38. See also Bennett, 'England: Women and Gender', p. 87.

[7] Evans, 'The Production of Space', p. 45.

[8] Dinshaw, *Getting Medieval*, pp. 100–12.

[9] Evans, 'The Production of Space', pp. 41–56.

[10] Cf. Evans, 'The Production of Space', pp. 49–50.

In relating how he had first dressed as a woman at the instigation of one Elizabeth Brouderer, Rykener continues the theme of dishonest trading. Elizabeth used her own daughter to lure male clients, but substituted Rykener during the night, telling the clients the following morning that they had in fact had sex with Rykener.[11] This Elizabeth Brouderer is probably to be understood as the Elizabeth Moring noted at length in the city's Letter Book 'H' ten years earlier.[12] Elizabeth was tried for operating a brothel under the cover of an embroidery business and for luring girls into prostitution under the guise of apprenticeships. The narrative again takes a sideswipe at incontinent priests and offers an account of one Joan who had complained to the mayor that her mistress had made her spend two nights with a priest under the pretext of lighting his way home. Joan's innocent abroad naïveté, reminiscent of the eponymous heroine of *Fanny Hill*, another male-authored narrative from a later era, serves as a foil for Elizabeth's deception.

These two apparently related cases co-exist with more conventional prosecutions for deception such as of a baker who inserted iron into his bread to increase the weight, a trader selling counterfeit spices, a scrivener who forged deeds, or a man who masqueraded as the Earl of Ormond.[13] Interestingly, these cases are all recorded in the Letter Books of the City; the kinds of cases recorded alongside the Rykener case in the Plea and Memoranda Rolls tend to focus on property and debt litigation.[14] The records insist on a moralizing discourse of deceit and falsehood discovered and punished which serves to reinforce the claim to moral authority of the civic governors. What the Rykener and the Moring cases specifically reveal, however, is a concern to enforce a conservative gender ideology which clearly distinguished men from women by dress and understood heterosexuality as normative.[15] An anxiety about women traders follows from this agenda. Such concerns may be contextualized in the understanding that society after the plague was in need of reform and that a divinely sanctioned social and gender hierarchy had to be restored.[16] Both cases also reflect an urban economy in which women were conspicuous as traders and apprenticeships were available to young women in much the same way as young men.[17] Like the mid-eighteenth-century world critiqued by Cleland in *Fanny Hill*, London is represented as a place of trade and commerce, where people bought and sold a very diverse range of commodities and services. Concern about honesty is here a specifically bourgeois concern that grows out of the needs of trade.[18]

Although Dinshaw and Evans both appreciate the fictive qualities of the narrative, no one to date has questioned the historicity of the actors or events described. Rykener's historicity

---

[11] That Brouderer's intention was to blackmail customers is suggested in Rexroth, *Deviance and Power*, p. 270.

[12] Rexroth argues that such an identification is 'speculation', but this is predicated on his understanding of the historicity of the Rykener case: *Deviance and Power*, p. 270, n. 14; *Memorials of London and London Life in the XIIIth, XIVth, and XVth Centuries*, ed. by H. T. Riley (London: Longmans, Green and Co., 1848), pp. 484–86.

[13] *Memorials of London and London Life*, ed. by Riley, pp. 496–98, 527–29, 536–37.

[14] I discuss below the Walpole case that is recorded immediately alongside that of Rykener and does not fit this pattern.

[15] For a discussion of the appropriateness of a modern discourse of homosexuality and heteronormativity etc. see T. Pugh, *Sexuality and its Queer Discontents in Middle English Literature* (New York: Palgrave Macmillan, 2008), pp. 1–19.

[16] Cf. J. Hatcher, 'England in the Aftermath of the Black Death', *Past and Present*, 144 (1994), pp. 3–35, especially 11–19, 27.

[17] Caroline M. Barron, 'The Education and Training of Girls in Fifteenth-Century London', in *Courts, Counties and the Capital in the later Middle Ages*, ed. by D. E. S. Dunn, The Fifteenth Century Series, 4 (Stroud: Sutton, 1996), pp. 139–53.

[18] Cf. Gervase Rosser's arguments respecting the value of guilds in an urban, commercial context: 'Crafts, Guilds, and the Negotiation of Work in the Medieval Town', *Past and Present*, 154 (1997), 3–31.

is indeed implicitly important to Judith Bennett, David Boyd and Ruth Karras, Shannon McSheffrey, Frank Rexroth and several other commentators in their discussions of the case.[19] That the text was created as the record of an actual case has always been presumed. Certainly the presence of the case in the Plea and Memoranda rolls initially appears unproblematic, though closer scrutiny reveals a slight inconsistency in the location of the entry at the very beginning of the second membrane of roll A34 alongside only one other case. This second case concerns one John Walpole, tailor, who had a longstanding grievance over his treatment in Ludgate jail. Its immediate interest here is that it references the issue of good governance by the mayor and aldermen and it is written up in a staged and dramatic way. It purports to give the findings of a jury of inquest dated 6 February 1395 concerning a verbal exchange in the vicinity of St Paul's between Walpole and John Fressh, the mayor, which had culminated in Walpole taunting the mayor with the threat, 'mayor, do me justice, or I will bring such a mob about you that you will be glad to do justice'. In response the mayor had ordered that he be taken to Newgate Prison, but as he was led away Walpole raised the hue and cry protesting that 'the mayor of London wants to have me falsely imprisoned because I sue for justice'. On arrival at Newgate, Walpole asserted that a number of earlier mayors had governed falsely. The jurors concluded that 'a great part of the uproar and rancour in the city from the time of Nicholas Twyford to the present day was made and spread by the ill-will of John Walpole, who was a great disseminator of discord'.[20] Introduced into this account at the point that the two men had entered St Paul's churchyard are the notorious Sir John Bushy and Sir William Bagot, both by this date closely associated with Richard II. They appear to play no part in the narrative other than to be present at this one moment, so their inclusion in the inquest account is very deliberate.

Somewhat unusually these two cases together occupy the whole of the recto of that membrane.[21] It is, however, the details of the Rykener case that raise the most immediate queries. First, as others have remarked, though Britby and Rykener are brought before the mayor presiding over the mayoral court and are made to answer questions put to them and though there is a clear statement that the two men were discovered engaged in sex, no

---

[19] Bennett, 'England: Woman and Gender', pp. 87–88, 100–1; S. McSheffrey, *Marriage, Sex, and Civic Culture in Late Medieval London* (Philadelphia: University of Pennsylvania Press, 2006), p. 149; Karras and Boyd, ' "Ut cum muliere" ', pp. 101–16; Rexroth, *Deviance and Power*, pp. 269–71. It is, of course, historians rather than literary scholars that have based their arguments on the assumed historicity of the case.

[20] *Calendar of the Plea and Memoranda Rolls of the City of London. Volume 3: 1381–1412*, ed. by A. H. Thomas (Cambridge: Cambridge University Press, 1932), p. 229. Twyford was mayor in 1388.

[21] The minutes of business in the mayor's court are not consistently recorded in the Plea and Memoranda Rolls. It would seem that certain more interesting cases were singled out for record in the City's Letter Books, which served as memoranda of the business of City government, whereas much routine court activity, often concerning property and debt litigation or administrative matters such as recording letters of attorney were documented in the Plea and Memoranda Rolls, albeit in rather loose chronological order. Other cases noted earlier (membrane 1) on the same roll (A34) as the Rykener case is found include a plaint by an apprentice whose master had failed to make him a freeman even after ten years (dated 4 November 1394) and a property dispute (dated 26 January 1395). On the verso of the second membrane there are again a couple of property and debt cases dated 18–19 October 1395. The cases on the third (and final) membrane of the roll also date to 1395. The previous roll (A33) contains cases from 1393 (membranes 1–3), 1394 (membranes 4–5r, 6–7r, 8), and stray cases from various years at the beginning of the fifteenth century (membranes 6v and 7v). None of the cases from 1394 on roll A33 is later in date than October, so the inclusion of the Rykener case on the following roll is logical, but its placement at the beginning of a new membrane is noteworthy. See *Calendar of the Plea and Memoranda Rolls, 1381–1412*, ed. by Thomas, pp. 205–32. For discussion of the mayor's court see *Calendar of Early Mayor's Court Rolls, 1298–1307*, ed. by A. H. Thomas (Cambridge: Cambridge University Press, 1924), pp. vii–xlv; C. Barron, *London in the Later Middle Ages: Government and People 1200–1500* (Oxford: Oxford University Press, 2004), pp. 154–56.

actual charges are recorded. Neither transvestism nor buggery were matters that are otherwise documented in English secular courts and the mayor's court of London would not have been considered competent to exercise jurisdiction at least in respect of sodomy.[22] Britby may have confessed to fornication, but this fell outside the competence of the court.[23] Prostitution, understood as the sale of sexual services — we are specifically told that Rykener demanded payment for his labour — was outlawed within the city of London and Soper Lane was very much within the city.[24] That said, there seems to have been little concern otherwise to prosecute or to punish individual sex workers; the main targets were the pimps and procuresses who controlled the trade. It may be that Rykener is an exception to this rule of thumb; he was no poor young woman forced or tricked into selling her body in order to get by, the pawn of the pimp or procuress who controlled her, nor was he offering vaginal sex.[25] But this does little to account for the questions posed to Rykener, nothing to explain his fulsome confession to numerous instances of both homosexual and heterosexual sex, almost all of which fell outside the boundaries of the court's jurisdiction (sometimes by many miles), nor the details of his work as an embroideress or a tapster (barmaid) which form part of his narrative. Even if we suppose — to confuse an historical Rykener with the textual Rykener — he was pathologically garrulous or a compulsive liar, the decision of the clerk making the entry to include so much detail irrelevant to the one specific transgression of prostitution within the city walls remains problematic.

Second, there is no record of a verdict or of punishment. Indeed, and quite exceptionally by the standards of the mayor's court, there is no further record of any response or action on the part of the court nor any further notice of Rykener. This is in essence a corollary of the first point. The absence of explicit charges and of any verdict or sentence is all the more striking a lacuna since, though the record is not an actual trial transcript, it still presents an unusually full account of what the two allegedly told the court. It ends abruptly with the last words of Rykener's reported testimony. No space is left before the next entry to suggest that such material was intended or that the clerk had left his task incomplete.

The discussion thus far draws attention to some peculiarities of the Rykener case, but of itself hardly disproves its historicity. I wish now to explore further evidence for the two

---

[22] The (?)early fourteenth-century English law compilation known as *Britton* indicates sodomy was punishable by death by burning. This would have made it a felony and so a matter reserved to the royal courts and beyond the jurisdiction of a borough court, though there is no evidence this was in fact the case: *Britton: The French Text Carefully Revised, with an English Translation, Introduction and Notes*, ed. by Francis Morgan Nichols, 2 vols (Oxford: Clarendon, 1865), I, 41. Helmut Puff has shown that towns within the German Empire and Switzerland, which historically often enjoyed rather greater autonomy, did act in sodomy cases, but not usually before the fifteenth century: H. Puff, 'Localizing Sodomy: The "Priest and Sodomite" in Pre-Reformation Germany and Switzerland', *Journal of the History of Sexuality*, 8 (1997), 165–95; H. Puff, *Sodomy in Reformation Germany and Switzerland, 1400–1600* (Chicago: University of Chicago Press, 2003), pp. 17–18. See also McSheffrey, *Marriage, Sex, and Civic Culture*, pp. 148–49; Karras and Boyd, ' "Ut cum muliere" ', p. 113, n. 10. Cf. the late fourteenth-century case of the hermaphrodite priest of Lübeck discussed below.

[23] This was a matter for the Church courts in their *ex officio* (or policing) capacity: Helmholz, *Marriage Litigation*, p. 70.

[24] R. M. Karras, *Common Women: Prostitution and Sexuality in Medieval England* (New York: Oxford University Press, 1996), pp. 14–15.

[25] Karras and Boyd argue that Rykener would not have been considered a prostitute because the medieval understanding of the prostitute 'was intimately tied up with femininity': Karras and Boyd, ' "Ut cum muliere" ', pp. 103–5. However, that the text clearly presents Rykener's interest in payment for sexual services and his promiscuity/availability, both crucial characteristics of medieval understandings of prostitution, suggests otherwise. There may be other reasons why the text is not in fact concerned with charges, verdicts, or punishments.

protagonists of the case, considering first John Britby. As a locative byname *Britby* (or obvious variant spellings) is obscure: there is a Britby in Cumberland and there are a small number of near-contemporary men named *Britby*. Of particular interest are a John Britby, clerk, noted in March 1384 and a John de Britby, recorded as the vicar of Stainton near Yarm (Yorkshire, North Riding), a church appropriated to Guisborough Priory, from 1410. It is possible these two references concern the same man towards the beginning and rather later in his career.[26] Given the apparent rarity of the name and the near coincidence of dates and of location — Britby is said to be from the county of York, i.e. Yorkshire, but not from a town or city that might be known in London such as York or Doncaster — it very possible that the John de Britby, subsequently vicar of an obscure Yorkshire parish, but perhaps only a clerk in minor orders some sixteen years earlier, was one and the same as the John Britby who propositioned Rykener. He may also have been at one time a royal clerk.[27] This does not absolutely confirm the historicity of the John Britby of the record, but it does make it likely. It certainly suggests at least that this is not a fabricated name.

If *Britby* is a very unusual name, then *Rykener* is no less. I have discovered only three other Rykeners, including two — perhaps one and the same — John Rykeners. A John Rykener of Bengeo (Herts.) is noted in 1403. Perhaps more interesting is John Rykener, clerk noted in January 1399 as having escaped from the Bishop of London's prison at Bishop's Stortford (Herts.) together with one Thomas Mareys, chaplain.[28] This prompts the question of why he was imprisoned in the first place. His clerical status no doubt explains why he was subject to the bishop's jurisdiction, but what serious matter led to him being held in an, albeit leaky, jail?[29]

[26] John Britby, clerk, was named with two other clerks, two knights and several other men as one of those enfeoffed with the manor of Powerstock (Dorset) by the (presumably) dying Sir William de Wyndesor, the husband of Alice Perrers: *Calendar of the Patent Rolls Preserved in the Public Record Office, Richard II–Henry IV*, 10 vols (London: H. M. Stationary Office, 1895–1909), *1381–85*, 390 (hereafter *CPR*). For John de Britby, vicar, see J. Graves, *The History of Cleveland, in the North Riding of the County of York* (Carlisle: Jollie, 1808), p. 479. This John appears to have been replaced as vicar in 1435, which would be compatible with this same John being a young man in 1394, but could also fit with his being a clerk, perhaps in minor orders, ten years earlier.

[27] Nicholas de Rounhey, one of the two other clerks named in the notice of the 1384 enfeoffment (note 25 above), can be identified with a chaplain of that name who was presented to the church of Debden (near Saffron Walden, Essex) by the king, the living being then temporarily in the king's gift. Rounhey would therefore appear to be a clerk in the king's service rewarded in the usual way with ecclesiastical preferment. This lends credence to the possibility that Britby was at some point a clerk in royal service, though — assuming he was the same man — his career seems not have been very successful. The vicarage he occupied latterly — valued at £5 14s. 2d. in the early sixteenth century — was not very lucrative and was dependent on Guisborough Priory and not royal patronage: *CPR 1374–77*, p. 130.

[28] *Calendar of the Close Rolls Preserved in the Public Record Office, Richard II–Henry IV*, 10 vols (London: H. M. S. O., 1914–1932), *1402–5*, 287 (hereafter *CCR*); *CPR 1396–99*, p. 461. John Rykener of Bengeo was associated with Sir Edward Benstead and Philip Thornbury, esquire, Hertfordshire landowners. There is a place called Rickney near Bengeo so the names may be related. Of John Rykener, clerk, nothing is otherwise known; the Patent Roll entry is concerned with the bishop of London's failure to keep his prison secure rather than the prisoners who escaped. The *Victoria County History* observes that the bishop's gaol at Stortford 'was used for all criminals within the liberty of the bishop in Hertfordshire, but the greater number of prisoners were convicted clerks'. It goes on to note that there were numerous escapes of prisoners during Bishop Robert Braybrooke's time. The propinquity of Bengeo and Bishop's Stortford — they are only a dozen miles apart — strengthens the possibility that these two Johns are one and the same. The third Rykener was a William Rykener, monk, recorded in the infirmary of St Swithun's cathedral priory at Winchester in 1382: *The Victoria History of the County of Hertford*, ed. by William Page, 5 vols (Westminster: Constable, 1902–23), III, 297–99; *Compotus Rolls of the Obedientiaries of St Swithun's Priory, Winchester*, ed. by G. W. Kitchin, Hampshire Record Society, 7 (London: Simpkin, 1892), p. 279.

[29] Simple fornication would not be a reason for a clerk to be held in a bishop's prison awaiting judicial process, but a variety of more serious matters would. This chance notice in the Patent Rolls could thus tally with the case from

Rykener is thus an actual, but uncommon name and the John Rykener of our text may well be identified with, or at least based upon, one or other (or both) of the men just noticed. He, like his client Britby, may have been a clerk or *clericus*, perhaps part of a larger subculture of men with clerical training drawn to the capital by the prospect of employment in royal service and the lure of ecclesiastical preferment. It is entirely possible that these two men came at some point to the attention of the city authorities. It follows that the entry in the Plea and Memoranda rolls at least names actual historical personages. It may even be that Rykener was known or suspected as practicing illicit sex. He may even have been caught with Britby.

Rykener may have been a real person, but his unusual name — as Carolyn Dinshaw has suggested — has some interesting resonances. She comments ' "Rykener" seems particularly appropriate for a prostitute (who reckons — counts — money) telling (reckoning — recounting, narrating) a story'.[30] Following Dinshaw's lead, we may note that the Middle English noun *rekenere* describes one who keeps accounts, precisely the kind of office a secular clerk might perform. Among the spellings found are those that substitute an *i* for the first *e*, taking us closer in sound to Rykener's name.[31] Dinshaw's discussion of the 'appropriateness' of Rykener's name references the Middle English *rekenen* — from which *rekener* derives.[32] The first meaning of *rekenen* — to count or to reckon — seems pertinent to trade generally rather than prostitution as such; the Bracton-author states that a burgess's son 'is taken to be of full age when he knows how properly to count money, measure cloths and perform other similar paternal business'.[33] The second meaning — 'to narrate' or 'recount' — seems especially pertinent in this instance. There may also be resonances of the verb *raiken*, which can mean to wander about at will.[34] The Rykener of the record relates an extraordinary narrative that takes him from London to Burford and back again. This logic would suggest his name may not just be happy coincidence, but deliberate choice if not actual fabrication.

Some other names noted in the narrative appear to signify actual persons. As already noticed, Elizabeth Brouderer or Elizabeth the embroideress, who employed Rykener and 'first dressed him in womanly garb', is probably one and the same as the Elizabeth Moring who appeared before the same court nine years earlier for running a prostitution racket masquerading as a legitimate embroidery business. She lured innocent girls by offering them apprenticeships only to prostitute them.[35] Moring at the time was living in All Hallows on the Wall parish, but she was expelled from the city by way of punishment. It is very possible that she subsequently resided at an address outside Bishopsgate, which is the location that Rykener attributes to Elizabeth Brouderer, being a matter of perhaps a couple of hundred yards distant, but, significantly, beyond the city gates.

A number of other named persons give every impression of being real personages, but I have only managed to identify one. Dns William Foxlee, scholar of Oxford, was very probably the same person as the Dns Foxle noted in 1410–11 as a chaplain of New College.[36] Philip,

---

the mayor's court, but hardly explains the five year interval between the two.
[30] Dinshaw, *Getting Medieval*, p. 103.
[31] *MED*, under *rekenere (n.)*.
[32] *MED*, under *rekenen*.
[33] *Bracton on the Laws and Customs of England*, ed. by George E. Woodbine, trans. by Samuel E. Thorne, 2 vols (Cambridge, MA: Belknap, 1968), II, 250.
[34] *MED*, under *raiken* 1c and 1d.
[35] Karras, *Common Women*, pp. 59–60 and 163, n. 49; Karras and Boyd, ' "Ut cum muliere" ', p. 114, n. 42. A translation of the case is published in *Memorials of London and London Life*, ed. by Riley, pp. 484–86.
[36] A. B. Emden, *A Biographical Register of the University of Oxford to A.D. 1500*, 3 vols (Oxford: Clarendon, 1957–

the rector of Theydon Garnon ought to be identifiable, but in fact other rectors' names are recorded for the pertinent date. I have been unable to find Brother John Barry of the Friars Minor, John Clerc of the Swan at Burford — with whom Ryckener claimed to have stayed for six weeks whilst employed in the capacity of a tapster or barmaid — and Joan, the daughter of John Mathew of Beaconsfield — with whom he claims to have lain like a man.[37] Dns. John, formerly chaplain at the Church of St. Margaret Pattens is also in principle identifiable.[38] The Oxford scholars Dns. John and Dns. Walter, and Brother Michael, another Franciscan, an anonymous Carmelite, and six foreign men, who encountered Rykener at Burford, together with two foreign friars minor, two chaplains, many nuns and many other women, married and single, all noticed in Rykener's account, are at best names. There is enough detail here to lend Rykener's account credibility, but we might also see this in part as a rhetorical strategy.[39]

Eleanor or Alianor is the name that Rykener adopted when dressed in women's clothing. It is not a rare name, but it is a name much more associated with royalty than the commonality.[40] It is, therefore, a name with pretensions, but it could well have satirical intent. Dinshaw suggests the name references Rykener's 'alienness' or 'otherness'. This may tell us more about modern scholarly interests in 'the other' than contemporary perceptions, though some resonance with the Middle English term for a foreigner cannot be overruled.

The final name to be explored is 'Anna meretrix quondam cuiusdam famuli domini Thome Blount' whom Rykener claimed first instructed him how to have sex as a woman. *Anna*, or *Ann(e)* in English, was rarely used as a given name as early as 1394.[41] Indeed easily the best known Anne was the recently deceased queen, Anne of Bohemia. It could be, therefore, that this Anne or Anna too was not a native Englishwoman — and perhaps Dutch or German since the name was more common in these regions.[42] *Meretrix* is here a slightly problematic term as

---

59), II, 720.

[37] A Thomas de Ulseby was presented to the rectory of Theydon Garnon in 1391 and a William Wasselyn in October 1394; no Philip is found: R. Newcourt, *Repertorium Ecclesiasticum Parochiale Londinense: An Ecclesiastical Parochial History of the Diocese of London*, 2 vols (London: Motte, 1708–10), II, 584. Barry is not found among the recorded graduates of either university. 'The Swan' at Burford is documented in 1629 by the bridge over the River Windrush. Swan Lane, which runs off Burford's High Street, was historically Mullender's Lane. 'The Swan' is not noticed among the medieval inns recorded in the recent 'England's Past for Everyone' study of Burford: R. H. Gretton, *The Burford Records: A Study in Minor Town Government* (Oxford: Clarendon, 1920), pp. 310, 370; A. Catchpole, D. Clark and R. Peberdy, *Burford: Buildings and People in a Cotswold Town* (Chichester: Phillimore, 2008), p. 47.

[38] John Stakbole was rector in 1379, but neither of the two chaplains named in that year was called John: *The Church in London, 1375–92*, ed. by A. K. McHardy, London Record Society, 13 (Woodbridge: Boydell, 1977), p. 11.

[39] Church court depositions include details designed to show that the deponent really witnessed the events they describe. Witnesses were sometimes specifically asked additional questions about the clothes people wore or the weather.

[40] The name *Alianor* or *Eleanor* is scarcely to be found in the extant nominative listings for the later fourteenth-century poll taxes. Using a sample of about 1,300 female names from the Suffolk poll tax of 1381, Sara Uckelman found only one instance: S. L. Uckelman, 'Index of Names in the 1381 Suffolk Poll Tax', pp. 1–25 (p. 7), published electronically at http://www.ellipsis.cx/~liana/names/english/suffolk1381.pdf (accessed 1 March 2011).

[41] Philip Stell counted the frequency of names of some 17,000 females from extant poll tax returns for Yorkshire in 1379 and 1381. Commenting that 'the names of the Holy Family ... were almost never used', he noticed the name Anne (Anna) only six times: P. M. Stell, 'Forenames in Thirteenth- and Fourteenth-Century Yorkshire: A Study Based on a Biographical Database Generated by Computer', *Medieval Prosopography*, 20 (1999), 95–128 (pp. 116 and 126). Uckelman found nine instances of *Anna* in the Suffolk 1381 poll tax returns: Uckelman, 'Index of Names', p. 6.

[42] Anna is found in sources of the period from the Low Countries: B. Brokamp, 'Female First Names in the Annual Accounts of Deventer 1337–1393', published electronically at http://www.deventerburgerscap.nl/studies/voornamen-vrouw-en.htm and S. L. Uckelman, 'Dutch Names

there is a tension between the Latin word for a prostitute that the recording clerk has chosen and Anne's former association with a servant/employee/retainer of Sir Thomas Blount; the translation 'whore' offered by Karras and Boyd probably gets us close to the English term that hides behind the Latin.[43] In modern English, it might also be rendered as *mistress*, though the Latin text could just as well have read *mulier*, *amazia*, or even *amica*. The juxtaposition of Anne and *meretrix*, however, begins to read like a formal appellation, Anne the Prostitute.

We know or may surmise four things about the textual Anne. First, she was most likely dead. The text describes her as formerly the mistress of an unnamed man, a formula that could perhaps imply that the relationship had ended, but much more likely indicates she was deceased.[44] Second, she was probably not English. Third, she is closely identified with the sex trade; it is implicitly as a professional sex worker that Anne taught Rykener to have anal sex like a woman. Fourth, she was at one time the mistress of someone in the service of Sir Thomas Blount. Evidently Blount's name is more important than that of the anonymous employee. Sir Thomas was a man of supposedly comparatively modest means who achieved a considerable degree of importance through devoted service to Richard II.[45] Anna was then very much the girl who danced with a man who danced with a girl who danced with the Prince of Wales — or in this instance the king himself. Once again, however, the historicity of Anne as a person is less than clear. The one-time attachment to an anonymous man who worked for one of the better known courtiers of the day hardly identifies her. Her given name is bound up with a work identity that lends her only a generic identity as a foreign, possibly Flemish sex worker. This is, of course, a plausible identity. Several of the women working as employees of the Southwark stews — in effect brothels — according to the 1381 poll tax returns were given the rather significant second name of Frowe, a version of the Dutch word for woman.[46] Ruth Karras indeed notes that 'Flemish, Dutch, and Low German women are particularly prominent in the records as prostitutes and bawds' and speculates that Flemish women may have been especially in demand as prostitutes.[47] What we can be more certain of is that women from the Low Countries were associated with the London sex trade in the contemporary imagination.

Thus far the evidence for the historicity of this case is ambivalent. The two principle protagonists are likely real persons. At least one of the men for whom Rykener provided sex in return for payment is also documented, though one is not. The case appears within the appropriate archive and is written in a form clearly informed by the conventions of the mayor's court. Magisterial concerns about dishonest trading — and women as dishonest traders —

1393–96', published electronically at http://www.ellipsis.cx/~liana/names/dutch/dutch14.html (all accessed 1 March 2011). Cf. also O. Leys and J. van der Schaar, *Vlaamse vrouwennamen en Hollandse naamgeving in de Middeleeuwen*, Anthroponymica, 10 (Amsterdam: Instituut voor Naamkunde, 1959), p. 28.

[43] Karras and Boyd, ' "Ut cum muliere" ', p. 111.

[44] Karras and Boyd render the Latin 'Anna meretrix quondam cuiusdam famuli' as 'Anna the whore of a former servant', but I read *quondam* to qualify Anne's status rather than that of Sir Thomas's employee: Karras and Boyd, ' "Ut cum muliere" ', p. 111.

[45] Sir Thomas Blount had remarried for the second time to a widowed heiress beyond childbearing age, in all probability, earlier in 1394: L. Clark, 'Sir Thomas Blount (*b*. after 1348, *d*. 1400)', in *The Oxford Dictionary of National Biography*, published electronically at http://www.oxforddnb.com (hereafter *ODNB*); 'Sir Thomas Blount (exec. 1400), of Laverstock, Wilts.', in *The House of Commons, 1386–1421*, ed. by J. S. Roskell, Linda Clark and Carole Rawcliffe, The History of Parliament, 4 vols (Stroud: Sutton, 1992), II, 261–62.

[46] *The Poll Taxes of 1377, 1379 and 1381*, ed. by C. C. Fenwick, Records of Social and Economic History, n. s. 27, 29, 37, 3 vols (Oxford: Oxford University Press, 1998–2005), II, 564. Two women named *Aughte Frowe* are recorded, where *Aughte* may represent a form of the modern Dutch girl's name *Aagtje*, a variant of Agatha.

[47] Karras, *Common Women*, pp. 56–57.

colour the way the narrative of the case is presented. To this we may add concerns about incontinent priests and, to use contemporary terminology, aliens or foreigners in modern English. These sorts of concerns are echoed in the extant wardmote court records of a generation later, but are here suggested by the regular notice of clergy, particularly friars, among Rykener's clients, including two alien Franciscans and six foreign men, and the resonances of the Anne or Anna just discussed.[48] There remains, however, much that is odd about the case, viz. its position on the extant rolls, the absence of either charge or outcome, and the entirely uncharacteristic trouble of the clerk to record events allegedly located outside the city of London and hence by any measure outwith the jurisdiction of the court.

In the section that follows I shall attempt to recover the possible meanings or resonances of Rykener's itinerary. Rykener's first named destination was Oxford. He stayed for five weeks in the guise of an embroideress and confessed to having frequently (*sepius*) committed sodomy there with three scholars, all described as *dominus* ('Sir'), the courtesy title for a priest. Oxford may not have been a serious rival to London, but it was county borough with a taxed population in 1377 of 2,357 suggesting, once clergy are added in, a total easily approaching 4,000.[49] In 1327 the town had been granted laws and liberties modelled on the city of London and this was confirmed in 1378.[50] Indeed only a year before, in September 1393, the mayor of Oxford had personally met with the then London mayor and aldermen to verify the pertinent entry in the city's Letter Book 'E'.[51] The authority of the borough's mayor, aldermen, and bailiffs to govern effectively through their officers and courts, however, was seriously undermined by the rival authority of the University. Since 1355 and the St Scholastica day riot between townsfolk and scholars, it was the University, not the town, that regulated the trade in foodstuffs, the cleansing of the streets, and the carrying of weapons in the streets. The Chancellor's court exercised jurisdiction over all transgressions, other than homicide and mayhem, involving clerks of the university, their families, or employees.[52] Oxford may constitutionally have been modelled on London, but in effect by the later fourteenth century its civic institutions were emasculated. Rykener's narrative implicates three scholars and in so doing casts aspersions on the capacity of the Chancellor of the university to regulate those under his authority. Oxford may have another resonance. Richard II's favourite Robert de Vere, who lived in exile following the rout at Radcot Bridge and had died in 1392, inherited the title of Earl of Oxford.[53]

Burford in the last years of the fourteenth century was a much smaller place having only 367 taxpayers in 1377.[54] A seigniorial borough enjoying limited civic autonomy, in the later fourteenth century it was one of the Cotswold boom towns associated with the wool trade and cloth manufacture.[55] 1394, however, was a date of some significance for Burford. In that

[48] Cf. the 1422 wardmote court: *Plea and Memoranda Rolls, 1413–37*, ed. by Thomas, pp. 115–41.
[49] *The Poll Taxes*, ed. by Fenwick, II, 287.
[50] *Calendar of Charter Rolls*, 6 vols (London: H. M. S. O., 1903–27), IV, 12–13; *A History of the County of Oxford. Volume 4: City of Oxford*, ed. by A. Crossley and C. R. Elrington (London: Institute of Historical Research, 1979), p. 51.
[51] *Calendar of Letter-Books of the City of London. H: 1375–99*, ed. by Reginald R. Sharpe (London: City of London Corporation, 1907), pp. 398–99.
[52] *A History of the County of Oxford*, ed. by Crossley and Elrington, IV, 54–57.
[53] Richard had specifically asked that Robert be allowed to return only months before his death. When his body was eventually brought back, Richard reportedly opened the coffin, 'looked long at his face and touched it with his finger, publicly showing to Robert, when dead, the affection which he had shown him previously, when alive': A. Tuck, 'Vere, Robert de, Ninth Earl of Oxford, Marquess of Dublin, and Duke of Ireland (1362–1392)', *ODNB*.
[54] *The Poll Taxes*, ed. by Fenwick, II, 290.
[55] Gretton, *Burford Records*, pp. 12–13, 165–66; Catchpole et al., *Burford*, pp. 19, 33–52.

year Thomas Despenser achieved his majority and gained control of the manor which had previously been held in wardship by the crown. Despenser effectively grew up at court with the young Richard II and, like Robert de Vere, became one of his intimates and most ardent supporters. Modern economic historians would doubtless point to Burford as an example of a community that flourished in the new climate after the Black Death. From the perspective of London's civic governors at the end of the fourteenth century, however, Burford must have looked like the wild west — unregulated crafts, the absence of guild structures that were subject to the oversight of civic government, little effective control over the training of craft workers or the quality of goods, little control over the market, and a court that was driven by a lord's concern with revenue rather than a magisterial concern with order.[56] Rykener's Burford was also a symbol both of aristocratic control of town government and of the court of Richard II. Here Rykener plied with impunity his trade under the guise of a barmaid of the Swan.[57]

Beaconsfield lies six miles north of Windsor halfway along the main road between Oxford and London, being some twenty miles or so — a day's journey — from each. Beaconsfield then may signify little more than a break in Rykener's journey.[58] A Nicholas Bekenesfeld, however, was made a buyer for the royal household in 1394.[59] Beaconsfield may thus allude to the extravagant ways of the royal court by reference to the royal buyer who bore its name. Even during this pause — the duration is not specified, but it might well be but a single night — Rykener still managed to have sex with a couple of foreign Franciscan friars whilst dressed as a woman and sex 'as a man' with John Mathew's daughter, Joan. That Joan is described in relation to her father would tend to signal that she was unmarried and possibly comparatively young. From the perspective of a clerical calculus of sin, simple fornication weighed much less heavily than buggery with a man in holy orders, but this is not a Church court record.[60] The concerns of a civic court and of civic governors are not identical. Joan is identified in relation to her father because her father is deemed to stand in authority over her. By managing to seduce Joan — implicitly on a single night and possibly using his disguise as a woman to approach her — Rykener is seen as threat to family life and patriarchal order.

Rykener's final destination on his circuitous excursion were the lanes located behind St Katharine's Hospital, to the east of the Tower and to the south of St Mary Graces, and so within the Liberty of St Katharine's, an area associated with the sex trade.[61] The hospital of

---

[56] Gretton, *Burford Records*, p. 83; T. B. Pugh, 'Thomas Despenser, Second Lord Despenser (1373–1400)', in *ODNB*. Martyn Lawrence comments: 'none of the six generations of Despensers were particularly concerned with local lordship. Notwithstanding their success at court, their estates were poorly managed': M. Lawerence, ' "Too Flattering Sweet to be Substantial"? The Last Months of Thomas, Lord Despenser', in *Fourteenth Century England, IV*, ed. by J. S. Hamilton (Woodbridge: Boydell, 2006), pp. 146–58, quoting p. 152.

[57] By analogy with a satirical poem from the end of Richard's reign edited as 'On King Richard's Ministers', the Swan could have been taken as an allusion to Thomas of Woodstock or indeed his wife Eleanor de Bohun, the swan being the Bohun badge: *Political Poems and Songs Related to English History*, ed. by T. Wright, Rerum Britannicarum medii aevi scriptores, 14, 2 vols (London: Longman, Green, Longman, and Roberts, 1859–61), I, 363–66.

[58] Beaconsfield had a tax population of 194 in 1377. It would appear to have been divided between a multiplicity of manors, but in 1394 much land was under the immediate control of Sir Hugh Berwick. The Victoria County History otherwise offers few clues to the community at the end of the fourteenth century: *The Poll Taxes*, ed. by Fenwick, I, 62; *The Victoria history of the county of Buckingham*, ed. by W. Page, 5 vols (London: Constable, 1905–28), III, 155–65.

[59] *CPR 1391–96*, p. 539.

[60] Cordelia Beattie represents the clerical tradition from the *Somme le Roi* in table form: C. Beattie, *Medieval Single Women: The Politics of Social Classification in Late Medieval England* (Oxford: Oxford University Press, 2007), p. 49, table 2.1.

[61] Cf. *Memorials of London and London Life*, ed. by Riley, pp. 487–88.

St Katharine had been refounded in 1273 by Queen Eleanor of Provence. Thereafter it was the queen who appointed masters and took an active interest in its running. It was the recipient of royal patronage and came to support a number of royal chantries even at a time it was struggling to support the poor persons for which it was founded.[62] St Mary Graces was also a royal foundation of 1350 and apparently still being built around this date.[63] The Tower was, of course, a royal palace. Rykener's encounter with the former chaplain of a London city church and two other anonymous chaplains within the shadow of the Tower, and on land associated with the queen, begins to look like a dramatic illustration of the sewer theory of prostituion.[64] In medieval thought prostitution was a necessary evil and its regulation the key to good order; in the words of the continuator of Thomas Aquinas' *De Regno*, 'take away the sewer and you will fill the palace with foulness'. The text goes on, 'take away prostitutes from the world and you will fill it with sodomy'.[65]

Although Rykner's itinerary to the west of London follows an established route, it contains at the very least some striking coincidences relating to recent events. Oxford sent a mayoral delegation to London in 1393. Thomas Despenser assumed by reason of his majority the lordship of Burford in 1394. Nicholas Bekenesfeld, who presumably hailed from Beaconsfield, was appointed a buyer for the royal household in 1394 — and Richard II was purchasing lavishly in London at this time; Caroline Barron has characterized the period 1392–94 as a 'spending spree' on the part of the royal wardrobe, much of this expenditure being made in the City.[66] The itinerary also continues the allusions to King Richard and the royal household suggested by the otherwise gratuitous reference to Sir Thomas Blount and, more tenuously perhaps, the recently deceased Queen Anne. Burford signifies Despenser, Oxford denotes Robert de Vere, Beaconsfield signifies Nicholas Bekenesfeld, the Swan at Burford may, as we shall see, denote Thomas of Woodstock and his wife Eleanor de Bohun, and the lanes by St Katherine's allude once again to the queen and more specifically to the royal palace of the Tower.

There is one further dimension to Rykener's narrative worth noticing. Not only does Rykener describe a peregrination punctuated by sex acts, he also offers information about how he made his livelihood. He first described how he stole ('*asportavit*') two gowns from the rector of Theydon Garnon, who had visited Elizabeth Brouderer's house and had had sex with him 'as with a woman'. When the priest demanded Rykener return the gowns, Rykener claimed that he was married; any claim in the courts would have to be made against Rykener's husband.[67] This was tantamount to blackmail since to sue Rykener alone risked exposing the true nature of the rector's misdemeanour.[68] When he stayed for five weeks in Oxford, Rykener

---

[62] *The Victoria History of London. Volume 1: Romano-British London, Anglo-Saxon Remains, Ecclesiastical History, Religious Houses*, ed. by William Page (London: Constable, 1909), pp. 525–30; *CPR 1377–81*, p. 559.

[63] Page, ed., *A History of the County of London: Volume 1*, pp. 461–64.

[64] This is indeed illustrated by the case a century later of one Alice who allegedly acted as 'a common bawd especially between gentlemen of the court and whores living in the precincts of St. Katherine': Karras, *Common Women*, p. 79.

[65] H. A. Kelly, 'Bishop, Prioress, and Bawd in the Stews of Southwark', *Speculum*, 75 (2000), 342–88 (p. 343, n. 3).

[66] C. M. Barron, 'The Quarrel of Richard II with London 1392–97', in *The Reign of Richard II: Essays in Honour of May McKisack*, ed. by F. R. H. Du Boulay and C. M. Barron (London: Athlone, 1971), pp. 173–201, at p. 197.

[67] It is possible that anxieties concerning dealings with married female traders lie behind this part of the narrative.

[68] Interestingly, if we may extrapolate from the example of Emma Northercote who sued a priest for non-payment for services, sex workers may have had less to fear from the secular courts than their clients. It may be that borough courts would welcome the opportunity thus presented of showing up a man in holy orders: M. Kowaleski,

tells how he dressed as a woman and, calling himself Alianor, worked as an embroideress. Implicitly Elizabeth Brouderer, who 'first dressed him in womanly garb', taught him also the craft of embroidery as a front for sex work. Needlework was very much associated with women. The seamstress and the dressmaker are both occupations readily found among women sex workers.[69] Embroidery or 'brouderie,' however, has high-status implications. The product of broiderers' workshops went to make ecclesiastical vestments or bed hangings and dress accessories for the very wealthy. The almost contemporary will of John of Gaunt, for example, includes a rich vestment said to have been purchased from a London 'brouderer'.[70] By working as a female brouderer during his stay in Oxford, therefore, Rykener was knowingly exposing himself to a clerical or a wealthy clientele.[71]

Whilst in Burford, Rykener was employed as a tapster (barmaid) at the Swan. The later medieval tapster was invariably seen as sexually promiscuous. Of Absolon, the amorous clerk in Chaucer's near-contemporary 'The Miller's Tale', it is said that

> In al the toun nas brewhous ne taverne
> That he ne visited with his solas
> Ther any gaylard tappestere was.[72]

A century later the tapster was specifically equated with the sex worker in a Coventry ordinance.[73] Indeed the pub was often understood as a place where assignations might be made and female employees might double as sex workers.[74] Perhaps there is also significance in the inn's identity. The Swan, a common enough name that, unlike the more explicit Cardinal's Hat, has remained popular, may yet be suggestive.[75] Hieronymus Bosch's 'The Wayfarer', otherwise 'The Prodigal Son', which dates to circa 1500, depicts an inn that clearly symbolises debauchery — a man conspicuously gropes a woman carrying a vessel for ale or wine in the

---

'Women's Work in a Market Town: Exeter in the Later Fourteenth Century', in *Women and Work in Preindustrial Europe*, ed. by B. A. Hanawalt (Bloomington: Indiana University Press, 1986), pp. 145–64 (p. 154).

[69] Goldberg, *Women, Work, and Life Cycle*, p. 152; Karras, *Common Women*, p. 54.

[70] *Testamenta Eboracensia, or, Wills Registered at York*, ed. by J. Raine, Publications of the Surtees Society, 4, 30, 45, 53, 79, 106, 6 vols (London: Nichols, 1836–1902), I, 227.

[71] We have here perhaps a resonance of a contemporary anxiety about the usefulness of some kinds of luxury production. This is most bluntly articulated in the last of the nearly contemporaneous Lollard *Twelve Conclusions*, which names the crafts of the goldsmith and the armourer as two examples of such 'nout nedful' occupations, citing 1 Timothy 6:8 to imply that in contrast victualling and clothing were 'nedful' trades. The Rykener case, a product of the same era and intellectual climate, is not, however, a Lollard text and its targets may be wider. As a product of London civic administration it may echo the fissures between the victualling trades and the non-victualling trades, including goldsmiths, drapers, and mercers, that at times polarized City politics in the later fourteenth century. Foreign merchants, including Lombards, may also be an implicit target since they monopolized the supply of silk thread and gold wire, necessary materials for the brouderer's craft. The primary target, however, was the royal court. The medieval crown was expected to manage from the revenues of the crown lands and raise taxes only at time of war, but in the early 1390s Richard II endeavoured to raise funds by various means whilst pursuing peace with France: *Selections from English Wycliffite Writings*, ed. by Hudson, pp. 28–29; Bird, *Turbulent London*; C. M. Barron, 'Richard II and London', in *Richard II: The Art of Kingship*, ed. by A. Goodman and J. L. Gillespie (Oxford: Clarendon, 1999), pp. 129–54 (pp. 141–49).

[72] 'The Miller's Tale', in *The Riverside Chaucer*, ed. by L. D. Benson (Boston: Houghton Mifflin, 1987), pp. 68–71 (p. 70), ll. 334–36.

[73] The contemporary marginal annotation reads 'For Tapsters & harlattes': *The Coventry Leet Book*, ed. by Mary Dormer Harris, Early English Text Society, o. s. 134–35, 138, 146, 4 vols (London: Kegan Paul, Trench, Trubner, 1907–13), 545.

[74] Karras, *Common Women*, pp. 71–72; Goldberg, *Women, Work, and Life Cycle*, pp. 116–17.

[75] The cardinal's hat suggests the engorged corona of the male phallus. It may be that the swan suggests the male genitalia.

open doorway; the inn sports a sign of a swan.[76] At much the same date one of the stews of Southwark that had its sign painted on the front of the building facing the river was the Swan.[77] The implication of Rykener's lodging at the Swan in Burford in the capacity of a tapster is that John Clerc knowingly engaged him as a sex worker.

It is in the context of his time at Burford that Rykener related not only the number of clients he had, but something of the payments he received. The Franciscan John Barry gave him a gold ring, but it is the monetary payments made by three of six anonymous foreign (*extranei*) men and a Carmelite friar that are of especial interest. As a clothing community in the heart of the Cotswold wool country, Burford attracted merchants, including Italian wool merchants, so Rykener may well have been tapping into such a clientele.[78] Rykener claims that he received variously 12d., 20d., and 2s. (= 24d.). These are not trivial sums, but probably not exceptional either. Karras cites a later example of a Lombard paying 12d. for sex with a woman in London, but otherwise her analysis indicates a considerable range of rates. No doubt the price reflected both the services demanded and the market that a sex worker operated within; Karras suggests that payments of 1d. 'were probably typical of the lower end of the trade'.[79] We can find numbers of examples of women who specialized in offering sexual services to priests or religious and Rykener is reported as claiming that 'he more often took priests than others because they liked to give him more than other men'.[80] Foreign merchants, however, were another market that probably paid well.[81] In identifying clergy, religious, and Lombards as clients and clients for gay sex, however, the text tapped into a current discourse. For example in 1376 Parliament had been petitioned to expel all Lombard brokers since they practiced usury and had introduced 'un trop horrible vice qe ne fait pas a nomer'.[82] In 1387 a former Austin friar and Lollard enthusiast provoked rioting by preaching at the London church of St Christopher le Stocks that friars were murderers, traitors, and sodomites. He subsequently turned these charges into a bill which he attached to the doors of St Paul's cathedral.[83] In 1395, and only a couple of months after the Rykener case, the Lollard *Twelve Conclusions* attacked clerical celibacy since it 'inducith sodomie in al holy chirche'.[84]

It should now be apparent that, regardless of the underlying historicity of the persons or events described, the Rykener narrative works to reference overlapping contemporary concerns with governance — a theme also reiterated in the Walpole case enrolled immediately

---

[76] The painting is in the Museum Boymans van Beuningen, Rotterdam. D. Wolfthal, *In and Out of the Marital Bed: Seeing Sex in Renaissance Europe* (New Haven: Yale University Press, 2010), pp. 88–90.

[77] *A Survey of London by John Stow*, ed. by C. L. Kingsford, 2 vols (Oxford: Clarendon, 1908), II, 55.

[78] T. H. Lloyd, *The English Wool Trade in the Middle Ages* (Cambridge: Cambridge University Press, 1977), pp. 51–53; G. Holmes, 'Lorenzo de' Medici's London branch', in *Progress and Problems in Medieval England*, ed. by R. Britnell and J. Hatcher (Cambridge: Cambridge University Press, 1996), pp. 273–85 (pp. 281, 283); Catchpole et al, *Burford*, pp. 40, 42.

[79] Karras's discussion is derived primarily from late fifteenth-century London evidence: Karras, *Common Women*, pp. 74, 79–80.

[80] Goldberg, *Women, Work, and Life Cycle*, p. 152; Karras, *Common Women*, pp. 75, 79.

[81] Karras, *Common Women*, 78; Goldberg, *Women, Work, and Life Cycle*, p. 154.

[82] *The Parliament Rolls of Medieval England, 1275–1504*, ed. by Chris Given-Wilson and others, 16 vols (Woodbridge: Boydell, 2005), II, 332; H. A. Kelly, 'Law and Nonmarital Sex in the Middle Ages', in *Conflict in Medieval Europe: Changing Perspectives on Society and Culture*, ed. by Warren Brown and Piotr Górecki (Aldershot: Ashgate, 2003), pp. 175–94 (pp. 188–89 and n. 67).

[83] Thomas Walsingham, *Historia Anglicana*, ed. by H. T. Riley, Rolls Series, Rerum Britannicarum medii aevi scriptores, 28, 2 vols (London: Longman, Green, Longman, Roberts, and Green, 1863–64), II, 157–59.

[84] *Selections from English Wycliffite Writings*, ed. by A. Hudson (Cambridge: Cambridge University Press, 1978), pp. 25, 150.

after — and with dishonest trading, foreigners, incontinent clergy, the royal court, gender and sexuality. In this context, sodomy functions as a metaphor for a range of social evils that may have had particular resonances from a magisterial and metropolitan perspective. I shall now try to locate the events of the case within the larger chronological context of the thwart relationship between the city of London and Richard II.

Two years before the Rykener case in June 1392, Richard II had suspended the City's liberties and imprisoned the then mayor and sheriffs on account of the City's alleged misgovernment which had resulted in rioting. According to (partisan) London chroniclers, a servant of the Bishop of Salisbury stole a loaf of horse bread in Fleet Street and stabbed the baker's man when he tried to snatch the loaf back. The thief then ran for shelter in the bishop's London residence of Salisbury Inn just yards away down Salisbury Alley. As one later chronicle puts it, 'then rose the streete, namely the youth' and tried to break into the Inn, threatening to burn it down, and not desisting until the mayor and aldermen had been summoned and ordered people to return to their homes.[85] Meanwhile word of the disturbance reached the bishop, John Waltham, the Treasurer, at Westminster who, supported by Archbishop Thomas Arundel of York, the Chancellor, complained to Richard II.

Waltham's plaint prompted the imprisonment of the mayor, the imposition of Sir Edward Dalyngrigge, builder of Bodiam Castle and a trusted courtier, as warden, and the appointment of a commission to investigate the alleged misgovernment.[86] Only when the City agreed to pay £10,000 were its liberties, conditional on good governance, restored. This restoration was elaborately enacted in August of that year.[87] The ceremony is described by Richard of Maidstone, in a contemporary letter, and in London chronicles. It saw Richard greeted on Tower Bridge and led into the heart of the City.[88] The culmination of the ceremonial, in which the City was likened to a bridal chamber, the citizens to a bride, and Richard to a bridegroom, was on Cheapside. Here a beautiful young woman (*formosaque virgo*) wearing a

---

[85] *The Brut or The Chronicles of England*, ed. by F. W. D. Brie, Early English Text Society, o. s. 131, 136 (London: Oxford University Press, 1906–8), I, 345–46; *Grafton's Chronicle; or, History of England* (London: [n. pub.], 1809), pp. 458–59; Bird, *The Turbulent London of Richard II*, pp. 105–7; Barron, 'The Quarrel of Richard II', pp. 180–84.

[86] Prominent members of this commission were the Duke of York, whose daughter was married to Thomas Despenser, and the Duke of Gloucester, who was married to Eleanor or Alianor de Bohun: Bird, *The Turbulent London*, pp. 102–4, 107–9; Barron, 'The Quarrel of Richard II', pp. 184–88.

[87] *CPR 1391–96*, p. 226; Bird, *The Turbulent London*, p. 104; Barron, 'The Quarrel of Richard II', pp. 194–95. Barron notes further smaller contributions by Londoners over the next couple of years. These included a gift of a large ornamental bird with a very wide gullet for Queen Anne and a boy upon a dromedary for Richard. It is tempting to read meanings into these outré Christmas presents. The boy might stand for the king. Paul Strohm argues that the bird was a pelican symbolic of the Queen's self-sacrificing sympathy for the City, but this does not obviously fit contemporary depictions of pelicans nor does the chronicler simply use the Latin word '*pelicanus*'. Perhaps the wide gullet indicates an insatiable appetite: ibid., pp. 195–96; *Polychronicon Ranulphi Higden, Monachi Cestrensis*, ed. by J. L. Lumby, Rolls Series, Rerum Britannicarum medii aevi scriptores, 41, 9 vols (London: Longman, Green, Longman, Roberts, and Green, 1865–86), IX, 278; P. Strohm, *Hochon's Arrow: The Social Imagination of Fourteenth-Century Texts* (Princeton, NJ: Princeton University Press, 1992), pp. 106–7: *The Medieval Bestiary: Animals in the Middle Ages*, published electronically at http://bestiary.ca/ (accessed 8 March 2011).

[88] Richard Maidstone, *Concordia (The Reconciliation of Richard II with London)*, trans. by A. G. Rigg and ed. by David R. Carlson, TEAMS Middle English Texts (Kalamazoo: Western Michigan University for TEAMS, 2003), <http://d.lib.rochester.edu/teams/publication/carlson-and-rigg-maidstone-concordia>; H. Suggett, 'A Letter Describing Richard II's Reconciliation with the City of London, 1392', *English Historical Review*, 62 (1947), 209–13; *The Brut*, ed. by Brie, pp. 347–48. The ceremonial was partly modelled on the 1377 coronation: Barron, 'Richard II and London', pp. 150–54.

crown, accompanied by a young man dressed as an angel (ll. 275–316), gave golden crowns to the king and queen.[89]

The payment of £10,000, the restoration of the City's liberties, and the election of a new mayor and sheriffs did not fully restore the status quo ante. The ceremonial was a staged charade that merely patched the relationship between the City and the king.[90] The terms of a statute of 1354, invoked to justify the earlier suspension of the City's liberties on the grounds of misgovernment, still applied. It must have seemed to Londoners and to the mercantile elite who ordinarily governed the City that Richard was moved not by a failure of civic government, but rather by his desire for money and his frustration that, immediately prior to the events of 1392, London merchants had proved unwilling to lend to him.[91] After 1392 Londoners felt compelled to furnish the king with money, however uncertain the prospect of repayment, lest Richard should again annul the City's constitution. This was the context for a loan of 10,000 marks (£6,666 13s. 4d.) by the City in December 1394.[92] In fact the December loan was repaid the following year, but this could hardly have been anticipated. It was in this context of impotence in the face of arbitrary royal government, fear of providing Richard with an excuse for renewed attack on the City's constitution and governors, anger at his repeated demands for money, frustration that there seemed no way out, but also a strong sense of the injustice of the events of 1392 that the account of the Rykener case was entered into the Plea and Memoranda Rolls of the City of London. Once again coincidence begins to appear more than coincidence. The loan was paid on Saturday 5th December. Britby and Rykener were supposedly arrested on Sunday 6th December.

The climate of fear that prevailed in London between 1392 and June 1397 when a charter confirming London's privileges in perpetuity was granted, albeit only after the payment of a further 10,000 marks, is illuminated by the case of Peter Mildenhall.[93] Before his death, Mildenhall had said that Richard II 'was not able to govern any realm' and had wished 'that he were in his *gong* (latrina), where he might stay for ever without further governing any'.[94] Mildenhall had also expressed a desire carry the king off, which he said would be easy because Richard regularly travelled from Sheen to the City with only a light guard. We know this only because his son was made to appear before Chancery for having concealed his father's

---

[89] This is Paul Strohm's reading, though the self-representation of the City as '*thalamus*' is clearly signalled in Maidstone's sexually charged account. Indeed as Richard returns to his marriage chamber, the citizens signify that they yield their bodies 'Et regat ad libitum regia virga suos' (ll. 207–14): Maidstone, *Concordia*; Strohm, *Hochon's Arrow*, pp. 105–11. The pageantry is further discussed in the first chapter of S. Federico, *New Troy: Fantasies of Empire in the Late Middle Ages*, Medieval cultures, 36 (Minneapolis: University of Minnesota Press, 2003). Of Maidstone's account of the marriage of Richard to London seemingly brokered by Richard's queen, Federico comments (p. 25) 'competing with the poem's portrayal of a just and good husband and king is the image of a sexual deviant, even a criminal'. Two other chronicle accounts indicate that the angel or angels were boys and specify that Richard was actually crowned by an angel: *The Westminster Chronicle 1381–94*, ed. and trans. by L. C. Hector and B. F. Harvey (Oxford: Clarendon Press, 1982), pp. 502–7; *The Brut*, ed. by Brie, pp. 347–48.

[90] Caroline Barron refers to the events as a 'pantomime': 'The Quarrel of Richard II', p. 190.

[91] Distrust of making loans to Richard was the legacy of the former mayor Nicholas Brembre, whose policy of lending to Richard and encouraging other Londoners to lend was intended to secure the king's favour. Brembre's support of the king made him a target of the appellants who early in 1388 had him tried for treason. Richard singularly failed to support his ally despite the weakness of the appellants' case and Brembre was consequently executed: A. Prescott, 'Sir Nicholas Brembre (*d.* 1388), Merchant and Mayor of London', in *ODNB*.

[92] Barron, 'The Quarrel of Richard II', p. 196.

[93] Barron, 'The Quarrel of Richard II', p. 199.

[94] *CCR 1389–92*, p. 527. *Dong* is a Middle English term related to the modern English *dung*, but from the Latin gloss presumably functions here as a colloquial term for a privy.

defamatory words. Such comments may have been commonplace, but only when voiced circumspectly. They will hardly ever enter the written record. Even in the case of Mildenhall we are told that 'he spake many other disrespectful words disparaging the king's person', but these words are left undocumented, as if too pernicious to be made textual.[95] Towards the end of Richard's reign, after the city's constitution had been fully restored, Londoners were, according to Jean Froissart, a little more openly critical, 'they hated hym so sore'.[96]

The issue supposedly at the heart of the rift between Richard and the City was that of good governance. The charge of misgovernment levelled in 1392 seems particularly to have rankled with the civic governors. The issue can be seen to have been played out symbolically. In answer to an earlier petition regarding the butchering of meat, Richard had ordered the cleansing of the River Thames between the Palace of Westminster and the Tower. A writ to that effect dated February 1393 is recorded in the City Letter Books.[97] The City asserted its own act of moral cleansing later the same year, requiring that 'proclamation be made, that no man, freeman or foreigner, shall be so daring as to go about by night in the City of London, or the suburbs thereof, after nine of the clock' unless he were 'a lawful man' about 'some real cause' and carrying a light. An earlier curfew of eight o'clock was declared for aliens. The ordinance goes on immediately to reiterate long-standing rules relating to prostitution:

> whereas many and divers affrays, broils, and dissensions, have arisen in times past, and many men have been slain and murdered, by reason of the frequent resort of, and consorting with, common harlots, at taverns, brewhouses of huksters, and other places of ill-fame, within the said city, and the suburbs thereof; and more especially through Flemish women, who profess and follow such shameful and dolorous life: — we do by our command forbid, on behalf of our Lord the King, and the Mayor and Aldermen of the City of London, that any such women shall go about or lodge in the said city, or in the suburbs thereof, by night or by day.[98]

The supposed encounter on Cheapside between John Britby, a visitor to London from Yorkshire, and John Rykener, a man in a woman's dress, between eight and nine o'clock on the night of Sunday 6 December 1394 begins to take on a new depth of meaning within the context just outlined. Most immediately it is an assertion of the good governance of the City: malefactors are swiftly detected and promptly brought to answer for their misdeeds. More specifically it is a demonstration of the City's vigilance in rooting out and suppressing 'the frequent resort of, and consorting with, common harlots', the cause of 'many and divers affrays, broils, and dissensions', even murders.

---

[95] There is a slight chance that such speech may be recorded or reported as in defamation actions or in depositions. In 1356 in the ecclesiastical Court of York, John Jordan undermined one William Theker, a key witness for the opposing party, claiming that Theker had said he would be willing to offer a halfpenny to St Mary of Lincoln if the saint would ensure the king had ill fortune in his activities: York, Borthwick Institute for Archives, cause papers, CP.E.70. For a useful discussion of slander against Richard II see M. Hanrahan, 'Defamation as Political Contest during the Reign of Richard II', *Medium Aevum*, 72 (2003), pp. 259–76.

[96] G. B. Stow, 'Richard II in Jean Froissart's *Chroniques*', *Journal of Medieval History*, 11 (1985), 333–45 (quoting p. 341). We may note here a tradition of veiled criticism of the crown and leading magnates in the more public form of chronicle writing: P. Maddern, 'Weather, War and Witches: Sign and Cause in Fifteenth-Century English Vernacular Chronicles', in *A World Explored: Essays in Honour of Laurie Gardiner*, ed. by Anne Gilmour-Bryson (Parkville: University of Melbourne, History Dept., 1993), pp. 77–98 (pp. 84–90).

[97] *Parliament Rolls*, ed. by Given-Wilson et al., III, 317; *Calendar of Letter-Books of the City of London: H*, ed. by Sharpe, p. 392; Barron, 'Richard II and London', pp. 143–44.

[98] *Memorials of London and London Life*, ed. by Riley, pp. 534–35.

A further context that may be tapped into is that of storytelling. There are elements of the Rykener narrative that are reminiscent of the fabliaux genre, but it is actually to chronicles that I now wish to turn. Four different chronicle sources from Danzig, Linköping, Lüneburg, and Hannover, tell the story of the anonymous hermaphrodite of Lübeck. The narratives are dated variously to 1382 and 1384 and were patently circulating within Hanseatic trading routes and so were very likely known in London around the same period.[99] Quite possibly we are tapping into a strong element of urban mythology; the anonymity of the hermaphrodite, the absence of documentation from Lübeck itself, and the uncertainty of date render the historicity of the case profoundly doubtful, but the tale is striking. The narratives tell of a hermaphrodite who by night dressed as a woman and sold sex to male clients from a wooden booth. Her/his undoing, however, was that by day s/he practiced as a priest and celebrated mass. One day one of her/his clients from the previous night entered the church in which s/he was celebrating and was shocked to recognize the person with whom they had had sex the previous night. Together with a friend he followed him/her back to the booth and subsequently discovered his/her male genitalia when having sex with him/her that evening. The authorities were summoned and the unfortunate hermaphrodite prostitute-priest was arrested, condemned, and subsequently burnt dressed in her/his women's clothes. The resonances with the Rykener case — cross dressing, dishonesty, the close association of priests with homosexual activity, and the eventual intervention of the city authorities — are highly suggestive and may have helped shape the Rykener account.[100]

I wish now to make an imaginative leap — one that no doubt not all will find convincing — and consider the Rykener narrative as political satire and what early modern scholars have dubbed 'political pornography'. (Medievalists may be uncomfortable with this usage and certainly the Rykener text itself is only pornographic in the technical sense that it is writing about one who sells sex commercially.) The actors in the narrative stand in for or allude to real personages who exercise political power or influence. Much political pornography of the French Revolutionary era, for example, targeted the clergy, the royal court, the queen, and even the king. Equivalent material from the reign of Charles II of England also satirized the king.[101] The Rykener text is highly critical of the clergy. It specifically alludes to the royal court in the person of Sir Thomas Blount and perhaps indirectly to Thomas Despenser and the late Robert de Vere by the mention of Burford and Oxford respectively. It also makes allusions to the events of 1392. Perhaps the most startling satirical reference – and the one most obvious to Londoners at the time — lies in Britby's initial encounter with Rykener. Britby we are specifically informed was from the county of York. Yorkshire, the city of York, and the house of York had particular and negative resonances for Londoners at this date. At the height of the crisis from June 1392 until January 1393 Richard had removed the major offices of

---

[99] 'Lübeck 1382/1384: Ein anonymer Falschpriester und Hermaphrodit', in *Quellen zur Verfolgungs und Alltagsgeschichte der 'Sodomiter' (Homosexuellen) im späten Mittelalter und der Reformatorischen Frühzeit*, published electronically at http://www1.uni-hamburg.de/Portal_BUH/index.htm (accessed 5 March 2011).

[100] A parallel phenomenon is suggested by Noël James's study of wardship in medieval culture. She demonstrates how on the one hand romance literature is informed by a knowledge of the law and on the other Church court depositions seem to resonate with narrative strategies derived from romances: N. J. Menuge, *Medieval English Wardship in Romance and Law* (Woodbridge: Brewer, 2001).

[101] L. Hunt, 'Pornography and the French Revolution', in *The Invention of Pornography, 1500–1800: Obscenity and the Origins of Modernity*, ed. by Lynn Hunt (New York: Zone, 1993), ch. 9; M. McKeon, *The Secret History of Domesticity* (Baltimore: Johns Hopkins University Press, 2005), pp. 303–12; R. Weil, 'Sometimes a Sceptre is Just a Sceptre: Pornography and Politics in Restoration England', in *The Invention of Pornography*, ed. by Hunt, ch. 3.

government to York.[102] Yorkshire was also associated with some of the major office holders of the day. One such was Bishop Waltham, whose appeal to Richard over the attack on his London inn precipitated Richard's seizure of the City's liberties. He was the then Treasurer and so was no doubt seen as complicit in Richard's money raising ventures, but had very close connections to Beverley in the East Riding of Yorkshire.[103] Bishop Waltham was supported in his appeal by the Chancellor, Thomas Arundel, the then archbishop of York. A key player in the inquiry into the City's supposed misgovernment was Edmund of Langley, Duke of York, who also happened to be the father-in-law of Thomas Despenser.

Once we begin to read the Rykener narrative as political satire, the critique of misgovernment contrasted to the good governance of the City of London — remember the events of 1392 were predicated on the City's supposed misgovernment — becomes sharper. The sodomy repeatedly committed without any sanction in the seigniorial borough of Burford, whose lord was Thomas Despenser, in the university borough of Oxford, where the mayor's authority was repeatedly eclipsed by that of the Chancellor of the university as a result of royal intervention, at seigniorial Beaconsfield, and in the royal liberty of St Katherine's contrasts with the immediate and decisive intervention of civic officers once Britby and Rykener were detected within the City. The sodomitical encounter in the lanes behind St Katherine's has already been shown to be a reference to the corruption at the very heart of the royal palace.

Within this satirical discourse, some of the names in the entry purporting to describe the proceedings against Britby and Rykener begin to take on new meanings. The aristocratic name of Alianor or Eleanor adopted by Rykener when dressed as a woman may have called to mind Alianor or Eleanor de Bohun, the wife of Thomas of Woodstock, Duke of Gloucester and uncle to the king, who may also be alluded to by reference to the Bohun badge of the Swan.[104] The deceased Anna or Anne, the whore, who was associated with the employee of Sir Thomas Blount who first instructed Rykener to practice anal sex now more plausibly fits a political pornographic rhetoric as a reference to Richard's recently deceased queen. Rykener, whose name means not so much teller of tales, but counter of money, and who turns tricks for cash, may well borrow the identity of an actual royal clerk, but it is hard not to notice the resonance of Ryk and Rick, a diminutive form of Richard. We have here a strong hint that Rykener is to be read as a parody of Richard.[105]

In Maidstone's prolix Latin encomium of the reconciliation ceremonial of 1392, Richard, accompanied by his queen, is invited to enter his *thalamus* or marriage chamber — itself symbolic of London, rhetorically described as the king's chamber — where we are told

[102] W. M. Ormrod, 'Competing Capitals: York and London in the Fourteenth Century', in *Courts and Regions in Medieval Europe*, ed. by S. Rees Jones, R. Marks and A. J. Minnis (Woodbridge: York Medieval Press, 2000), pp. 75–98 (pp. 97–8 and p. 81, table 1).

[103] R. G. Davis, 'John Waltham (*d.* 1395), Administrator and Bishop of Salisbury', in *ODNB*. There was an established tradition of men from the diocese of York, especially southern Yorkshire, including the East Riding, finding positions as royal clerks, some achieving senior offices in royal government: J. L. Grassi, 'Royal Clerks from the Archdiocese of York in the Fourteenth Century', *Northern History*, 5 (1970), 12–33 (see especially p. 26).

[104] A. Tuck, 'Thomas [Thomas of Woodstock], duke of Gloucester (1355–1397)', in *ODNB*; n. 56 above.

[105] Cecil Ewen noted that the name Richard is associated with such derivatives as *Rickard, Rickart, Rickert, Ricard*, and *Ricart*, and such pet forms as *Dick, Hick, Higg, Hitch, Hytche, Rich*, and *Rick*: C. L. Ewen, *A Guide to the Origin of British Surnames* (London: Gifford, 1938), p. 70. *Rykener* is not itself a derivative from *Richard*, but it is sufficiently analogous to derivatives then current that a contemporary audience could have made this link. Since Richard may have been Dickon to his friends, it follows that an allusion to Richard related to Rick would not have the same resonances of friendship.

Londoners were ready to yield their bodies and be directed by the regal rod (*'regia virga'*).[106] The climactic moment, took place on Cheapside. Here an angel and a virgin leant down from a celestial tower to present crowns to the king and his queen. The Rykener narrative offers a parodical mirror of this central moment. Rather than being offered a crown by an angel on Cheapside, Rykener is instead solicited by the lustful Britby. Instead of consummating his relationship with London in a bridal chamber, enabled no doubt by his royal rod, Rykener is instead buggered over a stall in a side street.

The text, as a fiction, necessarily incorporates contemporary understandings of the sex trade that are surely rooted in informed knowledge of late fourteenth-century London.[107] Similarly, the ideology of gender that underpins this text is a late fourteenth-century metropolitan ideology. The text constructs gender as performative because that was the understanding of the creators. It follows that to read this text as a source for gender and sexuality has some justification; Rykener may not be an example of practice, but he does speak to contemporary ideology. This, however, is to miss the text's rationale which was to offer a kind of samizdat criticism of King Richard on the part of people very close to the heart of the government of London.

We can locate the Rykener text within a broader contemporary tradition of critique of the king, which plays on the unmanliness and effeminacy of the court and its beardless and childless king and even presents Richard as, to use anachronistic terminology, a homosexual. Both Walsingham, who wrote of his 'indecent familiarity' with Robert de Vere, and the Evesham chronicler imply as much.[108] Walsingham further characterized Richard's favourites in 1387 as 'more soldiers of Venus than of Bellona ... more likely to defend themselves with their tongues than their spears' and blames these men for their influence over the king.[109] Londoners in 1399, Jean Froissart records, 'could hardly mention his name without adding, "Damn and blast the dirty bugger!" '[110] But we must beware of putting too much trust in evidence that was often written retrospectively after Richard's deposition. Nor should we

---

[106] Maidstone, *Concordia*, ll. 207–14; C. D. Liddy, 'The Rhetoric of the Royal Chamber in Late Medieval London, York and Coventry', *Urban History*, 29 (2002), 323–49.

[107] Cf. Karras, *Common Women*. It is likely that London as a major city and port provided a range of specialised sexual services including transvestite male prostitution such as is found in a number of historical (and contemporary) contexts. For London three centuries after the Rykner case see R. Trumbach, *Sex and the Gender Revolution. Volume One: Heterosexuality and the Third Gender in Enlightenment London* (Chicago: University of Chicago Press, 1998), pp. 6–8.

[108] 'Tantum coluit at amavit eundem ... familiaritatis obscoenae': E. B. Keiser, *Courtly Desire and Medieval Homophobia: The Legitimation of Sexual Pleasure in 'Cleanness' and its Contexts* (New Haven: Yale University Press, 1997), p. 150; J. M. Bowers, *The Politics of 'Pearl': Court Poetry in the Age of Richard II* (Cambridge: Brewer, 2001), pp. 173ff. Most criticism necessarily and inevitably dates to after his deposition, but as Sylvia Federico observes, by no means all: S. Federico, 'Queer Times: Richard II in the Poems and Chronicles of Late Fourteenth-Century England', *Medium Aevum*, 79 (2010), 25–47.

[109] '*Chronica Maiora*' of Thomas Walsingham, trans. by Preest, p. 248. Cf. W. M. Ormrod, 'Knights of Venus', *Medium Aevum*, 73 (2004), pp. 290–305. Mark Ormrod tellingly remarks in another essay that 'Edward III's own apparent determination to render the notion of the sodomitical king as uncompromisingly subversive ... contributed ... to the increasingly hostile public attitude to homosexuality that has often been seen as a feature of fourteenth-century culture, and thus gave additional negative force to allegations of sodomy when they recurred in the context of political opposition to Richard II in the 1390s': W. M. Ormrod, 'The Sexualities of Edward II', in *The Reign of Edward II: New Perspectives*, ed. by G. Dodd and A. Musson (Woodbridge: York Medieval Press, 2006), p. 47.

[110] Cited in Bowers, *The Politics of 'Pearl'*, p. 173.

assume that all Londoners were hostile to the king given, as Caroline Barron has pointed out, the extent of Richard's patronage of London merchants and specialist manufacturers.[111]

Christopher Fletcher has observed 'Richard's critics began with the themes of inconstancy and vice in condemning his unmanly morals'.[112] Richard/Rykener fully fits this model. He is unmanly. Indeed he even wears a dress and performs women's work. Though he engages in heterosexual sex 'as a man,' he also has sex with men 'as a woman' having been taught by one Anne, who may herself now be dead. He lacks all honesty or trustworthiness. He makes his money by his dealings with clergy, including the mendicant orders, and with foreign merchants.[113] These are two regular targets of hostility in later medieval London, but they have particular topicality in respect of the events of 1392.[114]

This then is a text fabricated by the Latin-literate clerks who serviced the mayor's court, who had access to and were versed in the diplomatic of the Plea and Memoranda rolls, and would have been unusually well informed in current events and the affairs of the city. Here we may see parallels with, for example, the Bazoche, the association of law clerks employed by the Parlement of Paris, who from the fifteenth century came to be famed for their public performance of satirical — and invariably misogynistic — farces. One particular farce from the end of the century even used dark humour around sodomy to target the monarch.[115] The earlier Rykener narrative, however, is an altogether much riskier document, certainly not for public performance, even for bill posting or more conspicuous record in the City's Letter Books. It was essentially for internal consumption among the clerks who serviced the mayor's court and perhaps not even the civic magistrates in whose name the court functioned.

In presenting the case of John Rykener as if the minutes of a real case, however, the authors may have been consciously courting danger. One matter left unresolved after the conditional restoration of London's constitution was whether royal courts could demand to see the actual records of cases heard in the city courts or, as the city asserted, merely hear an account of the proceedings by the Recorder. So long as this remained unresolved, there was a theoretical possibility that a royal court could demand access to the roll on which the Rykener case is entered. That this was in the compilers' minds is suggested by the fact that the anomalous

---

[111] C. Barron, 'The Deposition of Richard II', in *Politics and Crisis in Fourteenth-Century England*, ed. by J. Taylor and W. Childs (Gloucester: Sutton, 1990), pp. 133, 139–40.

[112] C. Fletcher, 'Manhood and Politics in the Reign of Richard II', *Past and Present*, 189 (2005), pp. 3–39 (p. 8). Fletcher's own thesis is that Richard's masculinity was in many ways very conventional and that contemporaries did not tend to present him as effeminate: C. Fletcher, *Manhood, Youth, and Politics, 1377–99* (Oxford: Oxford University Press, 2008). Cf. D. Rubery, 'The Five Wounds of Melibee's Daughter: Transforming Masculinities', in *Masculinities in Chaucer*, ed. by P. G. Beidler, Chaucer Studies, 25 (Cambridge: Brewer, 1998), pp. 157–71 (pp. 164–65).

[113] Helmut Puff, noting that instances of clergy convicted of sodomy are rare in Northern Europe before the later fifteenth century, comments that 'the "priest and sodomite" is not a pre-established social being. This type of marginal personality is first of all a discursive entity; it figures largely in defamatory literature of both lay and clerical origin, but comes to life in certain conflict situations'. This observation appears to fit the Rykener case remarkably well: Puff, 'Localizing Sodomy', p. 171. For a recent discussion of Chaucer's near-contemporary treatment of the friars see R. Epstein, 'Sacred Commerce: Chaucer, Friars, and the Spirit of Money', in *Sacred and Profane in Chaucer and Late Medieval Literature*, ed. by Robert Epstein and William Robins (Toronto: University of Toronto Press, 2010), pp. 129–45.

[114] Cf. S. McSheffrey, 'Whoring Priests and Godly Citizens: Law, Morality, and Sexual Misconduct in Late Medieval London', in *Local Identities in Late Medieval and Early Modern England*, ed. by N. L. Jones and D. Wolf (Basingstoke: Palgrave Macmillan, 2007), pp. 50–70.

[115] P. Crispin, 'Scandal, Malice and the Kingdom of the Bazoche', in *Medieval Sexuality: A Casebook*, ed. by A. Harper and C. Proctor (New York: Routledge, 2008), pp. 154–72 (esp. pp. 162–63); S. Beam, *Laughing Matters: Farce and the Making of Absolutism in France* (Ithaca, NY: Cornell University Press, 2007), pp. 45, 77ff.

case of John Walpole that appears immediately after had in fact prompted this constitutional dispute just a month before Richard stripped the city of its liberties.[116]

The Rykener text is not as elegantly written, but is in many ways a more interesting text than *Fanny Hill*. Cleland's fiction was created as an exercise in refined pornography and offers a (slightly tame) critique of the bourgeois values and morality of the nascent consumer society of mid eighteenth-century London.[117] The Rykener text was created in much more charged circumstances. It is a much angrier text. This is no elegant satire of the hypocrisy of bourgeois society. Rather it is a biting and dark parody of Richard II and the events of 1392. Unlike Cleland's creation, it uses a satirical discourse of sexual promiscuity not to titillate, but to give vent to suppressed anger and to pour scorn on Richard's rule.[118] Rykener's circuitous travels to Oxford, Burford and back via the lanes behind St Katherine's may be read as mimicking in duration, though not in location, Richard's itinerary during June to August of 1392.[119] A far cry from Maidstone's panegyric Latin verse, it is perhaps a more authentic response to the elaborate ceremonial of August 1392. The key moment of the ceremonial in Cheapside, located between the Conduit and the newly built Little Conduit which brought a supply of fresh water through the streets of the city, is here reduced to a sordid and clandestine encounter.[120] Rather than the City being symbolically cleansed, it is here polluted. Instead of Richard being welcomed into London as royal bridal chamber, Rykener retreats to a bare, wooden stall. Whereas at the culmination on Cheapside of the 'pantomime' fantasy of August 1392, Richard is crowned, at the apogee of the 1394 pornographic fantasy of poetic justice that masquerades as trial record, Rykener, the parody Richard, who practices the unmentionable vice of sodomy, is himself buggered.[121]

---

[116] Walpole tried to bring an action against the keeper of Ludgate Prison in the mayor's court, but claimed he had been badly advised in the drawing up of his written plaint or bill. He subsequently asked to be allowed to amend his original bill, but the mayor demurred and asked the Recorder to decided on the matter as a point of law. The Recorder subsequently ruled against Walpole, who consequently lost his case, but Walpole appealed to the royal justices sitting at St Martin le Grand. The justices then queried the custom on which the decision to reject Walpole's bill had been made. In May 1392 the Recorder answered in person that it had always been the custom of the City where bills were defective. In March 1393, however, the justices demanded to see the records of the case: *Calendar of Letter-Books of the City of London: H*, ed. by Sharpe, pp. 168, 374, 392–93.

[117] It is also a satirical response to Richardson's *Pamela*, likewise an epistolary novel that consciously contrived to convince its early readers of its supposed factual nature: Samuel Richardson, *Pamela; Or, Virtue Rewarded* (London: Rivington and Osborn, 1740).

[118] Federico observes that 'recent studies of Ricardian poetry have shown, the broadness of the category "sodomy" lent it an impressive metaphorical power that was used by several writers to talk about things even more disturbing, such as the violation of the body politic by the monarch or by treasonous advisers': Federico, 'Queer Times', p. 26. Cf. M. Hanrahan, 'Speaking of Sodomy: Gower's Advice to Princes in the *Confessio Amantis*', *Exemplaria*, 14 (2002), 423–46.

[119] N. Saul, 'Richard II, York, and the Evidence of the King's Itinerary', in *The Age of Richard II*, ed. by James L. Gillespie (Stroud: Sutton, 1997), pp. 71–92 (pp. 72–73).

[120] Barron, *London in the Later Middle Ages*, pp. 256–57.

[121] The timing of Rykener's supposed encounter with Britby and the payment of the 10,000 mark loan the previous day may suggest that the text was invented as imaginative wish fulfilment in which the City solicits Richard for the value of the loan and shortly after gets to bugger him.

Fiction After Felony

Innovation and Transformation in the Eland Outlaw Narratives

Sharon Hubbs Wright and Michael Cichon[1]

Introduction

In the mid-seventeenth century, John Hopkinson, a West Riding justice of the peace and antiquarian, copied 'The Death of Sir John Ealand of Ealand and his sonne in olde rymthe',[2] a stirring ballad about murder and revenge, into his otherwise mundane collections of pedigrees of the northern families.[3] Actually, he copied out several versions of the legend: two variants of the ballad, and two expanded prose narratives. How Hopkinson came by these variants of the Eland legend he does not say; however, he knew that the tale had a connection to medieval West Riding families because he placed the ballad and the longer narratives in his notebooks along with the pedigrees of the Elands, the Beaumonts, and the Saviles who figure prominently in the tale. As enthusiasts re-told the legend of the Eland feud even into the early twentieth century, it acquired embellishments that made for dubious historical record but entertaining fireside recitation: insults were tossed, vengeance promised, ambushes laid, and duplicitous maids their men betrayed. Despite the obvious flights of fancy, there was just enough evidence that the story might be based on real events that several respected eighteenth- and nineteenth-century historians[4] pursued the veracity of the legend until W. P. Baildon, writing in 1890, set the question in a new light with his publication of the King's Bench records relating to the 1350s murders of Sir John de Eland, former High Sherriff of York, and his son John de Eland

---

[1] The authors thank the Social Sciences and Humanities Research Council of Canada for their support of Dr. Wright's research on this project.

[2] *Rymthe*: an Old English word that passed into Middle English with the meaning 'space or space of time, time'. According to Angus McIntosh, M.L. Samuels, Michael Benskin and others, *A Linguistic Atlas of Late Mediaeval English*, 4 vols (Aberdeen: Aberdeen University Press, 1986), accessed from http://www.lel.ed.ac.uk/ihd/elalme/elalme.html, it was rarely used, and is attested in Norfolk and the north. Hopkinson likely meant to write *rythme*, which makes more sense.

[3] Bradford, West Yorkshire Archive Service, Hopkinson 32D86/12, ff. 11ᵛ–18ᵛ (for the ballad) and 41ʳ–45ʳ (for the prose narrative).

[4] For example, see the discussion of the sources of the legend in C. J. Davison Ingledew, *The Ballads and Songs of Yorkshire* (London: Bell and Daldy, 1860), pp. 66–86; <https://archive.org/details/balladssongsofyo00ingl> [accessed 15 September 2014]. In 1859 Ingledew was looking for information about Sir Hugh Quarmby: C. J. D. Ingledew, 'Ballad on Sir John Eland of Eland, co. York.', *Notes and Queries*, second series, 8 [191] (1859), 169, DOI:10.1093/nq/s2-VIII.191.169-h.

the younger.[5] Subsequent research by C. T. Clay in 1913, Philip Ahire in 1944, and J. M. Kaye in 1979 conclusively demonstrated that Eland and his felonious murderers were indeed flesh and blood and once upon a time dwelt in the West Riding.[6]

In recent years the ghost of Eland has become restless and no less than four new variants of the tale have come to light. Our own renewed interest in Eland's legend is occasioned by Wright's discovery in 2011 of three previously unknown witnesses: two variants of the ballad—one in London, British Library, Additional 56076 whose scribe is unknown and one in Bradford, West Yorkshire Archive Service, Hopkinson 32D86/12 whose scribe was John Hopkinson—and a variant of the prose narrative also recorded by John Hopkinson in London, British Library, Additional 26739.[7] A fourth manuscript containing the ballad and narrative was found in an Elizabethan commonplace book originating from Yorkshire (Additional 82370).[8]

Former scholarship has been preoccupied with authenticating the tale and reconciling its version of events to the legal record; the discovery of no less than four variants of the legend reminds us that the transformation of the Eland tragedies into legend has not received due consideration. Replete with law-breaking exploits, escape to the green forest, man-hunts, and proficiency in archery, the Eland legend issues from the same leafy haunts as the infamous outlaw Robin Hood.[9] Bearing strong similarities to other medieval tales and emerging in manuscripts around the same time as the True Tale of Robin Hood found in the Percy folios, it is time for the Eland tale to receive greater consideration alongside more commonly known medieval outlaw narratives.[10] Indeed, the Eland legend is singular among its fellow outlaw ballads because it can be anchored in space and time, providing a remarkable demonstration of the process of transformation from historical events to a more generic and innovative tale

---

[5] W. P. Baildon, 'The Elland Feud', *Yorkshire Archaeological Journal*, 11 (1890), 128–30, <https://archive.org/details/yorkshirearchae00socigoog> [accessed 15 September 2014].

[6] C. T. Clay, 'The Family of Eland', *Yorkshire Archaeological Journal*, 27 (1913), 225–48; J. M. Kaye, 'The Eland Murders, 1350–1: A Study of the Legend of the Eland Feud', *Yorkshire Archaeological Journal*, 51 (1979), 61–79 (pp. 61–79).

[7] The manuscript tradition of the Eland legend is fully discussed by Sharon Hubbs Wright, ' "The Death of Sir John Ealand of Ealand and his sonne in olde rymthe": Four New Eland Manuscripts and the Transmission of a West Yorkshire Legend', *Leeds Studies in English*, n. s. 45 (2014), 87–129.

[8] Steven W. May and Arthur F. Marotti, *Ink, Stink Bait, Revenge, and Queen Elizabeth: A Yorkshire Yeoman's Household Book* (Ithaca: Cornell University Press, 2014). See also Arthur F. Marotti and Steven W. May, 'Two Lost Ballads of the Armada Thanksgiving Celebration [with Texts and Illustration]', *English Literary Renaissance*, 41 (2011), 31–63, DOI:10.1111/j.1475-6757.2010.01079.x; Steven W. May, 'Matching Hands: The Search for the Scribe of the "Stanhope" Manuscript', *Huntington Library Quarterly*, 76 (2013), 345–75.

[9] The Percy Folio ballads of Robin Hood immediately come to mind, as does Martin Parker's 'True Tale of Robin Hood'. Parker's true tale is an early seventeenth-century version of the legend and was compiled from earlier ballads. The Percy Folio also contains non-Robin Hood outlaw tales, and other sixteenth- and seventeenth-century ballads dealing with characters operating outside accepted social norms abound — a cursory glance at *The English and Scottish Popular Ballads*, ed. by Francis James Child, 5 vols (Boston and New York: Houghton, Mifflin and Company, [1882–98]), verifies this.

[10] Students of medieval outlaws are fortunate to have at their disposal several very useful surveys of the field. See, for example: *British Outlaws of Literature and History: Essays on Medieval and Early Modern Figures from Robin Hood to Twm Shon Catty*, ed. by Alexander L. Kaufman (London: McFarland, 2011); Timothy S. Jones, *Outlawry in Medieval Literature* (New York: Palgrave, 2010); *Outlaws in Medieval and Early Modern England: Crime, Government and Society c. 1066–c.1600*, ed. by John C. Appleby and Paul Dalton (Burlington, VT: Ashagate, 2009); *Medieval Outlaws: Twelve Tales in Modern English*, ed. by Thomas H. Ohlgren (West Lafayette, IN: Parlor Press, 2005); *Robin Hood and Other Outlaw Tales*, ed. by Stephen Knight and Thomas Ohlgren, 2nd edn (Kalamazoo, MI: Medieval Institute Publications, 2000).

of rancour, revenge, and restoration of order. In short, with the Eland legend, we can do what many scholars of outlaw narratives cannot: navigate both legend and history in context.

We begin with an examination of the version of events in the ballad and then return to the legal record before considering the problem of audience. Unless otherwise stated quotations from the ballad are from for the variant in Additional 56076 transcribed by Wright.[11]

The High Sheriff Sir John de Eland murders the Good Sir Beaumont

As it survives in Additional 56076, the Eland ballad begins with six verses that describe a world in which men are driven to accumulate wealth and climb the social ladder:

> for when men walke in worldly wealth
> full few can have that grace
> long in the same to keepe themselves
> contentted with their place
> The Squire he must become a Knight
> the Knight a Lord must be
> Soe shall you see no worldlie wight
> content with his degree (st. 2–3).

In essence, the characters in this narrative desire to amass more riches and bigger titles. The world of this ballad is woefully deficient with respect to riches and titles, and unfortunately some people just cannot abide the successes of their neighbours. Moreover, the balladeer tells us that when this hankering for scarce resources both tangible and intangible is fuelled by egotism and self-importance, it can only lead to disaster:

> ffor pride it is that prickes the hearte
> & moves men to mischiefe
> all kinde of pittie sett apparte
> without any grudge or greive
> Some cannott suffer for to see
> & know their neighbours thrive
> like to themselves in good degree
> but rather seeke their lives (st. 4–5).

Even before the introduction of the main characters, the ballad describes an attitude that cultural historians and anthropologists readily identify as a hallmark of feuding societies: the aggressive social competition for scarce material and moral resources.[12] Interestingly, while the ballad does not overtly condemn social competition, it does criticize the personal motives that lie behind certain expressions of it: it is the haughty, ill-intentioned man who does not fear God who is decried. This statement sets the tone for the rest of the narrative, and will provide in part the moral justification for the series of murders the ballad relates.

---

[11] Wright, 'The Death of Sir John Ealand'.

[12] Literature on the feud abounds. For the concept of total scarcity, see Jacob Black-Michaud, *Cohesive Force: Feud in the Mediterranean and the Middle East* (New York: St. Martin's Press, 1975). For feud in general, see Christopher Boehm, *Blood Revenge: The Anthropology of Feuding in Montenegro* (Kansas: University Press, 1984). For feud in England, see Paul Hyams, 'Feud in Medieval England', *Haskins Society Journal*, 3 (1991), 1–21; Richard W. Kaeuper, *Chivalry and Violence in Mediaeval Europe* (Oxford: University Press, 1999); and *Violence and Medieval Society*, ed. by Richard W. Kaeuper (Woodbridge: Boydell Press, 2000).

Enter John Eland, who, as the balladeer puts it, 'with such foule faults was sore infecte' (st. 8) with misplaced envy and cupidity. As if his social ambitions and festering jealousy of the well-known and beloved Sir Robert Beaumont were not enough, Eland is descended from Cain himself (st. 12 and 44).[13] Why such a radical and vitriolic departure from the historical record (discussed below)? Eland is a sheriff, and as such in an outlaw narrative it is his function to be bad, regardless of whatever actions his historical counterpart may have undertaken. In his seminal study *The Outlaws of Medieval Legend*, Maurice Keen notes that the enemy *par excellence* of all outlaws in all the legends is the sheriff.[14] Moreover, he notes that 'ballad makers are always careful to particularize the abuse which these men have made of their position'.[15] The Eland Ballad tells us this plainly about Sir John: even before the murder, 'his doeinges makes him sore suspecte | in that to have delight' (st. 8). Afterward, the slaying is described as a mischief contrived in a wicked heart perpetrated by the wilfully ireful Eland (st. 37).

That the ballad departs from the historical 'facts' is not at all surprising. As Hugh Shields has observed, 'the old, early, oral, or Child ballad [...] is a song giving a report of a fulfilled action—information about a series of intelligibly motivated events in the past';[16] nevertheless, its historical message likely has been filtered through generations of artistic interpretation.[17] As a result, any historical message in a ballad has been re-interpreted for and by the 'contemporary' audience: 'the history contained in the oral ballad is a history of the contemporary situation in relation to the message, as well as a history of the events that the message describes'.[18]

In his study of the 'contemporary situation' of the ballad, Kaye essentially states that in so-called real life, the Elands were good and the Beaumonts bad, and the balladeer promulgated an historically inaccurate tale as a warning to contemporary sixteenth-century feuders (more on which below). There is certainly much more at stake here than the questionable historicity of the ballad and its admonition not to feud. In fact, although the ballad's narrative is not historically accurate—practically reversing the story recorded in the fourteenth-century legal records—it is nevertheless logically consistent and contains a number of features common to more or less all outlaw stories which help generate meaning: the protagonists operate outside legal norms and are at odds with institutionally acceptable modes of settling disputes; institutional authority is at best weak and at worst corrupt; and the agents of the law are even worse—the description of John Eland Senior in the ballad says it all: he is a local official, descended from Cain and on the devil's errands! It is important to note that in outlaw

---

[13] Cain has long-standing negative associations both in western European literature and English literature. Perhaps the best-known reference, at least to students of English literature, is the monster Grendel's descent from Cain. See *Klaeber's Beowulf and The fight at Finnsburg*, ed. by R. D. Fulk, Robert E. Bjork, and John D. Niles, 4th edn (Toronto: University Press, 2009). Timothy Jones observes that Christian and secular communities alike associate disreputable figures with outlawry in order to enhance the alienation of outlaw, and Cain is the prime example. See Timothy Jones, *Outlawry in Medieval Literature* (New York: Palgrave, 2010), pp. 27ff. For a variety of references in English to the first fratricide, see *A Dictionary of Biblical Tradition in English Literature*, ed. by David Lyle Jeffrey (Grand Rapids: Eerdmans, 1992).

[14] Maurice Keen, *The Outlaws of Medieval Legend* (New York, NY: Routledge, 2000), pp. 134–35.

[15] Ibid., p. 149.

[16] Hugh Shields, 'Popular Modes of Narration and the Popular Ballad', in *The Ballad and Oral Literature*, ed. by Joe Harris (Cambridge, MA: Harvard University Press, 1991), pp. 40–59 (p. 41).

[17] Charles Duffin, 'Fixing Traditions: Making History from Ballad Texts', in *The Ballad in Scottish History*, ed. by Edward J. Cowan (East Linton: Tuckwell Press, 2000), pp. 19–35 (p. 20).

[18] Ibid., p. 21.

narratives, the king's men are not hated because of the law they administer but rather because their administration of it is corrupt, without mercy, and entirely arbitrary.[19] The 'bad guys' of the historical record thus become the 'good guys' of the ballad who appeal to an older law, ancient rights, and heroic privileges:

> Lockwood as eldest unto them
> said frends I thinke it good
> wee went into our owne Countrye
> to venge our fathers bloud
> If Eland have this for well done
> he will slaye more indeed
> best were it then wee slewe him soone
> & cutt of Caines his seede (st. 43-44).

More than an admonition against feuding, the Eland ballad fits into the broader ballad literature of outlaws and feuds, where gentry discontent and a certain amount of self-help violence in the face of bad officials is celebrated.[20]

Almost all the markers of conventional, formulaic outlaw tales are present in the Eland ballad. In surviving outlaw tales, the social bandit's career is triggered by injustice and his goal is to right the wrong. Banditry in these narratives is not employed to achieve a major transformation but to restore the right order of things.[21] The Eland of fiction has a personal motive for hating Beaumont over and above Eland's bad pedigree and career-mandated nastiness: Beaumont flouted Eland's authority. In the ballad, Eland's response to this is to gather his forces, exterminate Hugh of Quarmby and Lockwood of Lockwood, Beaumont's chief men, and then wait outside Beaumont's castle until the maid lowers the drawbridge to collect water, at which point, 'a seege asalt they made | traiterously to the hall' (st. 21), the castle is stormed, Beaumont is killed, unarmed but having fought manfully, and Eland and his troops invite the two sons of Beaumont to join them for breakfast, literally over top of their father's decapitated corpse. As Helen Phillips notes, 'in fiction and popular tradition, bandit territory is moral territory'.[22] The ballad has built on the inherent badness of sheriffs by ascribing to John Eland a satanic malevolence:

> They had a guide that guided them
> that in their hearts did dwell
> which hereunto had movid them
> the verie Devil of Hell (st. 30).

---

[19] Richard Gorski reflects on outlaw ballads that 'the moral compass of common good and justice pointed directly away from the ill effects of administrative growth, notable among them being the arbitrary acts and corrupt habits of royal officials': 'Justices and Injustice? England's Local Officials in the Later Middle Ages', in *Outlaws in Medieval and Early Modern England*, ed. by Appleby and Dalton (Burlington, VT: Ashgate, 2009), pp. 55–74 (p. 63). Later, he notes that ballad sheriffs preserve 'past recollections and current fears of royal authority gone bad' (p. 73).

[20] Like Gorski, A. J. Pollard points out that in stories, righteous and violent defence of justice is taken for granted in the same way as in reality, violence was justified in terms of law enforcement. 'When the "representative hierarchy" failed, direct action in defence of the common weal was believed to be justified.' A. J. Pollard, 'Political Ideology in the Early Stories of Robin Hood', in *Outlaws in Medieval and Early Modern England*, ed. by John C. Appleby and Paul Dalton (Burlington, VT: Ashgate, 2009), pp. 111–28 (p. 117–18).

[21] *Medieval Outlaws: Twelve Tales in Modern English Translation*, ed. by Thomas Ohlgren (West Lafayette, IN: Parlour Press, 2005), pp. xxvi–xxvii.

[22] Helen Phillips, 'Bandit Territories and Good Outlaws', in *Bandit Territories: British Outlaws and Their Traditions*, ed. by Helen Phillips (Cardiff: University of Wales Press, 2009), pp. 24–43 (p. 10).

Such malevolence extends well beyond any reasonable excuse for a feud, essentially making the revenge of Beaumont's kin a holy enterprise motivated not by greed, envy or desire to climb the social ladder but rather by a completely understandable need for redress as well as a social obligation to protect others from Eland's depredations. The outlaw, when deprived of his rightful place in society, must resort to self-help because the very people or agencies designed to protect one's rights are those committing the crime—the surviving sons of the wronged houses of Beaumont, Quarmby and Lockwood do exactly this when, after fifteen years of martial training to 'weald their weapons well' in 'feates of fence' (st. 42), 'to venge [their] fathers blood' (st. 43) and 'cut off Cain his seed' (st. 44), they return to reclaim their patrimony. Far from warning people against feuds, the narrative again reinforces the idea that extra-legal means are acceptable when wicked lawmen wrongfully deprive people of their rightful inheritance, place in society, and the like. The balladeer makes it absolutely clear that the initial murder was such

> [...] a cruel deed
> who could their hands refraine
> for to finde out such wicked weeds
> though it were to their paine (st. 45).

And thus it is that the surviving Beaumonts vow to return to their lands, and in keeping with many an outlaw ballad, they set an ambush in the woods.

When they catch Eland, the Beaumonts isolate him and then kill him.[23] The gang then immediately seeks refuge in the forest. It is a commonplace that in outlaw ballads protagonists take to the woods, so much so that Keen coined the phrase 'the Matter of the Greenwood' and proposed it as a fourth 'matter' alongside the traditional Matters of Britain, France and Rome.[24] Literary outlaws operate from the woods, using ambush, deception, and trickery to achieve their revenge, and not surprisingly the Beaumont gang does exactly this. The ballad recounts that they operate out of well-known local forests: Brereton Green, Cromwellbottom Woods, Furness Fell, and Annely Wood. A forest locale is an obvious choice of setting both literarily and practically, but it is more than 'a useful and engaging stage-prop' as in a chivalric romance. For the literary outlaw, the forest is 'an asylum from the tyranny of evil lords and a corrupt law'.[25] More importantly, the life of the forest is free and one in which one chooses one's own law.[26] This impulse to freedom, whether literary or real, can be understood in terms of Robert Merton's characterization of extra-legal behaviour as a form of innovation.[27]

The outlaw narrative and innovation

Merton, a sociologist, was interested in patterns of deviation, and he observed that some 'social structures exert a definite pressure upon certain persons in the society to engage

---

[23] They also plot the murder of John Eland Junior, a stratagem made all the more interesting because John Eland Senior spared Beaumont's heirs — given his fate, a gross tactical blunder. Perhaps this narrative detail is designed to diminish the Beaumont gang in the readers' or listeners' opinion, but the outlaws' decision is a very practical one in terms of limiting the number of potential avengers they might have to later confront should the Elands decide to riposte.

[24] Keen, p. 1.

[25] Keen, p. 2.

[26] Ibid., p. 148.

[27] Social scientist Robert Merton defined 'innovation' as one of five patterns of individual adaptation whereby people accept or reject cultural goals and the means to achieve them. Merton's five patterns are conformity, where one accepts both the goals and the means; innovation, where one accepts the goals but rejects the means; ritualism,

in non-conforming rather than conforming conduct'.[28] He also noted that this is a normal response to the social situation in which the individual finds him or herself.[29] Societies have culturally defined goals that are deemed legitimate objectives for society's members, and cultural structure 'defines, regulates and controls the acceptable modes of reaching out for these goals'.[30] Moreover, 'cultural goals and institutionalized norms operate jointly to shape prevailing practices'.[31]

When people seek the goals of the society but are denied the opportunity to compete for them, or choose not to compete in conventional ways, we are dealing with innovation, and this is the sentiment that underlies many outlaw ballads. As Merton puts it, 'aberrant behaviour may be regarded sociologically as a symptom of dissociation between culturally prescribed aspirations and socially structured avenues for realizing these aspirations'.[32] Our literary outlaws, then, represent cultural heroes who break taboos and violate norms but do this to re-affirm traditional values of freedom and justice, all the while challenging a closed political and economic system;[33] and because of this institutional weakness or failure, the protagonists cannot help but operate outside officially sanctioned behavioural norms.

Our ballad begins with six verses that set out succinctly the goals of the Eland feuders—wealth, prestige, and social advancement. When these goals are obviated, we see the players turn to extra-legal means. The sheriff feels slighted, his prestige and social standing suffer, and so he gathers an army and makes war on his rival. His victims are slighted by this excessive attack and dispossessed, but because the very person who was to enforce the laws that were to protect them was himself corrupt (Sheriff John Eland), the survivors resort to ambush and highway robbery. Cultural emphasis on the goal, whether it be land, wealth, a title, or power, and limited access to the means to achieve the goal due to a corrupt royal officials and the condition of being outlawed, prompt innovation.[34]

This is problematic in that late medieval people seem to have had what Keen calls a 'stubborn conservatism in social thinking. Ancient usage and the established order of things, hallowed by time, were sacrosanct; custom had the force of law. In such a world, revolutionary ideals were disreputable, and lawlessness of itself could command no admiration.'[35] How then can we reconcile the actions of innovators with a society Merton would call a 'tradition-bound, "sacred" society marked by neophobia'?[36] In general, outlaw tales reinforce the status quo

---

where one rejects the goals but accepts the means; retreatism, where one rejects all goals and means; and rebellion, where one rejects all goals and means and replaces them. Robert Merton, *Social Theory and Social Structure* (New York, NY: Free Press, 1968), p. 194.

[28] Ibid., p. 132.
[29] Ibid., p. 185-6.
[30] Ibid., p. 186-7.
[31] Ibid., p. 187.
[32] Ibid., p. 188.
[33] Ohlgren, p. xxxiii.
[34] Merton, p. 199.
[35] Keen, 7. For a recent and more nuanced interpretation of this, see Mark Leahy's 'Where Shall we Rob? Fantasies of Justice in the Early Robin Hood Ballads', *British Outlaws of Literature and History*, ed. by Alexander I. Kaufman (Jefferson, NC: McFarland & Company, 2011), pp. 204–18 (p. 204–6). Leahy highlights the contradictions of a so-called 'good' outlaw who both challenges and upholds laws, who remedies injustice but at the same time ensures the conditions which make it possible endure, and suggests that this indicates a 'peculiar ideological fantasy' of a privileged group's desire for both justice and an unjust world.
[36] Merton, p. 188.

rather than upset it because they assume that the outlaws want to be restored.[37] In outlaw stories, some sort of recovery or restitution occurs at the end of the tale: 'it was the urgent and necessary desire of all outlaws to be readmitted to the benefits and protection of the king's peace'.[38] The legend of the Eland feud also conveys this urge. In the prose narrative, following the extermination of the Eland males, Quarmby is killed, Lockwood is caught and slain while visiting his paramour, and Adam Beaumont goes off to join the Knights of Rhodes—a mainstream, socially sanctioned, monastic crusading order.[39] After the Eland male line has been extinguished, a surviving sister marries Henry Savile, to whom the Eland lands pass. In the ballad, all the principal feuders are out of the picture; nevertheless, the text conveys an appeal for charity from the balladeer to Savile, the new lord of Eland, and in reality someone who benefited from his relationship with the crown. With a lord once more in Eland hall and both sides having slaked their thirst for vengeance in the blood of their enemies, both the ballad and prose versions narrate a return to the state of affairs that existed before Sir John's murderous rampage and the Beaumont gang's multiple reprisals.

The ballad's appeal to Savile is curious in terms of both feud and recovery and restitution:

> learne Savile heare I yow beseech
> teach your posteritye
> to shewe such meanes that Eland us'd
> & be full of charitye
> ffor by good meanes youre eldres came
> to knightly dignitye
> where Eland first forsooke the same
> and came to misirye (st. 115–16).

The specific admonition to the new lord is to be a better man than his namesake, whose pride and pitilessness are condemned in the direct address to Savile. The outlaws themselves cannot be readily readmitted into society—in the ballad, one is dead and the others have disappeared—but the plea for gentleness and benevolence obviously reflects a desire to recover the state of affairs which presumably existed prior to the feud.

In combination with the appeal to Savile, the Eland ballad also exhibits its social conservatism and desire for the socio-political status quo by relating the downfall of the Beaumont gang, and this presents a particular take on outlaw stories. The outlaws, who have been living the lives of highwaymen, ambush John Junior on his way to church on Palm Sunday, and after they kill him, again take to the woods. Tactically, this is sound as it eliminates a future avenger, but the Beaumont gang is punished for the killing. While John Senior is clearly horrible, the ballad seems to disapprove of the murder of the son as excessive—the tone of the ballad is markedly different at this instance than at the point of the initial revenge killing. Beaumont, Lacy, Lockwood and Quarmby 'by fond deceipte there did they frame | their craftie cruelty' (st. 75), a cruelty that involved the abuse of a miller and his wife as well as the stealthy slaying of an innocent man on a holy day! Our ballad tells us that the entire countryside was roused, that the locals raised a hue and cry in order to bring

---

[37] Ruth Evans, Helen Fulton, and David Matthews, 'Introduction: Stephen Knight and Medieval Cultural Studies', in *Medieval Cultural Studies: Essays in Honour of Stephen Knight*, ed. by Ruth Evans, Helen Fulton, and David Matthews (Cardiff: University of Wales Press, 2006), pp. 1–8 (p. 4).

[38] W. M. Ormrod, 'Robin Hood and Public Record: The Authority of Writing in the Medieval Outlaw Tradition', in *Medieval Cultural Studies: Essays in Honour of Stephen Knight*, ed. by Ruth Evans, Helen Fulton, and David Matthews (Cardiff: University of Wales Press, 2006), pp. 57–74 (p. 70).

[39] London, British Library, Additional MS 26739, f. 82^r.

the outlaws to justice (st. 102), and pointedly relates that 'but as for Beaumont and the rest | undone were utterly' (st. 96).

In addition to social conservatism and the drive toward reconciliation prevalent in outlaw narratives, the ballads themselves offer insight into reconciling the tension of praising self-help violence while subsequently condemning those innovators who practice it. In her study of seventeenth-century crime drama, Joy Wiltenburg observes that ballads invite their audience to imagine the inner life of the condemned.[40] She asserts that even though ballads can be read as urging compliance to law in word and deed and feeling, they allow much room for ambiguity.[41] Wiltenberg and others have observed the continuation of feuding into the seventeenth century, citing specifically the execution of Robert Devereux, the second Earl of Essex, and the ballad that recounts the event. In 1601, Devereux led what has been called the last honour revolt, and when it failed miserably, he 'justified his degree of autonomous action in the honourable pursuit of a private feud'.[42] The Earl vociferously maintained his right to feud and openly mourned the perceived injustice of his sentence.[43] Devereux insisted that natural law allowed for the use of force against force, that he had in no way acted against the queen herself or God, and that he was merely a traitor to an unjust law.[44] Even though he abandoned this tack on his way to the scaffold, nevertheless the sentiment that drives both outlaw narratives and the feud cultures that revel in them persists in his arguments. Moreover, in the literature at the very least, 'the appeal of active deviance breaks through the penitential gloss'.[45] Emotion, says Wiltenburg, is used in ballads to evoke, reproduce, and solidify core cultural assumptions, and 'audience imagination of criminal experience, for all its ambiguity, enabled a vicarious participation in deviant lives.'[46] Again, this correlates well with Merton's take on innovation and the sentiment that informs both feuding behaviour and innovative means of accessing culturally significant goals. Wiltenburg's assessment of the later ballad material also helps account for the about-face in terms of the outlaws' standing within the ballad and the shifting legitimacy of their actions in the Eland Ballad as it has been transmitted.

The murder of Sir John de Eland: what the legal sources say

Now let us consider the demise of the Elands as attested in legal records.[47] In October of 1350, a group of outlaws lay in wait along the road that ran from Elland to York; in due course came their chosen prey, Justice of the Peace Sir John de Eland.[48] Sir John undoubtedly knew the men who brought him down on that road and knew that they planned his untimely departure

---

[40] Joy Wiltenburg, 'Ballads and the Emotional Life of Crime', in *Ballads and Broadsides in Britain 1500–1800*, ed. by Patricia Fumerton and Anita Guerrini (Burlington, VT: Ashgate, 2010), pp. 173–88 (p. 173).
[41] Ibid.
[42] Richard W. Kaeuper, *Chivalry and Violence in Medieval Europe* (Oxford: University Press, 1999), p. 300.
[43] Wiltenberg, p. 182.
[44] Kaeuper, p. 300.
[45] Wiltenberg, p. 175.
[46] Ibid., p. 174.
[47] To this point discussed most fully in Kaye in 1979.
[48] On July 6, 1351 the crown commissioned William de Plumpton and others to arrest 'Adam Beaumund, Wiliam de Lokwode and very many other felons indicted of the death of John de Eland'. See *Calendar of Patent Rolls*, Edward III, 1350–1354, 156; <http://sdrc.lib.uiowa.edu/patentrolls/e3v9/body/Edward3vol9page0156.pdf> [accessed 15 September 2014].

from this world; he made a will only one month before he was slain.[49] Eland's son, who was also named John, attempted to prosecute his father's murders at King's Bench. The accused felons looked unfavourably upon this initiative of the younger John de Eland, and they shot him down likewise in an ambush, mortally wounding him along with his young son, Sir John's grandson, bringing an abrupt end to the Eland male line. As we learn from the indictment made by Sir John's fellow justices following John Junior's death, all this occurred before the Justices Itinerant had arrived in York to hear the case. The Eland estates, including Eland Hall, passed with Sir John's grand-daughter Isabelle de Eland upon her marriage to Sir John Savile. The family was henceforward known as the Saviles of Eland Hall.[50] The response to the Eland murders was pronounced, but ultimately ineffectual. For years to come, King's Bench refused to issue pardons for felony in the West Riding without attaching the exclusion 'except for the murder of Sir John de Eland'.[51] Nevertheless, it came to pass that not a single one of the indicted murderers was brought to justice, although a handful of lesser men who received them were tried and convicted.[52]

Having laid out the bones of the case, we must add flesh to provide context for the murders and the legend. Sir John was a knight, as the antiquarian Dodsworth wrote *circa* 1621, 'of great account, and High Steward to the Earl of Warren, of the Manor of Wakefield, and other lands in the north parts: and was lord of Elland, Tankersley, Fulridge, Hinchfield and Ratchdale'.[53] In 1309, after inheriting his father's estates, he swore fealty to John de Warenne, Earl of Surry, in the Wakefield manor court. In 1317, while in the service of the Earl de Warenne, he obtained a royal grant to hold a weekly market at Eland.[54] During the fallout of the Earl of Lancaster's rebellion against Edward II, Eland's lucrative lands were seized by royal agents, but the lands were returned in 1322 when Sir John proved the agents' accusations of disloyalty were false.[55] In fact, Sir John de Eland became a trusted and frequently appointed royal servant: chosen as justice of Oyer and Terminer in the years 1327, 1330, and 1333; a commissioner of Array in 1325 and 1335; High Sheriff of Yorkshire in 1341; aid collector for the Black Prince's knighting in 1347; and finally, justice of the peace for the West Riding of Yorkshire in the late 1340s until his murder in 1350.[56]

With such a resume, Sir John de Eland fits easily within the fourteenth-century squirearchy, defined by Richard Gorski as that group of 'resident knights, esquires, and those who would be soon reckoned as gentlemen', whose private interests ran alongside royal service and who

---

[49] Originally recorded in the registers of Archbishop Zouche, a copy of Eland's will appears in York (Province), *Halifax Wills: Being Abstracts and Translations of the Wills Registered at York from the Parish of Halifax*, ed. by J. W. Clay and E. W. Crossley, 2 vols (Leeds: Whitehead, [1904]), II 214–15; <https://archive.org/details/halifaxwillsbein02york> [accessed 15 September 2014].

[50] Clay, 'The Family of Eland', pp. 225–48.

[51] For examples of pardons issued to both Yorkshire and non-Yorkshire residents with this blanket exclusion, see the *Calendar of Patent Rolls* for the years after Eland's murder. Numerous examples may be found in C. P. R. *Edward III*, vol. 9, 1350–1354: see pp. 64, 168, 171, 214, 229, 238, 242, 244, 269, 293, 305, 321, 364; <http://sdrc.lib.uiowa.edu/patentrolls> [accessed 30 May 2015].

[52] Baildon, p. 128.

[53] Oxford, Bodleian, MS Dodsworth 145, f. 107, for which there is a nineteenth-century transcription in an appendix to Joseph Hunter, 'Antiquarian Notices of Clay House in Greet Land', *Yorkshire Archaeological Journal*, 2 (1873), 129–70 (p. 163).

[54] *Calendar of the Charter Rolls Preserved in the Public Record Office*, 6 vols (London: HMSO, 1903–27), III, 24 February 1317.

[55] Philip Ahier, *The Legends and Traditions of Huddersfield and its District*, 2 vols (Huddersfield: The Advertiser Press, 1940–45), II 109.

[56] Ahier, II 110.

used office-holding as both a measure and proof of elevated status.[57] Although belonging to the squirearchy meant work, especially for responsible office-holders, it also opened the way to political patronage and to opportunistic oppression of rivals and lesser folk. As Gorski's study of the fourteenth-century sheriff emphasizes, petty day-to-day shrieval corruption was standard fare, with some real overachievers, notably in Yorkshire and Nottinghamshire, providing outstanding examples of misconduct, extortion, and tyranny.[58] Sir Peter de Nuttele, sheriff of Yorkshire, among his other serious malpractices, took bribes throughout the 1350s to release known felons from York castle while at the same time falsely confining petty offenders until they paid undeserved fines. In like manner and time, Sir Thomas de Bekerying, sheriff of Nottingham, virtually made sport of false imprisonment, extortion, and unwarranted purveyance.[59] Small wonder with examples such as these, that sheriffs were cast as villains. Was Sir John de Eland a sheriff of similar moral calibre to these men? Probably not!

Eland certainly had a long career of enforcement and financial management within Yorkshire; his one-year shrieval appointment, however, was a short one. This would suggest that he did not have a strong inclination for systematic abuse of authority or for playing the shrieval patronage game to its fullest extent, as Nuttele and Bekerying did. Gorski's research suggests that a short stint as sheriff without reappointment was rather more typical than a long run, precisely because of royal concerns over corruption. However, Yorkshire, along with a number of the northern counties (especially Cumberland and Northumberland), falls into the less typical group, with a very high shrieval reappointment rate and a small number of career administrators dominating the county offices. Eland's long presence among the dominant squirearchy of the county, particularly in the West Riding, speaks to his ambition; holding the office of sheriff only once where it was clearly possible to do so for much longer suggests that Eland was not driven to opportunistic excess.[60] Nothing in his record of service suggests he should be ranked among the infamous sheriffs of his era.

Nonetheless, we can reasonably guess that Sir John de Eland was disliked for his work by those whom he fined, indicted, or imprisoned. Long serving officials, through their legal or illegal activities, could easily build up scores, which invited forceful settlements that bypassed the justice system. Assaults on county officials, usually against the bailiffs and often by means of ambush on the road, were quite common and were part of the risk of the job.[61] Occasionally, conflicts erupted into open acts of defiance at court sessions or resulted in the murder of royal justices.[62] However, the murders of Sir John de Eland in 1350 and his son in 1351 seem particularly vicious, a point which may have contributed to the early preservation of the story in popular memory as well as among the crown justices.

What of the felons who murdered Sir John and his son? As with Sir John, these men seem to have belonged to a select group, a kind of squirearchy of misrule interested in disordering

---

[57] Gorski, 'Justices and Injustice?', pp. 56–57.
[58] Richard Gorski, *The Fourteenth-Century Sheriff: English Local Administration in the Late Middle Ages* (Woodbridge: Boydell, 2003). See in particular Chapter 4, 'Shrieval Corruption'.
[59] Gorski, *The Fourteenth-Century Sheriff*, pp. 102–3.
[60] Gorski, *The Fourteenth-Century Sheriff*, pp. 45–50. 'Yorkshire, where the reappointment rate exceeded fifty percent, demonstrates most emphatically the potential for small-group domination at the apex of the administrative hierarchy. Affairs in this vast shrievalty were left to a few administrative veterans like Sir john Bygod, sir John de Dependen, Sir Ralph de Euer, Sir James de Pykering, and Sir John Saville' (p. 50).
[61] Gorski, 'Justices and Injustice?', p. 72.
[62] A Yorkshire example: Sir Ralph de Hastynges was assaulted in Beverley in 1338 while holding inquisitions. Gorski, *The Fourteenth-Century Sheriff*, p. 95.

rather than upholding the business of the shire. Two of them, William of Hornby son of William of Quarmby (a. k. a. William Quarmby), William son of Thomas of Lockwood (a. k. a. William of Lockwood), had been outlawed earlier in 1350 for various felonies and trespasses committed in the West Riding. William of Lockwood had a string of indictments and had been outlawed for failing to appear after five summonses in 1349. The third man, Adam de Beaumont, a member of the bellicose Beaumont family, also had been outlawed some years earlier. Sir John de Beaumont, head of the Beaumont family and probably Adam's father, was feared throughout the county for threatening, beating, and extorting chattels and payments from county men.[63] From the court records, it is clear that Sir John de Eland and the Beaumonts had offered one another good reason for mutual hatred. While Sir John was High Sherriff (1341), he heard and indicted several cases of felony and trespass against members of the Beaumont and Lockwood families.[64] In 1344 Thomas de Eland, Sir John's elder son from his first marriage, was murdered at the Eland estates in Tankersley by Hugh of Tankersley, who had ties to the Beaumont family.[65] Within eight years of Thomas de Eland's killing, all the Eland men were dead, with their blood unavenged and their murderers roaming free. This is where the legal trail ends and the transformation of Eland from victim to villain begins.

Context and audience for the legend

To this point we have considered the nature of the Eland legend, arguing that it must be read as a member of the family of outlaw ballads that flourished in the late medieval and early modern period. Also, we have looked at the mid-fourteenth century origins of the story from the legal side of things, which look rather more like a feud between local strong men than an isolated case of murdering a crown official. Our question at present is twofold and moves into debated territory: when did the story become written in the form known to us now and for whom was it written? These are questions about context and audience and will naturally require some attention to the manuscripts. However, the manuscript tradition for the ballad is unnecessarily convoluted because so many of the antiquarians who published versions of it identified the manuscripts by their current owners' names; when the manuscripts changed hands so did their identifiers, with the result that the same manuscripts were often known by different names. As noted above, a full discussion of the lost and extant manuscripts, along with transcriptions of two new variants of the ballad, has been published by Wright.[66]

For many years John Hopkinson's copies of the ballad and prose narrative made around 1650 were the oldest known manuscripts. However, previous researchers working on the legend had evidence of manuscripts before that date. On a visit to Kirklees Hall in 1621, the genealogist Roger Dodsworth had seen a written version of the Eland story and recorded that it was known in the county because it had been performed thereabouts as a play as well as

---

[63] Kaye, pp. 64–65.
[64] Ibid., p. 71.
[65] Although it is not entirely clear how Sir John de Eland's offspring were ordered, it seems he had been married twice. He had at least two sons from his first marriage, Thomas and Hugh, and a third son, John Jr., from his second marriage. It's possible that Thomas was killed because he was the sheriff's son. The office of sheriff, because it was a royal office, included paid protection. It would have been difficult for robber knights like Beaumont to murder the sheriff, but extended family were vulnerable, as was Sir John himself after his tenure of sheriff was over. Royal protection did not extend to the office of Keeper of the Peace. See Clay, 'The Family of Eland', p. 245.
[66] See fn. 7 above.

a song.[67] Although there is no way of knowing, Dodsworth may have seen our new variant of the ballad in Additional 56076, which dates from around 1600. Or perhaps it was the slightly earlier variant from around 1580 in Additional 82370 discussed by Marotti and May. The point is we have a collection of witnesses around the end of the 1500s, some 250 years after John de Eland was laid in his grave. Over three centuries some grafting to the narrative is to be expected; however, the nearly complete reversal of events from those recorded in the fourteenth-century courts raises many difficult questions. Aside from the problem of when the ballad became a written text, there is also the question of audience; for whom was this outlaw ballad composed and sung and why?

The origin of the legend is indisputably in the 1350s. At some point the version of the legend was recorded that still survives in the earliest extant texts which date to the late sixteenth century. The language of the ballad, along with what seem to be references to Sir Henry Savile (who died *circa* 1555), suggests that the written source for the later sixteenth- and seventeenth-century manuscripts originated in the first quarter or half of the sixteenth century.

Following Thomas Whitaker, Kaye made a strong, if brief, argument that the ballad was recorded in the early part of Henry VIII's reign to admonish Sir Henry Savile not to repeat the sins of his ancestor Sir John de Eland. In the second quarter of the sixteenth century, Savile was engaged in a public power struggle with Sir Richard Tempest.[68] Looking again at the state of the West Riding during this period, one can easily see why a contemporary balladeer might use the Eland legend as a cheeky jab at a local big man. The Savile-Tempest conflict bore a strong resemblance to the events of the ballad and their quarrel was well known.

So bitter was the rancor between Sir Henry Savile and Sir Richard Tempest that the Earl of Surry spoke of it in a report to Cardinal Wolsey.[69] Henry Savile's father and most of his forefathers back to Sir John de Eland (who was his seventh-great grandfather) had served at some point in the office of High Sheriff.[70] The Saviles lost their hold on the office because Sir Henry's father died prematurely in 1505 and Richard Tempest, who was twenty years older than Henry, had the advantage of time to form the political alliances necessary to gain influential local offices. Tempest was appointed as Sheriff of York in 1516 and afterward to the position of steward of the large royal manor of Wakefield in 1521.[71]

In 1528, Sir Henry Savile was appointed Commissioner of the Peace due to his good relations with Cardinal Wolsey.[72] Savile was removed from office immediately after Wolsey's fall. He also asserted his hereditary claim to the mesne lordship of at least seven townships

---

[67] Oxford, Bodleian, MS Dodsworth 145, f. 107^r.

[68] Here Kaye is following Whitaker's assertion that the Savile of the ballad had to be Sir Henry Savile who died in the mid 1550s and could not be his son and heir who was *non compos mentis*. See Thomas Dunham Whitaker, *Loidis and Elmete; or an Attempt to Illustrate the Districts Described in those Words by Bede and Supposed to Embrace the Lower Portions of Airedale and Wharfedale, Together with the Entire Vale of the Calder, in the County of York* (Leeds: Robinson, son, and Holdsworth, 1816), p. 395.

[69] R. B. Smith, *Land and Politics in the England of Henry VIII: The West Riding of Yorkshire: 1530–46* (Oxford: Clarendon Press, 1970), p. 48. See also London, National Archives (P.R.O.) SP/1/88/ff. 119–20.

[70] Sir Henry Savile was a direct descendant of Sir John Savile of Eland Hall and his wife Isabelle de Eland, daughter of the unfortunate Sir John de Eland. There is an interesting connection between the Saviles and Robin Hood. Robin, as all the tourists who come to see his grave in Kirklees know, was murdered by his kinswoman, the Prioress of Kirklees, and is buried at the abbey, in the manor of Wakefield, near Eland Hall. Sir John de Savile, who married Isabel de Eland, was the nephew of the Prioress of Kirklees. J. W. Clay, 'The Savile family', *Yorkshire Archaeological Journal*, 25 (1918–20), 1–47.

[71] Smith, p. 147.

[72] Smith, p. 148.

in the northern part of the manor of Wakefield, a claim that put him in direct conflict with Richard Tempest, who as Wakefield steward had to defend the crown's interest. In a series of cases between 1530 and 1536 in Star Chamber, Richard Tempest accused Henry Savile of encroaching in the royal mesne, protecting known murders and coiners, maintaining retainers, hunting deer in the King's park, and stealing from Sir Thomas Tempest (Richard Tempest's son).[73] For his part Henry Savile always denied the charges made by Tempest and brought a series of counter charges, accusing Tempest of abusing his position as steward, taking bribes, claiming conduct money for soldiers whom he had never conducted to Scotland, maintaining the murderers of five men, and keeping men in his fee and livery that were not household servants.[74]

The ballad, as it was cast by its sixteenth-century scribe, may well have been intended as a caution for a specific man, as Kaye believed. We would argue, however, that the balladeers' use of the tale in this way illustrates perfectly how outlaw narratives themselves were altered, in an ongoing process of composition, to provide anonymous social commentary for many ears to hear and interpret. Local interest in tempering wider social conflict must not be underestimated. Savile and Tempest's fight had long tendrils, reaching both up and down the social ladder of allegiances within and without their immediate households. The Saviles of Eland Hall, for example, were among the prominent pro-royal families during the Pilgrimage of Grace. Sir Richard Tempest died while imprisoned in the Fleet; falling on the losing side of Henry VIII's wrath, Tempest had been allied with Lord Darcy who was beheaded as a traitor.[75]

We need not focus only on the Pilgrimage of Grace. The West Riding offered almost unlimited opportunity for the Eland feud to entertain and admonish audiences who lived in a violent and hierarchical milieu. The rancour between Savile and Tempest was merely one feud in a long conflicted region. From Sir John de Eland's day to the reign of Henry VIII, the West and North Ridings provided ideal conditions for the production of real outlaws and songs of their exploits. Before the great plague of 1348–49, the feuding lords of Wakefield and Lancaster dominated local politics and drew their followers into their conflicts. After the Warrene and Lancastrian lands had reverted to the crown, no one family emerged (as the Percys did in Northumberland) to fill the vacuum. The crown used stewards to manage royal demesnes, frequently drawing on local magnates or gentry to fill that role. Unlike magnates in other parts of England, many magnates of the region retained ancient privileges that allowed them to remain surprisingly independent of crown control even into the day of the Tudors. More than a few powerful men maintained households that amounted to small private armies. Lord Darcy, who held a crown stewardship, maintained a household with 80 men in fee.[76]

In 1534 local officials wrote to Lord Cromwell complaining about the deplorable state of affairs in the Riding, with so many barons claiming liberties and interfering in crown courts by arriving at the sessions with their own juries or with armed companies, that it was impossible to administer royal justice adequately.[77] Sir William Gascoigne, for example, had arrived at the court in Wakefield with one hundred men to prevent a case against him from turning in

---

[73] Smith, p. 149.
[74] Smith, p. 149.
[75] Smith, p. 150.
[76] Smith, p. 137.
[77] National Archives, (P.R.O.) SP/1/88/ff. 119–20.

a direction of which he disapproved.[78] The records in Star Chamber indicate that Gascoigne was little more than a robber knight who terrorized the lesser men of the county. If the records are true, he was just one of a long line of such men, with Sir John de Beaumont, enemy of Sir John de Eland being an earlier version of the same.

Conclusion

We have considered here the evolution and appeal of the legend of the murder of Sir John de Eland, sheriff of Yorkshire, particularly in relation to its acquired theme of innovative resistance to authority, a theme which it shares with many English outlaw narratives. Outlaw narratives, and especially ballads, are culturally didactic[79] and have a moral function as well as entertainment value. Moreover, ballads represent a particular way of telling a particular story[80] whereby a 'culturally significant past is ushered into the present'.[81] In short, the legend of the Eland Feud re-tells history to suit its own purpose, namely, to emphasize innovative resistance to unjust expressions of authority by narrating to its contemporary audience the rationale, actions, and consequences of an historic feud in light of on-going regional struggles.

A full-on fight was not the only way to conduct a feud. The singing and reciting of local tales of murder that were part of common memory were sideways pokes at one's enemy, particularly if that enemy was related to original participants. Helen Phillips notes that good bandits command respect, especially in times when authority is distrusted or seems unable or unwilling to uphold justice.[82] The Eland ballad's clear expression of local dissatisfaction with royal officials and actions goes some distance to explaining its survival through the turbulent final centuries of the Middle Ages culminating in the Pilgrimage of Grace. Ballads record not objective or factual history, but rather 'the kind of culture-bound "truths" that emphasize group consciousness and cement the world view of a traditional, oral community'.[83] In this light, the ballad does not have to conform to so-called real history of actual events to have found their way into the ballad because those events spoke so strongly to chords of justice at play among yeomen and knights and barons. Indeed, as Joy Wiltenburg notes, ballads constantly emphasize common human feelings that bind an audience with the inner experience of the felon.[84]

The Eland ballad, then, conveys a particular sentiment which correlates with what social scientist Robert Merton has observed with regard to extra-legal behaviour. Merton uses the term *anomie* (normlessness) to describe the process by which society becomes unstable when people use the most efficient means, not the institutionally prescribed means, of netting the culturally approved value.[85] Faced with barriers to acquiring a culturally approved goal, one innovates. In the literature, the use of disguise, trickery, and triumph by means of humiliation

---

[78] Smith, p. 146.
[79] Flemming G. Andersson, 'Technique, Text and Context: Formulaic Narrative Mode and the Question of Genre', in *The Ballad and Oral Literature*, ed. by Joseph Harris (Cambridge: Harvard University Press, 1991), pp. 18–39 (p. 32).
[80] Ibid., p. 38.
[81] Duffin, p. 20.
[82] Phillips, pp. 1, 5.
[83] Duffin, p. 21.
[84] Wiltenburg, p. 186.
[85] Merton, p. 189.

alongside conventional ways of feuding creates an alternative realm to the 'orthodox' one.[86] Still, the Eland ballad, like other outlaw ballads, preserves the idea that one can be respectful of higher authority and simultaneously attack the corrupt 'middle management'. When our feuders go too far, they themselves are exterminated, and the ballad ends with a declaration of hope for peace and good government on the part of the ruling Saviles even after praising the men who took down John Eland. More generally, the very existence of families and strong men in the West Riding who could muster one hundred or more men to intimidate one another, speaks strongly of a society still bound up in the old feudal ties of lord and vassal, knight and retainer. For this society, stories of entrapment, murder and vengeance still had appeal because they directly spoke to men's conditions.

---

[86] Phillips, p. 2.

'The Death of Sir John Ealand of Ealand and his sonne in olde rymthe'

Four New Eland Manuscripts and the Transmission of a West Yorkshire Legend

Sharon Hubbs Wright[1]

Introduction

Somewhere between a deadly fourteenth-century arrow and a sixteenth-century pen, the demise of Sir John de Eland was transformed from court record into legend. Remembered even now as a local ghost story, the late medieval tale of the West Riding Eland murders recounted the exploits of young outlaws who dwelt in the forest and exacted bloody vengeance upon the sheriff Eland. The tale was sufficiently well known to survive in eight manuscripts before the middle of the seventeenth century. Whereas a great deal of ink has been spilled on the question of the origins of the Robin Hood stories, the Eland legend, although much less well known, provides an important contemporary example of events that began as an act of violence, became a matter of law, and eventually grew into something rather more fabulous in the retelling. This article discusses the discovery of four new manuscripts of the Eland story; it provides a history of the lost and extant Eland manuscripts, many of which survive due to the seventeenth-century antiquarian John Hopkinson's interest in the tale; and it includes semi-diplomatic transcriptions of two of the newly discovered variants of the ballad (Additional 56076 and Bradford, Hopkinson 32D86/12 ff. 11 v–18 r).

Four new Eland manuscripts, containing three ballad variants and two prose narrative variants, have come to light since J. M. Kaye's reexamination of the legend in 1979. Of the three manuscripts which I have identified (Bradford, West Yorkshire Archive Service, Hopkinson 32D86/12; London British Library, Additional 26739; London, British Library, Additional 56076), Additional 56076 (transcribed below) is especially interesting since it appears to have been prepared for recitation: unlike the other newly identified manuscripts, it is not bound as part of a book, but contains two loose folios which were once bound along the top. The fourth manuscript, found by Marotti and May (London, British Library, Additional

---

[1] Research for this project was supported by the Social Sciences and Humanities Research Council of Canada.

'The Death of Sir John Ealand of Ealand and his sonne in olde rymthe'

MS 82370) is discussed at length in their recent book *Ink, Stink Bait, Revenge, and Queen Elizabeth.*[2]

Before discussing in detail the individual manuscripts, both lost and extant, a general overview of the manuscripts' context will be useful. To begin with, we know the Eland story, which I have examined at length elsewhere, cannot pre-date the events of the 1340s and 1350s.[3] We know of Sir John, who met his fate on the Eland road in October of 1350, from his lengthy service to the crown. At various points in his career, Sir John was Steward of the Manor of Wakefield for the Earl of Warrene;[4] Justice of Oyer and Terminer in the years 1327, 1330, and 1333; a commissioner of Array in 1325 and 1335; High Sheriff of Yorkshire in 1341; aid collector for the Black Prince's knighting in 1347; and finally, justice of the peace for the West Riding of Yorkshire in the late 1340s until his murder in 1350.[5] John de Eland was the sort of knight who would easily have gathered enemies as a result of performing his official duties, including those whose names still appear in the Eland legend: William Quarmby, William of Lockwood, and Adam de Beaumont son of Sir John de Beaumont. Beaumont senior was feared throughout the county for threatening, beating, and extorting chattels and payments from county men.[6] During his short stint as sheriff (1341), Eland heard and indicted several cases of felony and trespass against members of the Beaumont and Lockwood families.[7] In 1344 Thomas de Eland, Sir John's elder son from his first marriage, was murdered at the Eland estates in Tankersley by Hugh of Tankersley, who had ties to the Beaumont family.[8] Within eight years of Thomas de Eland's killing, Sir John and all the Eland men were dead, murdered in ambushes in the high street. The whole affair has the odor of feud about it, and the survival of a ballad and a longer prose narrative suggests a depth to the story which the legal records do not convey.

The legal records tell a version of events quite different from those recorded by the ballad and the prose narrative, which was most likely composed later than the ballad as it contains

---

[2] Steven W. May and Arthur F. Marotti, *Ink, Stink Bait, Revenge, and Queen Elizabeth: A Yorkshire Yeoman's Household Book* (Ithaca: Cornell University Press, 2014). See also Arthur F. Marotti and Steven W. May's book concerning Additional 82370 is forthcoming with Cornell University Press. See also Arthur F. Marotti and Steven W. May, 'Two Lost Ballads of the Armada Thanksgiving Celebration [with Texts and Illustration]', *English Literary Renaissance*, 41 (2011), 31–63; Steven W. May, 'Matching Hands: The Search for the Scribe of the "Stanhope" Manuscript', *Huntington Library Quarterly*, 76 (2013), pp. 345–75. The authors generously shared with me their transcription of the ballad before publication of their book.

[3] Sharon Wright and Michael Cichon, 'Fiction After Felony: Innovation and Transformation in the Eland Outlaw Narratives', *Leeds Studies in English*, n. s. 45 (2014) 71–86.

[4] Sir John de Eland held lands from Warrene and Lancaster and he was lord of Eland, Tankersley, Fulridge, Hinchfield and Ratchdale. See Oxford, Bodleian Library, MS Dodsworth 145, f. 107, of which there is a nineteenth-century transcription in an appendix to Joseph Hunter, 'Antiquarian Notices of Clay House in Greet Land', *Yorkshire Archaeological Journal*, 2 (1873), 129–70 (p. 163). See Wakefield Court Rolls, CXI, 58 for the licence for Eland Market.

[5] Philip Ahier, *The Legends and Traditions of Huddersfield and its District*, 2 vols (Huddersfield: The Advertiser Press, 1940–45), ii 110.

[6] Wright and Cichon, 'Fiction After Felony'. See also J. M. Kaye, 'The Eland Murders, 1350–1: A Study of the Legend of the Eland Feud', *Yorkshire Archaeological Journal*, 51 (1979), 61–79 (pp. 64–65).

[7] Kaye, p. 71.

[8] Although it is not entirely clear how Sir John de Eland's offspring were ordered, it seems he had been married twice. He had at least two sons from his first marriage, Thomas and Hugh, and a third son, John Jr., from his second marriage. It's possible that Thomas was killed because he was the sheriff's son. The office of sheriff, because it was a royal office, included paid protection. It would have been difficult for robber knights like Beaumont to murder the sheriff, but extended family were vulnerable, as was Sir John himself after his tenure of sheriff was over. Royal protection did not extend to the office of Keeper of the Peace. See C. T. Clay, 'The Family of Eland',

a much expanded and embellished version of the tale including references to the Knights of Malta. By the time the story emerges in writing, Sir John de Eland is the villain, the Beaumonts and Lockwoods the persecuted outlaws. All the fourteenth-century records are legal in nature, and there is no physical evidence of gests, ballads, or narratives before the late sixteenth century, which is the date of the earliest extant manuscripts (Additional 82370 and 56076 both date between 1580 and c. 1600).

Filling in the gap from the fourteenth century to these early extant manuscripts must involve some speculation. Without question, the ballads of the earliest extant manuscripts were being copied from earlier written sources. This is clear from standard copying errors. For example, the scribes of Additional 56076 have corrected skipped lines in stanzas 29 and 105 and also made interlinear additions of dropped words in stanzas 76 and 89. On two occasions, the first scribe dropped a whole stanza, only to realize the error and insert the stanza back in to the ballad at the moment the error was detected, placing the dropped stanza in the wrong place entirely, viz. stanzas 30 and 49. Additional 82370 has corrections to skipped lines in stanza 105 and miscopied lines in stanza 29, as well as a tangle with stanza numbering from that point on. These are clear signs of copying rather than the encoding of oral tradition.

The extant ballad manuscripts are all written in Early Modern English with some late Middle English terms present throughout. Discussed more fully under the entry for Additional 56076, linguistic evidence points to an early to mid-sixteenth-century capturing of the ballad in writing. Internal references in all but one of the texts to one Savile, possibly Sir Henry Savile (d. 1558), add weight to a date of recording prior to his death.

Comparison with other legends recorded by Child or Percy is also helpful. Leaving aside the well known example of the *Gests of Robin Hood*, there are other late medieval West Yorkshire and Lancashire legends which offer a comparable trajectory to Eland. The Cumbrian legend of the outlaws Adam Bell, Clym of the Clough, and William of Cloudesley was known before 1435. These names were enrolled in a parliamentary return for Wiltshire along with those of Robin Hood, Little John, and Much the Miller's son. Knight and Ohlgren suggest this was done in the 'spirit of satire'; although, given the political climate at the time, defiance seems a likely motive as well.[9] Whether satire or defiance, the point would be lost without common understanding of the message, which of necessity locates the stories attached to these names further back in time. Like the Eland legend, the first ballads concerning Adam Bell, Clym of the Clough and William of Cloudesley appear in the sixteenth century; but in this case—unlike Eland—there are written fragments surviving from 1510.[10]

A Lancashire ballad, recorded in the Percy folios, relating to the murder of Sir John Butler of Bewsey (d. 1430) is also of interest when thinking about the transformation of the Eland murders into ballad form.[11] As with Eland, the legend of Butler of Bewsey recalls the murder of a local knight and landholder.[12] The Butlers were an established family residing primarily in

---

Yorkshire Archaeological Journal, 27 (1913), 225–48 (p. 245).

[9] Stephen Knight and Thomas H. Ohlgren, 'Adam Bell, Clim of the Clough, and William of Cloudesley: Introduction', in *Robin Hood and Other Outlaw Tales*, ed. by Stephen Knight and Thomas H. Ohlgren, TEAMS, Middle English Texts Series (Kalamazoo, Mich.: Medieval Institute Publications, 1997), <http://d.lib.rochester.edu/teams/text/adam-bell-clim-of-the-clough-william-of-cloudesley-introduction> [accessed 18 November 2014].

[10] Roger Chambers, *Outlaws of Inglewood: A Cumbrian Legend* (Liskeard: Exposure, 2007), pp. 93–94.

[11] Thomas Percy, *Bishop Percy's Folio Manuscript*, ed. by John W. Hales and Frederick J. Furnivall, 3 vols (London: Trubner, 1868), iii 205–14.

[12] John Harland, 'The Bewsey Tragedy and its Legend', in *Ballads and Songs of Lancashire* (London: Routledge,

the parish of Poulton-le-Fylde, Lancaster.[13] In their ballad Butler's hall is breached and he is murdered in front of his daughter Ellen in the middle of the night. As with Eland again, there are surviving legal records which anchor the ballad to recorded violent events, including the abduction, rape and forced marriage of Sir John Butler's widow Isabelle.[14] The surviving heir married into the Savile clan. John's heir, also John Butler (d. 1462), married Anne Savile.[15]

The preservation and memorialization of these tragic stories served a larger purpose than simply telling a good tale. However different the later preserved form of the tales, which perforce changed with the passage of time, their first composition was undoubtedly significant for the family and networks of the people involved, possibly serving to maintain family cohesion or to speak their truth to the wider community. This may explain why the Eland legend is so altered from the fourteenth-century legal narrative. It may well have been composed to tell the Beaumont clan's side of the events. For whomever it was composed, the Eland legend remained relevant into the fifteenth and sixteenth centuries because so many descendants of the original feuding parties were still living in the West Riding. Stories like Sir John Butler's and Sir John de Eland's also remained relevant in a West Riding whose social conditions had changed very little from the fourteenth to the sixteenth century.[16]

The lost manuscripts, arranged by last recorded date of viewing

The lost Kirklees Hall MS, last seen 1621

In 1629, the Yorkshire antiquarian Roger Dodsworth summarized a version of the tale of the murders of the Elands and Beaumonts, which he says he saw some years earlier in 1621 among the papers and pedigrees of Sir John Armitage of Kirklees Hall. Dodsworth provides no physical description of the documents that he saw. Significantly, he did record that 'they have a Play and Song thereof in the country still', demonstrating a longer local tradition for the story.[17] Dodsworth understood that the Eland feud with the Beaumonts was the result of a 'hurly-burly' between the retainers of the region's two great lords of the mid-fourteenth century, the Earl John de Warren and the Earl of Lancaster.

The lost Broomhead Hall MS, last seen 1743

According to J. H. Turner, a version of the Eland legend was seen by the Rev. Joseph Hunter when he catalogued the collection of Mr. Wilson of Broomhead Hall, Sheffield, at the time of

---

1875), pp. 14–22. It is also number 165 of the Child Ballads: *The English and Scottish Popular Ballads*, ed. by Francis James Child, 5 vols (Boston and New York: Houghton, Mifflin and Company, [1882–98]).

[13] Henry Fishwick, *History of the Parish of Poulton-le-Fylde in the County of Lancaster*, Remains, Historical and Literary, Connected with the Palatine Counties of Lancaster and Chester, new series, 8 ([Manchester]: Chetham Society, 1885), pp. 10, 68.

[14] National Archives, Special Collections, 8/27/1305; *Transactions of the Historic Society of Lancashire and Cheshire*, third series, 3 (1875), 123; *Index to the Rolls of Parliament, Comprising the Petitions, Pleas, and Proceedings of Parliament from ann. 6 Edw. I to ann. 19 Hen. VII (A.D. 1278.–A.D. 1503.)*, ed. by John Strachey, John Pridden, and Edward Upham (London: [n. pub.], 1832), p. 28.

[15] John Pilkington, *The History of the Lancashire Family of Pilkington and its Branches from 1066 to 1600* (Liverpool: Brakell, 1894), p. 18, accessed from <https://archive.org/stream/thehistoryoflanc00pilk#page/n47/mode/2up/search/Butler>.

[16] Wright and Cichon, 'Fiction After Felony', pp. 85–86.

[17] MS Dodsworth 145, f. 107.

the hall's sale to Sir Thomas Phillips, in 1743.[18] The sale of Wilson's collection and Hunter's list of its contents were noted in the *Gentleman's Magazine* of 1843.[19] Hunter's complete hand list of the manuscripts may be among his notes on the Wilson family.[20]

The lost Hopkinson MS transcribed by Watson in 1775

A ballad of 124 stanzas.

In 1775, the Reverend John Watson transcribed and published a variant of the ballad, which he titled the 'History of Sir John Eland, of Eland, and his Antagonists'.[21] This is the first printed version of the ballad and the one most copied by other authors, including Whitaker, Ingledewe and Turner.[22] Based on Watson's discussion of the ballad, it appears that he copied it from among the papers of John Hopkinson (1612–81), which he writes were at North Bierley when he saw them.[23] Forty years on, Thomas Whitaker, who in 1815 copied Watson's transcription into his history of Leeds and environs, states that Watson copied the ballad from Hopkinson's manuscripts, which were in the library of Frances Mary Richardson Currer (1785–1861) of Eshton Hall.[24] Whitaker, however, must have used Watson's 1775 transcription and never carefully compared it with the ballad he says was in the library at Eshton Hall because it is impossible that the variant of the ballad transcribed by Watson is one and the same Eshton Hall variant which found its way to its current location in the Bradford Library Archives (see the discussion of Hopkinson 32D86/12 below).[25] In the first place, Watson's transcription possesses 124 stanzas while the former Eshton Hall Hopkinson has only 120 stanzas; second, when compared with Watson's transcription, the Hopkinson 32D86/12 variant uses different words, word order or whole phrases on more than 100 occasions.

How may we account for such a difference? It is clear that there were Hopkinson papers at Bierley for Watson to consult in the 1770s. In the Eshton Hall Library catalogue entry which describes the 41 Hopkinson volumes held there, the cataloguer records correspondence of June of 1753 from a Mr Wilson to a Mr Richardson of Bierley: 'I have sent you your ancestor

---

[18] *The Elland Tragedies, Viz: the MURDERS of Sir ROBERT BEAUMONT, of CROSLAND; HUGH DE QUARMBY, of QUARBY, Esquire; JOHN DE LOCKWOOD, of LOCKWOOD, Esquire; Sir JOHN ELAND, Senior, at BRIGHOUSE; Sir JOHN ELAND, junior, AND HIS SON, at ELAND; And others. With the exploits of Wilkin de Lockwood, at Cannon Hall, and of Adam de Beaumont, at Honley, and in Rhodes and Hungary, as Recorded in Ancient Manuscripts in Prose and Verse, with Notes, Pedigrees, and Evidences Recently Brought to Light*, ed. by J. Horsfall Turner (Bingley: Harrison, 1890), p. 6.

[19] 'The Wilson Manuscripts', *The Gentleman's Magazine*, new series, 20 (1843), 185–86 (p. 185).

[20] London, British Library, Additional 24467. See also Joseph Hunter, *Hallamshire: The History and Topography of the Parish of Sheffield in the County of York: with Historical and Descriptive Notices of the Parishes of Ecclesfield, Hansworth, Treeton, and Whiston, and of the Chapelry of Bradfield* (London: Lackington, Hughes, Harding, Mavor, and Jones, 1819), pp. 275–79.

[21] John Watson, *The History and Antiquities of the Parish of Halifax, in Yorkshire* (London: Lowndes, 1775), pp. 170–76.

[22] Thomas Dunham Whitaker, *Loidis and Elmete; or an Attempt to Illustrate the Districts Described in those Words by Bede and Supposed to Embrace the Lower Portions of Airedale and Wharfedale, together with the Entire Vale of the Calder, in the County of York* (Leeds: Robinson, son, and Holdsworth, 1816), pp. 396–401; C. J. Davison Ingledewe, *The Ballads and Songs of Yorkshire* (London: Bell and Daldy, 1860), pp. 66–86; Turner, *The Elland Tragedies*, pp. 59–82.

[23] Watson, *History and Antiquities of the Parish of Halifax*, p. 178.

[24] Whitaker, *Loidis and Elmete*, p. 395.

[25] Whitaker's copy of Watson's transcription has dropped Watson's verse 116, probably a typesetting error since in every other respect the copy is exact.

Hopkinson's MSS. Out of respect to Mr Hopkinson, I took a walk to Rothwell; and in the church choir, on the left hand of the door, pretty high on the wall, is a neat white marble monument, with a Latin inscription, being an encomium of his learning in history, antiquities, and heraldry'.[26] Hence, it is probable that Watson transcribed the 'History of Sir John Eland, of Eland, and his Antagonists' from a manuscript in Hopkinson's hand that was still in Bierley in 1775.

The Mr Richardson in Bierley of 1753 to which the cataloguer referred was Dr Richard Richardson, Esq., M.D., F.R.S., of Bierley, a botanist, antiquary, and classical scholar, whose grandmother was John Hopkinson's sister Jane Hopkinson Richardson.[27] Richard Richardson's son was the Rev. Henry Richardson (1758–84), Rector at Thornton in Craven, who in 1783 married Margaret Wilson of Eshton Hall, the seat of the Wilson family since the mid-seventeenth century. Their bibliophile daughter and sole heir, born posthumously to Richardson, was Frances Mary Richardson Currer.[28] The Hopkinson manuscripts must have come into her possession through the Richardsons of Bierley.

Although this solves the problem of where some of Hopkinson's manuscripts travelled, it does not sufficiently explain the differences between Watson's transcription of Hopkinson's 'History of Sir John Eland, of Eland, and his Antagonists' and the variant found in Hopkinson 32D86/12 which bears so many differences including the title 'The death of Sir John Ealand of Ealand & his Sonne in old rymthe'. A search of the estate papers of Eshton Hall, which have been housed since 1976 at the Leeds University Library, Special Collections, MS 417, has not revealed any papers in Hopkinson's hand. It may be that the Lost Hopkinson-Watson variant was among the portion of the Hopkinson papers that went to J. G. F. Smyth of Heath, near Wakefield, who was also descended from Jane Hopkinson.[29] This is perhaps the most likely explanation since Additional 26739 (discussed below), which contains a previously unknown variant of the prose narrative, was acquired by the British Library from the collections of John Smyth of Heath House. The journey of the Hopkinson papers from Richardson Currer's library to the Bradford Archives is discussed below in the entry for Bradford, West Yorkshire Archive Service, Hopkinson 32D86/12 ff. 12–18.

The lost Holroyd–Exley MSS transcribed by Turner in 1890, last seen 1943

A ballad of 111 stanzas and a prose narrative.

In 1887, John Horsfall Turner found and transcribed a variant of the ballad accompanied by the longer prose narrative among the papers of John Baker Holroyd, Earl of Sheffield (1735–1821), both of which he published in 1890 as part of *The Elland Tragedies* in a comparative edition with the variant transcribed by Watson in 1775.[30] Turner dated the manuscript to the late sixteenth or early seventeenth century and argued for a date before

---

[26] C. J. Stewart, *A Catalogue of the Library Collected by Miss Richardson Currer, at Eshton Hall, Craven, Yorkshire* (London: Moyes, 1833), p. 432, <https://archive.org/details/catalogueoflibra00rich> [accessed 18 November 2014].

[27] Edwin Butterworth, *Historical Sketches of Oldham* (Oldham: Hirst, 1856), p. 33.

[28] Colin Lee, 'Currer, Frances Mary Richardson (1785–1861)', in *The Oxford Dictionary of National Biography* (Oxford, Oxford University Press, 2004), s. v., <http://www.oxforddnb.com/view/article/6951> [accessed 1 April 2014].

[29] William Arthur Jobson Archbold, 'Hopkinson, John (1610–1680)', in *Dictionary of National Biography*, 63 vols (London: Smith, Elder, and Co, 1885–1900), XXVII, 340–41.

[30] Turner, *The Elland Tragedies*, pp. 59–82.

1620. The manuscript of the ballad was last seen in the private collection of Arthur Exley of Gerrards Cross in 1943. There is a picture of the manuscript, unfortunately of rather poor quality, in Philip Ahier's *Legends and Traditions of Huddersfield*.[31] Judging from the picture, the hand is clearly seventeenth-century secretary. According to Ahier, Exley purchased the manuscript at Sotheby's in 1938. The fate of the manuscript is currently unknown. Arthur Exley of Queden Cottage, Marsham Way, Gerrards Cross, Buckinghamshire, died in 1944 and his widow Margaret Exley died in 1952.[32] The manuscript may still be in private hands.

Assuming that Turner's transcription is accurate, the most interesting feature of the lost Holroyd-Exley MS is the stanzas which it does *not* possess. At 111 stanzas long, it is the shortest variant of the ballad. Hopkinson 32D86/12 (transcribed below) is second shortest with 120 stanzas. Additional 56076 (also transcribed below) has 123 stanzas and Additional 82370 (transcribed by Marotti and May) is longest with 126 stanzas. In general, the stanzas that are absent from the lost Holroyd-Exley MS are those which depart from the action of the tale, shifting to a didactic explanation. For example, Holroyd-Exley does not have the didactic stanzas 4, 5 or 6, present in all other variants of the ballad, which sequence begins 'for pride it is that prickes the hearte | & moves men to mischief'. It does not have some of the stanzas which use the authorial voice, such as stanzas 12 and 13 in Additional 56076:

> But now I blushe to singe for dreade
> skowing my owne Country
> soe stoutly stanid with Caines bloud
> there springe in plentiouslie
>
> Alas such store of wittie men
> as art now in theise dayes
> were then unborne ungotten both
> to staye such wicked wayes.

Nor does it contain stanzas, such as those just quoted, which directly link the actions of the characters with demonic forces. It lacks Additional 56076's stanza 30 ('They had a guide that guided them [...] the verie Devil of Hell') and stanzas 67 to 69 which theatrically invoke 'curell Mars' and 'Cains seed'. Most significantly it does not have the warning to Savile to show 'charitye' lest he come to 'misirye' that is present in all other variants of the ballad. This warning to Savile has been used by Kaye to date the antecedents of the extant manuscripts to the early portion of the sixteenth century.[33]

Although Additional 82370 has fifteen more stanzas (126 in total) than the Lost Holroyd-Exley variant (111 stanzas), in terms of spelling and word usage, Holroyd-Exley more closely resembles Additional 82370 (next entry below) than any of the other variants of the ballad. Both ballads begin 'What wealthy wights can here attaine' ('what welthye wyghtes can here attain' in Additional 82370), using the word 'wealthy' where all the other variants use 'worldly'. Both manuscripts use the older term 'esquire' where the others use 'squire' in the third stanza and the archaic word 'appay'd' (last line of stanza 13 in Lost Holroyd-Exley and stanza 18 in Add 82370) to mean 'satisfied' where the others use the word 'afraid' to complete the rhyme.

---

[31] Ahier, II, pt. 1, p. 5.
[32] 'Deaths', *The Times* [London, England], 29 May 1944: 1; 'Deaths', *The Times* [London, England] 4 Nov. 1952: 1. <http://www.thetimes.co.uk/tto/archive> [accessed 30 June 2014].
[33] Kaye, pp. 77–78.

'The Death of Sir John Ealand of Ealand and his sonne in olde rymthe'

Without seeing the manuscript, it is difficult to say what all this means in terms of locating its antecedent. It could be evidence of a late medieval variant not yet expanded as a cautionary tale to the Saviles—making it a very early version of the legend—or could be evidence of a seventeenth-century copyist excising the stanzas that seemed too Catholic.

The extant manuscripts, arranged by date

London, British Library, Additional MS 82370

The 'Stanhope' Manuscript of John Hanson, circa 1580s–1590s: 126-stanza ballad, ff. 33r–42r, and a prose narrative ff. 12r–18v.

Additional 82370, described as a commonplace book, is the focus of a study by Arthur F. Marotti and Steven W. May. At 126 stanzas, Additional 82370 is the longest of the ballad variants. The manuscript was found among the Spencer-Stanhope family's papers acquired by the British library in 2005. In addition to the Eland legend, Additional MS 82370 contains several unrelated texts including two ballads concerning the Armada defeat, which Marotti and May published in 2011.[34] In 2013, May also published a study of the Stanhope MS identifying the scribe as John Hanson, as had been suggested by A. M. W. Stirling in 1910.[35] May provides a detailed description of the dating of the manuscript and its attribution to John Hanson, who was a descendant of the West Riding Saviles.[36] Prior to being purchased by the BL, the Hanson manuscript of the ballad was last noted in 1910 in the possession of J. Montague Stanhope of Cannon Hall by Stirling, who wrote in her *Annals of a Yorkshire House* that the manuscript was kept together with a second copy of the prose narrative.[37] John Hanson (d. 1621) was the grandson of John Hanson de Woodhouse, buried in Eland in 1599, and whose mother was Agnes Saville (eldest daughter of John Saville of Eland).[38] Moreover, members of John Hanson's family were under-stewards to the Saviles and had access to all their family papers.[39] Personal interest in the tale may go some way to explaining why there were two copies of the prose narrative and a ballad all kept together. Stirling transcribed a portion of the narrative (the third chapter relating to Canon Hall) and a picture of the manuscript is included at the end of the transcription.[40]

---

[34] Marotti and May, 'Two Lost Ballads of the Armada Thanksgiving Celebration'.
[35] May, 'Matching Hands', pp. 345–75.
[36] J. Horsfal Turner, *Biographia Halifaxiensis. Or, Halifax Families and Worthies: A Biographical and Genealogical History of Halifax Parish* (Bingley: Harrison, 1883), p. 230.
[37] A. M. W. Stirling, *Annals of a Yorkshire House: From the Papers of a Macaroni & His Kindred*, 2 vols (London: Bodley Head, 1911), i, 7: 'For a dark legend hangs over the old house, the story of which is still preserved among the muniments there in an ancient manuscript in the handwriting of John Hanson; while kept with the original document is a copy of it, together with a less accurate ballad version, contained under the same cover and evidently dating from some generations later.' Stirling provides no explanation for her dating of the ballad.
[38] Turner, *Biographia Halifaxiensis*, p. 230.
[39] J. Horsfal Turner, *Halifax Books and Authors: A Series of Articles on the Books Written by Natives and Residents, Ancient and Modern, of the Parish of Halifax (Stretching from Todmorden to Brighouse), with Notices of their Authors and of the Local Printers; Comprising Materials for the Local and Literary History of the Parish, Including Antiquity, Genealogy, Biography, Topography, Natural History, Scientific Research, Political and Economic Progress, Parliamentary and Municipal Matter, Theology, Romanism, Anglicanism, Congregationalism, Quakerism, Unitarianism, Methodism, Moravianism, Baptist Denominatinationalism, Poetry, Hymnology, Law and Ethics, Fiction, &c.; Lists of Vicars, Nonconformist Ministers, Portraits, &c.* (Brighouse: The 'News' Office, 1906), p. 148.
[40] Stirling, pp. 15–19.

London, British Library, Additional 56076

Ballad only, 123 stanzas, circa 1600.

Till now Additional 56076 was unknown to scholars, having been acquired at auction from Dawsons of Pall Mall in the fall of 1969 and not foliated until 1984.[41] It was evidently unknown to Kaye, who does not cite it. This new variant of the Eland ballad is quite interesting because it is not part of a larger codex but is unbound. It bears the title 'Sir John Eland' and is copied out in two mid-seventeenth-century secretary hands with the first scribe ending at stanza 85 and the second copying for 37 more stanzas to finish at stanza 123. There is no evidence that the leaves were ever bound into a codex. The ballad was copied onto three loose leaves of eight-by-twelve-inch paper that were at some point folded to half width at four inches and then folded along the length at three, six and nine inches, which would fit nicely into a pocket, envelope or book board. There is no address or seal to suggest it was posted. On the verso of folio three, in the location of the third fold, 'Verses about Beaumonts of Crosland Elland of Elland etc.' is written in an eighteenth-century hand. The three leaves are currently bound along the top; however, this binding is not the original one. The leaves appear to have been bound at the top in the centre of the page by two thongs approximately two centimeters spaced.

The text was clearly meant to be opened toward its head because the verso text is reversed 160 degrees to the recto, making it easy to flip the pages vertically and continue reading. This is worth noting because, quite unlike the other versions of the ballad, Additional 56076 provides headings at transition points in the ballad in addition to using the verse to signal a change. Between its stanzas 34 and 35, Additional 56076 has the heading 'The first fraye endid | Murder | The Second Fraye Begineth' with the word *Murder* underlined several times. The ending of the second 'fraye' is similarly indicated between stanzas 65 and 66. For all these reasons, it seems quite reasonable to infer that the MS was intended for recitation.

An interesting difference between Additional 56076 and the other versions of the ballad is the date offered for the letters patent to Eland for a market. Additional 56076 (st. 11) says that the market was granted under Edward III's seal, whereas both Watson's transcription of the lost Hopkinson MS (st. 11) and Turner's transcription of the lost Holroyd-Exley MS (st. 8) give the date of Edward I. In the margin of Additional 56076 in a later hand is written '15° E: 3'. This is a regnal date which signifies the fifteenth year of the reign of King Edward III (1341/1342), which is actually quite close to the date of the Eland legal case in 1350.

The assessors at Dawson's compared this manuscript with Watson's and Turner's transcriptions and declared it 'more interesting than either of these versions in that it is the longer version in old spelling and, though closer in text to Turner's shorter version, it shows many different readings'.[42] As for dating the source text, the assessors caution that 'old spelling' leaves much room for evaluation. Yin Liu notes that several features of the rhyme suggest a date of composition after 1500 and probably before 1600.[43] Stanzas 6 (*peare : where*) and 39 (*were : appeare*) both use a rhyme on /ɛ:/ which has been lowered from Middle English /e:/ by the /r/ which follows. Lowering in this way began in the fifteenth century, but was more common in the sixteenth century and becomes less common the further one moves into

---

[41] London, British Library, Archives and Manuscript Catalogue, Additional 56076, 'Ballad of Sir John Elland'.
[42] Dawson's of Pall Mall, *Catalogue 200* (London: Dawson, 1969), p. 35.
[43] I am indebted to my colleague Dr. Yin Liu, Department of English, University of Saskatchewan for her advice and evaluation of the language of the ballad.

the seventeenth century.[44] Stanza 61 appears to use a rhyme on /oː/ (*loe : to*) which could only occur in the 1500s at the earliest, after the raising of Middle English /ɔː/ to /oː/ as in *lo*. According to Dobson, this use of /oː/ is attested into the last half of the seventeenth century.[45] The rhyme in stanza 118 (*backe : betake*) works in *back* on the fronted vowel /æ/ and in *betake* on the vowel /aː/, which began fronting in northern dialects around 1400[46] (although this shift was more commonly found after 1500).[47]

Significant items in the lexis are highly unlikely much after 1600; whereas a seventeenth-century scribe might admit them as archaisms, a poet writing after 1600 is quite unlikely to have used them spontaneously. The term *vail* (st. 57) meaning 'avail, help' is attested in the *OED* from 1300–1608; it tended to be replaced by *avail* after 1600. *Kind* (st. 64) in *OED*'s sense 3a 'character or quality derived from birth or native constitution; natural disposition, nature', as it is used in the ballad, is well attested only c. 1600. *Slo* for *slay* (confirmed by rhyme in st. 64) is attested only to c. 1585. The earliest known use of *extreme* (st. 68) is c. 1460. Use of the term *Palmison* (st. 76) is more frequent in the North but becomes rarer after c. 1600. Although revived by Sir Walter Scott, the term *boun* (st. 83) was obsolete c. 1600. The phrase *brim as boares* (st. 101) follows *OED breme* sense 5b, where the idiom (brim meaning 'fierce') is attested c. 1400–c. 1600. *Ride* (st. 114) is probably 'rid'; both the Lost Hopkinson-Watson MS and the transcription of the Holroyd-Exley MS have *dispatched*, which is attested in this sense from 1530. Without further internal dating evidence, these features of rhyme and word use seem to point to a date of c. 1600, possibly a little earlier.

Bradford, West Yorkshire Archive Service, Hopkinson 32D86/12.

A 120-stanza ballad (ff. 11v–18r, transcribed below) and a prose narrative (ff. 41r–45r).

As with Additional 56076, Hopkinson 32D86/12 contains a previously unidentified and untranscribed variant of the Eland ballad. It also contains a previously unidentified variant of the prose narrative. The ballad variant (below) is presented below following the transcription of Additional 56076, and is also compared through the apparatus with the previously published transcription of the lost Hopkinson-Watson MS.

In 1986, forty-one volumes of Hopkinson's papers came to WYAS Bradford from the Bradford Reference Library where they had been since 1920. Held at one time in the collection of the antiquarian William Cudworth (fl. 1874–99), the volumes were donated to the Bradford Reference Library in 1920 by Dr J. Hambly Rowe who was their last private owner.[48] At present, it is not clear how the volumes, which match their description in the catalogue of Richardson Currer's library, came into Cudworth's collection.[49] With an exact match to Richardson Currer's catalogue, there is no question that they are one and the same volumes. As described above, many of Hopkinson's papers came to Richardson Currer

---

[44] E. J. Dobson, *English Pronunciation 1500–1700*, 2nd edn, 2 vols (Oxford: Clarendon Press, 1968), ii, 201.
[45] Ibid., ii, 4.
[46] Dobson, ii, 98.
[47] Richard Jordan, *Handbook of Middle English Grammar: Phonology*, trans. and rev. by Eugene J. Crook (The Hague: Mouton, 1974), p. 276.
[48] *Bradford Archives 1974–1995: An Illustrated Guide to Bradford District Archives* (Wakefield: West Yorkshire Joint Services Committee/West Yorkshire Archive Service, 1996).
[49] Stewart, p. 432.

through her father, Henry Richardson (1758–84), who was John Hopkinson's great grand-nephew.[50]

Hopkinson must have copied out the ballad around 1650 into his larger collection of West Yorkshire pedigrees, more or less at the same time as the Lost Hopkinson-Watson variant. He either gave or copied the title "The death of Sir John Ealand of Ealand & his Sonne in old rymthe." Hopkinson's use of the word *rymthe* in his title is a puzzle. Possibly he meant to write *rythme*, for, spelled as it is, it would be a very late use of the Middle English term meaning a measure, a space of time or leisure time, which is not attested after the early sixteenth century.[51] It is curious, though, that the word *rymthe* is attested in the north, particularly in Norfolk, and we know that Hopkinson was asked by Henry, Duke of Norfolk, to examine the great collection of papers and documents belonging to his estate, which included holdings in Yorkshire.[52]

Turner, commenting on the Lost Hopkinson-Watson ballad, says that Hopkinson regularized the language in his version of the ballad for his mid-seventeenth-century audience.[53] In some cases, this seems to be true of Hopkinson 32D86/12 as well—for example, the word *squire* instead of *esquire* (stanza 3), or *bridge* rather than *brigg* (stanza 19). However, there are some places where Hopkinson 32D86/12 continues to use the older forms: *murther* instead of *murder* (stanza 31). What this suggests about the relative dates at which the two Hopkinson MSS were copied is very difficult to say, especially with only one of them surviving.

The prose narrative in Hopkinson 32D86/12 will be discussed along with other prose narrative variants in the entry for Additional 26739 below.

London, British Library, Additional 26739, ff. 78v–82r

Prose narrative only.

Additional 26739 came to the British Library with other volumes from the library of John Smyth, of Heath House, near Wakefield.[54] Smyth was a descendant of John Hopkinson and evidently some of Hopkinson's papers went to him instead of traveling to Hopkinson's other descendant Frances Mary Richardson Currer, whose library at Eshton Hall has been described above. Additional 26739 is a bound volume of Yorkshire West Riding pedigrees in John Hopkinson's hand. It contains only a prose narrative.

Hopkinson recorded three variants of the Eland prose narrative: the newly identified variant in Additional 26739, the narrative in Hopkinson 32D86/12 and the variant printed by Turner from the Lost Hopkinson-Watson MS. All these manuscripts would seem to be linked to the same exemplar, perhaps separated by one iteration of copies. Although all the texts do vary, their variations are not significant in terms of changes to the story line. A few

---

[50] Butterworth, p. 33.
[51] *Middle English Dictionary* (Ann Arbor: University of Michigan Press, 1952–2001), s.v. rimth(e), <http://quod.lib.umich.edu/m/med/> [accessed 30 May 2015].
[52] See Joseph Stevenson, 'Preface', in *Selections: Unpublished Manuscripts in College of Arms and the British Museum Illustrating the Reign of Mary Queen of Scotland, MDXLIII–MDLXVIII* (Glasgow: Maitland Club, 1837), pp. ix–xvi, <http://www.archive.org/details/selectionsfromu00stevgoog> [accessed 18 November 2014].
[53] Turner, *The Eland Tragedies*, p. 15.
[54] On the Smyths of Heath Hall see Wakefield, West Yorkshire Archive Service, Smyth of Heath, Family & Estate Records, C547: <http://www.nationalarchives.gov.uk/a2a/records.aspx?cat=201-c547&cid=0#0> [accessed 18 November 2014].

'The Death of Sir John Ealand of Ealand and his sonne in olde rymthe'

comparative passages will suffice to demonstrate the nature of the variations between the two newly identified manuscripts.[55]

Additional 26739	**Hopkinson 32D86/12**
[…] afterward coming to Crosland hall & finding noe waye to gitt in there they hidd them selves in bushes untill such tyme as they perceived a mayde of the house litt downe the drawbridge to passe over & doe some houshold busnies; and forthwith they came to the bridge & passed over into the hall where Sir Robert Beaumond & his family being in bedd nothing suspected them […] (f. 78v)	[…] & afterward came to Croslandhall & finding noe waye to gitt in, they hidd themselves in bushes until such tyme as they perceived a maide of the house did lett downe the drawebridge to passe over to doe some houshold busines and therewith they came to ye bridge & passed over into the hall where Sir Robert Beaumont & his familye being in bedd nothinge suspected the matter […] (f. 41r)
After all these thinges itt chanced that Lockwood fell in love & was enamored of a woman dwelling {als: abbrev} Camell ate Canon Hall nere Cawthorne, & according to the appointment bitwixt them; they often mett in Emley parke, at a great hollowe oak, which the keeper observing, betrayed & discovered their doeings. (f. 81r)	Afte all these thinges itt chanced that Lockwood was enamored of a woman dwelling at Camell {als: abbrev} Canonhall nere Cawthorne and according to the appointment betwixt them they mett often in Emley parke at a great hollowed oake, which the keeper seeing, betrayed & discovered their doeings. (ff. 43v–44r)
(Discussing the fate of Lockwode) […] perceiving they culd not have their will of him, threatned to burne the house over his head, which Lockwood feared not; his woman seeing him very busy in defending hiselfe (he having most trust & confidence in her) she sodainely fell upon him & with her knife cutt his bowstringe, & runne away from him: then said Lockwood, ffye on the whore, that ever thou wase ordained to be the distuction of mans blood, for by the & such like may all men take example. (f. 81r)	(Discussing the fate of Lockwode) […] perceiveng they culd not have their will of him, threatned to burne the house over his head, which Lockwood nothinge feared, his woman perceiving him most busye in defending himselfe (he having most truste in her) she sodainely leaped upon him & with her knife she cutt his bowestringe, & runne away fast from him: Then said Lockwood flye on the whore that ever thou wast ordained to be the distruction of mens blood, for by the & such like may all men take example. (f. 44v)

---

[55] Additional 26739 has two sets of foliation numbers, which suggests rebinding or reassembly of the codex. The most recent foliation is the one cited here.

(Discussing the fate of Beaumont) And at the last partly for this cause & partly because there came downe from London diverse proces to attache him, being of himselfe out of quietness, & his friends fearfull of him nor durse entertain him, he was constrained to flee into France, soe went forwards & continued amonge the Knights of the Rhodes & in Hungare, where his valiant acts were had in good estimation, & was appointed to serve & fight against the Heathens, from whence he directed his letters into Yorkshire. (f. 82r)	(Discussing the fate of Beaumont) And at the last partly for this cause & partly for as much as there came downe from London divers proces directed to the sheriffe & divers other noblemen for to attache him & being out of quiettnes of himselfe & his frends he was constrayned to flee into ffrance, & soe continued amongst the knights of the Rhodes & in Hungarie where his valiant Acts were had in estimacoun & was appointed to fight with the Heathens, from whence he directed his letters into Yorkshire […] (ff. 44v–45r)

As popular tales go, the Eland legend in both its ballad and embellished prose form are not the most compositionally exciting examples of the late medieval outlaw genre. The *Gests of Robin Hood* are much better known and more appealing as a narrative. What makes the Eland story compelling is exactly what Robin Hood lacks. It has a beginning that we can pinpoint in time and a trajectory that illustrates well how popular tales may tell some truth. For cultural historians such a window into the past is invaluable and quite rare.

The ballad transcriptions: conventions and collation

The transcriptions of Additional 56076 and Hopkinson 32D86/12 are semi-diplomatic. Scribal contractions are expanded and supplied letters have been italicised. Scribal insertions are indicated with \…/, editorial insertions with […], and expunged text < …>. Brevigraphs have been preserved. Lineation and indentation of the ballad stanzas have been preserved. In the case of Hopkinson 32D86/12 lineation has been inserted by the editor. Text in engrossing hand has been emboldened.

Hopkinson 32D86/12 has been collated with the Lost Hopkinson Manuscript that was published in 1775 by John Watson in *The History and Antiquities of the Parish of Halifax, in Yorkshire*.[56] The Watson transcription is discussed above.

---

[56] Watson, *History and Antiquities of the Parish of Halifax*, pp. 170–76.

'The Death of Sir John Ealand of Ealand and his sonne in olde rymthe'

London, British Library, Additional 56076

[Folio 1r]

Sir John Eland

[Column 1]

1. No worldly wight can here attaine
allwayes to have their will
Sometime in ioye sometime in paine
their course they must fullfill

2. for when men walke in worldly wealth
full few can have that grace
long in the same to keepe themselves
contentted with their place

3. The Squire he must become a Knight
the Knight a Lord must be
Soe shall yow see no worldlie wight
content with his degree

4. ffor pride it is that prickes the hearte
& moves men to mischiefe
all kinde of pittie sett apparte
without any grudge or greive

5. Some cannott suffer for to see
& know their neighbours thrive
like to themsleves in good degree
but rather seeke their lives

6. for some must needs be putte[57] alone
and such must have no peare
like to themselves the would have none
dwell nigh them any where

7. where pride doth reigne within the heart
& wickednes in will
the feare of God then sett aparte
themselves they must be ill

8. with such foule faults was sore infecte
one Sir John Eland Knight
his doeinges makes him sore suspecte
in that to have delight

---

[57] *puste* (looks like *st* ligature corrected).

9   Sometimes there dwelt at Croslandhall
    a kinde & Curtious Knight
    it was well knowne that he with all
    Sir Roberte Beaumont height

10 Att Eland Sir John Eland dwelt
    within the mannor hall
    the Towne his owne the parishe held
    most parte upon him all

11 The markett towne was Eland then
    the Patent hath been seene
    under kinge Edward Seale certeyne[58]
    the third Edward I weene

12 But now I blushe to singe for dreade
    knowinge my owne Countrye
    soe stoutly stanid with Caines bloud
    there springe \in/ plentiouslie

[Column 2]

13 Alas such store of wittie men
    as art now in theise dayes
    were then unborne ungotten both
    to staye such wicked wayes

14 Some saye that Eland Sheriffe was
    by Beamont disobeyed
    which made him for the same trespasse
    to be the worse apaid

15 Hee raised the Countrie round aboute
    his friends & tenants all
    men for that purpose picked out
    stoute sturdie men & tall

16 To Quarmbye hall they came by night
    & there the Lord they slue
    That time Quarmby of Quarmby hight
    before the Countrie knowe

17 To Lockwood then the selffe same night
    thei came & there they slewe
    Lockwood of Lockwood that wylie wight
    which stirred the strife anewe

18 When they had slaine thus suddenly

---

[58] '15° E: 3:' is written in left margin. This corrects the Holroyd (Watson) text which says the first Edward.

'The Death of Sir John Ealand of Ealand and his sonne in olde rymthe'

        Sir Roberte Beaumonts aide
        they came to Crosland craftyly
        of nought were they afraide

19   The hall was wattered well aboute
      no wight coulde enter in
      till time the bridge were well laid out
      they durst not enter in

20   Before the hall they could invade
      in Bushment they did ligge
      & watched a mayde wylie trade
      till she litt downe the brigge

21   They laid a seege asalt they made
      traiterously to the hall
      the Knights Chamber they did invade
      & slue the knight withall

22   Yet have I reade most certainely
      that slaine before he was
      he fought against them manfully
      Unarmed yea alas

23   His servants stroake & still withstood
      & fought with might & maine
      in his defence they shed their bloud
      yet all was but in vaine

24   The Ladie skreakte & cryed withall
      from her when as they ledd
      her deare husband into the hall
      & there stroke of his heade

[Folio 1v]

[Column 1]

25   But all in vaine the more pittye
      that pittie had no place
      for craftie mischeife & crueltie
      theise men did most imbrace

26   See here in what uncyrteyntie
      this wretched life is ledd
      att night in his prosperitie
      tomorrow slaine in bedd

27 I wis a woefull house there was
  the Lord laye slaine & deade
  their foes did eate before thier face
  their meate all wine & breade

28 Twoe Boyes Sir Robert Beaumont had
  then lefte alone unslaine
  Sir John of Eland he then bad
  come eate with me certeyne

29 The one did eate with him [exp: I thinke] \truily/
  the younger it was I thinke
  Adam the other sturdily
  would neither eate nor drinke

30 They had a guide that guided them
  that in their hearts did dwell
  which hereunto had movid them
  the verie Devil of Hell

31 See how this boy said Eland see
  his fathers death can take
  if any be it wilbe hee
  his death can venge or wrake

32 But if that he may wild anon
  I shall for him foresee
  and cutt them of by one & one
  as time shall then serve me [exp: me]

33 The first fraye here now have yow heard
  The second shall ensue
  & how much mischeife afterwards
  upon this murder grewe

34 And how the mischeife afterwards
  their wicked hearts within
  light on themselves shalbe discribed
  marke now for I begin

~~~

The first fraye endid

murder [Underlined many times decoratively.]

[Column 2]

The Second Fraye Begineth

'The Death of Sir John Ealand of Ealand and his sonne in olde rymthe'

35   The same morning a messenger
       was sent to Lancashire
       To Mr. Townley of Brackton hall
       his help for to require

36   Unto the mount beneath Marsden
       Now came they there indeed
       but hearing that their friends were slaine
       they turned again with speed

37   when Eland in his willfull ire
       thus Beaumont bloud had sheade
       into the coasts of Lancashire
       the Ladie Beaumont fledd

38   With her shee tooke her children
       att Brearton to remaine
       sometime also at Towneley hall
       they soiourned certeyne

39   Breareton & Townley frends they were
       to her & of her bloud
       as presently it did appeare
       they fought to doe her good

40   They kepte the boyes till they increast
       in person & in age
       their fathers death to have redresse
       still kindled their courage

41   Lacye & Lockwood were with them
       brought up at Brearton greene
       & Quermby kinsman unto them
       at home durst not be seene

42   The feates of fence they practized
       to weald their weapons well
       till 15 yeares were finished
       and then so it befelle

43   Lockwood as eldest unto them
       said frends I thinke it good
       wee went into our owne Countrye
       to venge our fathers bloud

44   If Eland have this for well done
       he will slaye more indeed
       best were it then wee slewe him soone

      & cutt of Caines his seede

45   O Lord this was a cruel deed
      who could their hands refraine
      for to finde out such wicked weed
      though it were to their paine

46   To this the rest then all agreed
      deviseinge all a daye
      of this their purpose how to speed
      which was the readiest waye

[Folio 2r]

[Column 1]

47   Two men that time from Quermby came
      Dawson & Haigh indeed
      with them consulted on the same
      in this how to proceed

48   Theise countriemen of course onely
      said Eland keepes allwaye
      the Turne of Brighouse certeynly
      & yow shall know the daye

49   I saw my father Lockwood slaine
      & Quermbye in the night
      & last of all they slew certeyne
      Sir Roberte Beaumont Knight

50   The day was sett the Turne was kept
      at Brighouse by Sir John
      little wist he was besett
      then at his cominge home

51   Dawson & Haighe had plaid their \partes/
      & brought from Brearton greene
      yonge gentlemen with hardye heartes
      as well were knowne & seene

52   Adam Beaumont there was laid
      Lacy with him also
      & Lockwood who was nought afraid
      to fight against his foe

53   In Crombwelbothom wood they laye
      a nomber with them moe
      arayed they were in good aray

'The Death of Sir John Ealand of Ealand and his sonne in olde rymthe'

        a spye they had alsoe

54   To spye the time when Eland came
        from Brighouse Turne that daye
        who plaide their partes & shewd the same
        to them whereas they laye

55   Beneath Brookfoote there was a hill
        to Brighouse in the waye
        forth came they to the topp of this
        there pryeinge for their [exp: pey] prey

56   from the lane end came Eland then
        & spyed theise Gentlemen
        sore wondred hee who they should be
        & vayled his Bonnett then

57   Thy Curtisie vailes thee nought sir K*nigh*t
        thou slewe my father deare
        sometime Sir Rob*er*te Beaumont height
        & slaine thou shalt be here

[Column 2]

58   Said Adam Beaumont w*i*th the rest
        thou has our ffathers slaine
        whose bloud we hope shalbe redrest
        on thee & thine certeyne

59   To strike at him still did they strive
        but Eland still w*i*thstood
        w*i*th might & maine to save his life
        but still they shedd his bloud

60   They cutt him from his companie
        belike at the lane [exp: heade] end
        & there they slewe him certeynlie
        & thus he made his end

61   Marke here the end of Crueltie
        such end has falsehood loe
        such end himselffe loe here hath he
        who brought others to

62   Yet Beaumont here was much to blame
        though here he plaid the man
        his p*ar*te he plaid yet in the same
        of a right Christian man

63   A pure conscience could men finde
an heart to doe that deed
though he himselffe had bene assigned
his owne hearts bloud to bleed

64   But kinde in theise younge gentlemen
crept where it could not goe
& in such sorte inforced them
theire fathers bane to sloe

65   The second fraye lo here yow have
the third now shall yow heare
of your kindnes no more I crave
but still for to give eare
here endeth the second fraye

~~~

The third fray

66   When Sir John Eland thus was slaine
indeed the storie tells
both Beaumont & his [exp: freants] friends certeyne
fledd all t[exp: he]o fournes ffells

67   O cruell Mars why art thou nought
contented yet with this
to sheade more bloud but still thou fought
for such thy nature is

68   Thy [exp: yonge] owne conscinece corruptid thee
indeed could never staye
till unto extreame miserye
it run the ready waye

69   ffor Cains seed on every side
with wicked hearts disgract
for to shew mercie hath denied
which needs must be displaste

[Folio 3v]

[Column 1]

70   In fournes ffells longe time they were
boasting of their misdeed
more mischeife still contriveinge there
how yet they might proceed

71   They had their spyes in this countrie

'The Death of Sir John Ealand of Ealand and his sonne in olde rymthe'

        ny Eland than whoe dwelt
        where Sir John Eland dwelt truely
        & there his muse he held

72   Mo gentleman then was yet there
        in Eland *pa*rishe dwelte
        save Savile halffe *pa*rte of the yeare
        his house at Rishmouth helt

73   Hee kept himselffe from such debate
        removinge there w*i*thall
        twice in the yeare in Savills gate
        unto the Bothomhall

74   Adam of Beaumont then truelye
        Lacye & Lockwood eeke
        & Quermby came to this Countrye
        theire purpose for to seeke

75   To Crombwelbothom hall they came
        there kept them secretly
        by fond deceipte there did they frame
        their craftie cruelty

76   This was the end the soothe to saye
        on Palmison even at night
        to Eland \halle/ they tooke the waye
        about the darke midnight

77   Into the Milnehouse then they brast
        they kepte them secretly
        thus by deceipte there did they frame
        their craftie cruelty

78   The morninge came the milner sent
        his wife for corne in haste
        theise gentlemen in hand her hent
        & bound her very fast

79   The miller said shee should repent
        her stayinge there so longe
        a good cudgell in hand he hent
        to chastice her w*i*th wronge

80   With haste into the milne came he
        & most w*i*th her to strive
        but they him bound ymedyatly
        & laid him by his wife

81	The yonge K*nigh*t [exp: hean] dreaminge the selffe same \night/
	with foes he was bested
	that secretly fetled him to fight
	against them in his bedd

[Column 2]

82	he shewed his Lady soone of this
	but as a thinge most vaine
	shee weighed it light & said I wis
	to Church wee must certeyne
83	And serve God this *present* daye
	the knight he made him boune
	and by the milnehouse laye the waye
	that leadis unto the Towne
84	The drought had made the water small
	the stakes appeared drye
	the knight his wife & servants all
	came downe the dame therebye
85	When Adam Baumont this beheld
	out of the milne came hee
	his bowe with him in hand he held
	& shott at him sharplie

[Hand changes here]

86	He shot the knight over the breast plat
	wherewith the shaft did slide
	William of Lockwood wroth thereat
	saide Cozen yow shoot wide
87	He shot himselfe & hit the knight
	but nought was hurt with this
	whereat the knight had great delight [59]
	& had not yet bene slaine
88	In case my father had bene clad
	in such armor certeyne
	your wicked hands escapid he had
	& had not yet bene slaine
89	O Eland town alacke saide he
	if thou but knew of this
	these fooes of myne full soone \would/ flee

---

[59] 'X' in the left hand margin of this column, closer to the right hand column than the left. No other significant marks.

'The Death of Sir John Ealand of Ealand and his sonne in olde rymthe'

            & of their purpose misse

90   By stealth to worke needs must they goe
        else had it bene too much
        the towne knowinge their lord bene \sloe/
        for them & twentye such

91   William of Lockwood was a dread
        the towne should rise indeed
        he shot the knight quiet through the \heade/
        & slue him quiet with speed

92   his sonne & heire was wounded then
        & yet not deade at all
        into the howse convayed he was
        & died in Eland hall

93   A full sister forsooth had he
        an halfe brother alsoe
        his full sister his heire must be
        his halfe brother not soe

[Folio 3r]

[Column 1]

94   His full sister heire she was
        & Savile wed the same
        thus lord of Eland Savile was
        & since in Saviles name

95   Looe here the end of all mischeife
        Eland Elands name
        displaced was to their great greif
        well worthye of the same

96   But as for Beaumont & the rest
        undone were utterly
        thus simple virtue is the best
        & cheife ffelicitye

97   What time theise men such fraye did frame
        died have I redd & heard
        that Eland came to Saviles name
        in Edward dayes the third

98   By Whittell lane end they tooke their \flight/
        and soo to the ould earth yate
        then take they wood as well they might

        & spied a privie gate

99   Themselves convayeinge craftilye
       to aneley wood that waye
       the Towne of Eland manfully
       pursued them that daye

100   The Lords servants throughout the towne
       had cried with might & maine
       up gentle yeomen get *your* bowne
       this daye your Lord is slaine

101   Whittle Smith & Rymington
       Burney with many more
       as brim as boares they made them bowne
       their Lords enemies to slooe

102   And to be short the people rose
       through all the towne about
       theane secretly followinge on their \fooes/
       with hue & crie & shoute

103   All sort of men shou'd their good will
       some bowes some stavies did beare
       some brought forth clubes & rusty bills
       that sawe no sunes that yeare

104   To church now as the *pa*rish came
       they ioyned with the towne
       like hardye men to stand all same
       to fight now were they bowne

105   Beaumont & Lockwood saw all this
       [exp: they fetled them to bowe I wis
       & shote as they were wood.]
       & Quermby where they stood
       they fetled them to bowe I wis
       & shote as they were wood.

       [Column 2]

106   Till time that all their shaftes were \spent/
       of force needs must they fly
       they had dispatched their intent
       & lost the victorye

107   The hardiest man of them that was
       was Quermby that is true

'The Death of Sir John Ealand of Ealand and his sonne in olde rymthe'

          for he would never turne his face
          til Eland men him slue

108   Lockwoode he bore him on his backe
          & laide him in Aneley wood
          to whome his purse he did betake
          of gould & silver good

109   Take here this gould to y*ow* saide he
          & to my cozen deare
          & in your mirth remember me
          yet when y*ow* make good cheare

110   Give place w*ith* speed & fare y*ow* well
          god sheilde y*ow* from mischance
          in case it otherwise befell
          it would be my greevance

111   Their fooes soe fearcely followed on
          it was no bideinge there
          Lockwood w*ith* speed he went away
          to his freinds where they weare

112   With hast they toward Huddersfield
          did take the readiest waye
          Adam of Beaumont the way he \held/
          [exp: h] To Croslandhall that daye

113   When Eland men returned home
          through Aneley wood that waye
          there found they Quermby then alive
          scarse dead as some men saye

114   But then they slue him out of hand
          & ride him out of paine
          the late death of their Lord Eland
          inforced them certeyne

115   learne Savile heare I y*ow* beseech
          teach your posteritye
          to shewe [exp: she] such meanes that Eland us'd
          & be full of charitye

116   ffor by good meanes yo*ure* eld*res* came
          to knightly dignitye
          where Eland first forsooke the same
          & came to misirye

117	mark here the breach of charitye
how wretchedly they end
makre heare how cheife felicity
doth charity attend

[Folio 3v]

[Column 1]

118	A wesh it is to every wight
please god that maye we can
it wins allwayes with great delight
the harte of many a man
119	O wrathull ire o worst the
then wrought this wretchedness
theise gentlemen brought here onely
to greife & great distresse
120	Wheare charitye withdrawes the heart
from sorrow & sighinge deep
right heavey makes it many a \man/
& many an eye to weep

[Column 2]

121	yow gentlemen love one annother
love well the yeomanrye
let every christian love his brother
& dwell in charitye
122	So shall it come to pas truely
that good men shall us love
& after death soe shall yow be
in life with god above
123	To whome allwayes of every wight
through all yeares & dayes
in heaven & earth both daye & night
be honoure laud and praise.

Finis ./.

'The Death of Sir John Ealand of Ealand and his sonne in olde rymthe'

Bradford, West Yorkshire Archive Service, Hopkinson 32D86/12

[Folio 11v] **The death of Sir John Ealand of Ealand & his sonne in old rymthe**

[1] noe worldly wight cann here attayne
alwayes to have his[60] will
sometymes in ioye[61], sometyes in paine
his[62] course he must fullfill.

[2] ffor when that menn doe growe in wealth[63]
full few can have that grace
long in the same to keepe themselves
contented with their place

[3] But the Squire must[64] become a Knight
the Knight a Lord wold bee
Thus shall yow have[65] noe worldly wight
content with his degree.

[4] But pride itt is that pricks menns hearts[66]
& moves them[67] to mischeife
All kind of pittye sett apart
without all grace or greife.[68]

[5] Some cannot suffer for to see
& knowe their neighbours thrive
Like to themselves in good degree
but rather seekes their lives.

[6] And some muste be possest alone,
and such wold have noe peere
Like to themselves they wold have none
dwell nighe them any where.

[7] With such like faults fouly[69] infect
was[70] Sir John Eland Knight

---

[60] his] Watson *their*
[61] sometymes in ioye] Watson *But now in grief,*
[62] his] Watson *their*
[63] ffor when that menn doe growe in wealth] Watson *For when men live in worldly wealth*
[64] But the Squire must] Watson *The Squire must needs*
[65] have] Watson *see*
[66] But pride itt is that pricks menns hearts] Watson *For pride it is that pricks the heart*
[67] them] Watson *men*
[68] Watson 1775 has another stanza: *Where pride doth reighn within the heart, |And wickedness in will, |The fear of God quite set apart, |Their fruits must needs be ill.*
[69] faults fouly] Watson *faults was foul*
[70] was] Watson *one*

>   His doeings make menn[71] much suspect
>   therein he tooke delight
>
> [8]   Sometymes there dwelt at Crosland hall
>   a kind & curteous knight
>   Itt was well knowne that he withall
>   Sir Robert Beau-mont[72] hight

[Folio 12r]   **The murder of Eland, Beaumont etc**

> [9]   Att Eland Sir John Eland dwelt
>   within the mannor hall
>   The towne his owne, & parish halfe[73]
>   the greater part, were all[74]
>
> [10]   The markett towne was Ealand then
>   the patent hath beene seene
>   Under Kinge Edwards seale certaine
>   The first Edward I weene.
>
> [11]   But now I blushe to sing for dread
>   knoweing mine owne Countrye
>   Soe basely stor'd with Caines seed
>   there springing plenteouslye.
>
> [12]   Alacke such store of wittye menn,
>   as now are in these dayes
>   were both unborne & gotten then
>   to staye such wicked wayes.
>
> [13]   Some say that Ealand sherrife was
>   by Beau-mont disobeyed
>   which might to[75] him for that trespasse
>   make[76] him the worse appayd.
>
> [14]   He raised the Country round about
>   his freinds[77] & tennants all
>   menn[78] for the purpose picked out
>   stout, sturdy, strong,[79] & tall.
>
> [15]   To Quarmby hall they came by night

---

[71] menn] Watson *it*
[72] Hopkinson seems to have inserted a hyphen between *Beau* and *mont*. Perhaps a slip of the pen?
[73] & parish halfe] Watson *the parish held*
[74] the greater part, were all] Watson *Most part upon him all*
[75] to him for that] Watson *him make for that*
[76] make] Watson *with*
[77] Hopkinson wrote *freinds* for *friends*
[78] menn] Watson *and*
[79] strong] Watson *men*

'The Death of Sir John Ealand of Ealand and his sonne in olde rymthe'

                    and there they Lord they slewe
                    All that tyme hugh of Quarmby height
                    before the Countrye knewe.

[16]   To Lockwood then the selfe same night
           they came & there they slewe
           Lockwood of Lockwood that wilye wight
           which spread[80] the strife anew

[Folio 12v]   **The murther of Ealand, Beau-mont &ct.**

[17]   when they had slayne thus sudainely
           Sir Robert Beau-monts ayde
           To Crosland they came craftilye
           of naught they were afrayd.

[18]   The hall was watered well about
           noe wight cold enter there[81]
           untill the bridge was letten downe[82]
           they durst not venture nere[83]

[19]   Before the house they cold invade
           in ambushe they did lodge
           They watch'd a wench with wilye trade
           till she lett downe the bridge.

[20]   A seige they sett, assault they made
           most stoutly[84] to the hall
           The knights chamber they did invade
           and tooke the knight withall

[21]   And this is for most certaintye
           before that slaine[85] he was
           he fought amongst[86] them manfully
           unarmed as he was.

[22]   His servants rose & still withstood
           and strucke with might & maine
           in his defence they shedd their blood
           yett[87] all this was in vaine

---

[80] which spread] Watson *That stirr'd*
[81] culd enter there] Watson *might enter in*
[82] unitl the bridge was
    letten downe] Watson *till that the bridge was well laid out,*
[83] nere] Watson *in*
[84] most stoutly] Watson *Heinously*
[85] before that slaine] Watson *That slain before*
[86] amongst] Watson *against*
[87] yett] Waton *But*

[23] The Ladye cride & sreacht withall
from her when[88] as they ledd
her deare husband[89] into the hall
and there straike[90] of his head

[24] But all in vaine, the more pitye
for pitye had noe place
But crafte, mischeife & crueltye
These menn did most imbrace

[Folio 13r] **The murders of Ealand Beau-mont &c**

[25] They had a guide which guided them
and in their hearts did dwell
The which to that had[91] moved them
the very devile of[92] hell[93]

[26] I wisse a wofull house there was
the Lord laye slaine & dead
Their foes then eate before their face
their meate, ale, wine, & bread.

[27] Two boyes Sir Robert Beaumont had
ther lefte alive unslaine
Sir John of Ealand he them bade
come[94] eate with him certaine

[28] The one did eate with him trulye
the younger itt was I thinke
Adam thelder sturdilye
wold nether eate nor drinke

[29] See how this boye said Eland, see
his fathers death doth take
If any be itt wilbe hee
that will revengement make

[30] Bit if he doe waxe[95] wild anone
I shall him oversee[96]

---

[88] from her when] Watson *When as from her*
[89] Her deare husband] Watson *Her dearest knight*
[90] straike] Watson *cut*
[91] to that had] Watson *to this that*
[92] of] Watson *in*
[93] Watson has another full stanza here: *See here in what uncertainty |This wretched world is led |At night in his prosperity, |At morning slain, and dead,*
[94] come] Watson *to*
[95] if he doe waxe] Watson *if that he wax*
[96] oversee] Watson *soon foresee*

'The Death of Sir John Ealand of Ealand and his sonne in olde rymthe'

                      And cutt them of by one & one
                      as time shall then serve mee

[31]   The first fray now here yow have heard
           and[97] the second shall ensue
           And how much mischeife afterward
           upon this murther[98] grewe

[32]   And how the mischeife he contriv'd
           his wicked heart within
           Light on himselfe, must[99] be describ'd
           marke now for I beginne

[Folio 13v]   **The murther of Ealand Beau-mont &c**

[33]   The same morning two messingers
           were sent to Lancashire
           To Townley & Brearton there[100]
           their helpe for to require

[34]   unto the mount beneath marsden
           then were they comed with speed
           But heareing that their frends were[101] slaine
           they turnd againe indeed.

[35]   when Ealand thus with[102] wilfull ire
           now[103] Beaumonts blood had shedd
           Into the coaste of Lancashire
           the Lady Beaumont fledd

[36]   With her she tooke her children all
           att Brearton to remaine
           Sometimes also at Townley hall
           they soiourned certaine

[37]   Brearton & Townleye freinds they were
           to her & of her blood
           And presently itt did appeare
           they sought to doe her good.

[38]   They kept there still[104] till they increast

---

[97] and] Watson ommitted
[98] this murther] Watson *these murders*
[99] must] Watson *shall*
[100] Townley & Brearton there] Watson *Mr. Townley and Brereton*
[101] frendes were] Watson *friend was*
[102] thus with] Watson *with his*
[103] now] Watson *thus*
[104] there still] Watson *the boys*

	in person & in age
	Their fathers blood to have redrest
	Still kindled their courage.
[39]	Lacye & Lockwood was with them
	brought up at Brearton greene
	And Quarmbye kinsman unto them
	att home durst not be seene.
[40]	The feats of fence they practised
	to weald their weapons well
	Till fifteene yeares were finished
	and then soe itt befell

[Folio 14r] **The murthrs of Ealand Beaumont &c**

[41] Lockwood the eldest of them all
said freinds I thinke itt good
wee went into our Country all
to avenge[105] our fathers blood

[42] If Ealand have this for well done
he will slaye more[106] indeed
Best where itt then see slew him soone
and soe cutt of Cains seed[107]

[43] I sawe my father Lockwood slaine
and Quarmbye in the night
And last of all they slew certaine
Sir Robert Beau-mont knight

[44] O now[108] this was a cruell deed
who cold his[109] hands refraine
But to cutt of[110] such wicked weed.
Thoughe itt were to their paine

[45] To this then[111] all the rest agreed
deviseing day by day
of this their purpose how to speed
what was the readiest waye.

[46] Two menn that tyme from Quarmby came

---

[105] avenge] Watson *venge*
[106] more] Watson *mo*
[107] soe cutt of Cains seed] Watson *cut off Cain his seed*
[108] now] Watson *Lord*
[109] his] Watson *their*
[110] But to cutt of] Watson *For to pluck out*
[111] this then all the rest] Watson *this the rest then all*

'The Death of Sir John Ealand of Ealand and his sonne in olde rymthe'

                      Dawson & Haighe indeed
                      who then consulted of the same
                      of this how to proceed

[47]   These Countrymenn of course onely
        Said Ealand kept alwaye
        The Turne at Brighouse certainly
        and yow shall knowe the daye.

[48]   To Cromwelbothome yow must then[112] come
        in the wood there for them[113] wayte
        soe yow may have them all & some
        and take them in a straite.

[49]   The day was sett, the turne was kept
        att righouse by Sir John

[Folio 14v]   **The murthrs of Ealand Beaumont &c**

        But litle wiste he, how he was besett[114]
        then att his comeing home.

[50]   Dawson & Haighe had playd their parts
        and Brought from Brererton greene
        yonge Gentlemenn with hardye hearts
        as well was[115] knowne & scene.

[51]   Adam of Beaumont there was layd
        and Lacye with him also
        And Lockwood who was naught afeard
        to fight against his foe.

[52]   In Cromwelbothom woods there[116] laye
        a number with them more
        Armed they were in good arraye
        a spye they had also.

[53]   To spye the tyme when Ealand came
        from Brighouse turne that day
        who playde his part & shewd the same
        to them where as they laye.

[54]   Beneath Brookfoote a hill there is
        to Brighouse in the waye

---

[112] then] Watson ommitted
[113] for them wayte] Watson *to wait*
[114] But litle wise he, how he was besett] Watson *Full little wist he was beset,*
[115] was] Watson *were*
[116] there] Watson *they*

             forth \came/ they to the topp of this
             there spyeing[117] for their prey.

[55]   And[118] from the Lane end came Ealand then[119]
             and spyed these Gentlemenn
             Sore woundred he who they should[120] be
             and vayld his bonnett then.

[56]   Thy curtesie avayles the naught Sir knight
             thou slew my father [exp: dead] deare
             Sometymes Sir Robert Beaumont knight
             & slaine thou shalt be here.

[57]   Said Adam Beau-mont with the rest
             thou hast our father slaine
             whose death wee weane[121] shalbe redrest
             of the & thine certaine.

[Folio 15r] **The murthur of Ealand Beau-mont &c**

[58]   To strike at him they all did[122] strive
             and[123] Ealand still withstood
             with might & maine to save his life
             but yet they shedd his blood.

[59]   They cutt him from his companie
             belike at the lane end
             And there they slewe him certainly
             even[124] thus he made his end.

[60]   marke here the end of all mischeife[125]
             such seeds hath false seed loe[126]
             Unto such end himselfe forsooth[127]
             as he brought others to;

[61]   yett Beaumont he[128] was much to blame
             though there[129] he playd the man

---

[117] spyeing] Watson *prying*
[118] And] Watson ommitted
[119] then] Watson *then Eland came,*
[120] should] Watson *could*
[121] weane] Watson *mind*
[122] they all did] Watson *still did they*
[123] and] Watson *but*
[124] even] Watson *and*
[125] of all mischeife] Watson *of cruelty*
[126] seeds hath false seed] Watson *fine hath falshood*
[127] Unto such end himself forsooth] Watson *Such end forsooth himself had he*
[128] yett Beaumont he] Watson *But Beaumont yet*
[129] though there] Watson *Tho' here*

'The Death of Sir John Ealand of Ealand and his sonne in olde rymthe'

                this partye cold not playe the part[130]
                of a true[131] christian.

[62]   A pure conscience cold never find
       in[132] heart to doe this deed
       Though he this day shold be assign'd
       hos owne hearts blood to bleed.

[63]   But kind in thise yonge Gentlemenn
       crept where it cold not goe
       and in such sort inforced them
       their fathers bane to sloe.

[64]   The second fraye now here yow have
       the third now shall yow heare
       of your kindnes noe more I crave
       but onely to give eare.

[65]   When Sir John Ealand thus was slane
       indeed the storye tells
       Both Beau-mont & his fellowes eke[133]
       fledd downe[134] to ffournes fells.

[Folio 15v]   **The murthr of Ealand Beaumont &c**

[66]   O cruell mars why was thou not
       contented yet with this
       But yett did looke to shedd more blood[135]
       for such thy nature is

[67]   Their yonge conscience corrupt by the
       indeed cold never staye
       Till into extreame miserie
       itt came the rediest waye.[136]

[68]   In ffournes fells long tyme they were
       boasting of their misdeeds
       In more mischeife contreiveing there
       how yett they might proceed.

[69]   They had their pies in this Countrye

---

[130] this partye cold not playe the part] Watson *The part he play'd not in the same*
[131] true] Watson *right*
[132] in] Watson *an*
[133] eke] Watson *then*
[134] downe] Watson *into*
[135] But yett did looke to shedd more blood] Watson *To shed moe blood, but still thou sought,*
[136] Watson has a stanza here: *For Cain his seed on ev'ry side |With wicked hearts disgrac'd |Which to shew mercy hath denied, |Must needs be now displac'd*

                nighe Ealand then who dwelt[137]
                where Sir John Ealand dwelt[138] truly
                & there his household held

[70]   Moe Gentlemen then was not there
        in Ealand parishe dwelt
        Save Savile halfe part of thie yeare
        his house at Rishworth held.

[71]   He kept himselfe from such debate
        removeing thence withall
        Twice in the yeare by Saviles gate
        utno the Bothom hall.

[72]   Adam of Beau-mont then truly
        Lacye & Lockwood eke
        And Quarmbye came to this Countrye
        their purpose for to seeke

[73]   To Cromwellbothome woods they came
        there kept them secretlye
        By fond deceite there did they frame
        their craftye crueltye

[Folio 16r]   **The murthur of Ealand & Beau-mont &c**

[74]   This is the end in soothe to saye
        on Palmison Even at night
        To Ealand milne they tooke their[139] waye
        about the murke midnight

[75]   Into the millhouse then[140] they brake
        & there kept[141] secretlye
        Thus by deceite there[142] did they seeke
        the yonge knight for to slaye

[76]   The morneing came the miller sent
        his wife for corne in haft
        These Gentlemenn in band her bent[143]
        & bound her hard & fast.

[77]   The miller said[144] she shold repent

---

[137] then who dwelt] Watson *who then dwell'd*
[138] dwelt] Watson *liv'd*
[139] their] Watson *the*
[140] then] Watson *there*
[141] Watson omits *them*
[142] Thus by deceite there] Watson *By subtilty thus*
[143] band her bent] Watson *hands her hent*
[144] said] Watson *sware*

'The Death of Sir John Ealand of Ealand and his sonne in olde rymthe'

                    she stayed[145] there soo long
                    A good cudgell in hand he tooke[146]
                    to chastice her, though[147] wrong.

[78]   Into the milne with hast came he[148]
         & ment with her to strive
         But they him bound[149] imediately
         & layd him by his wife

[79]   The yonge knight dreamed ye selfe saime night
         with foes he was bested
         who secretly setled[150] them to fight
         against him in his bedd

[80]   He told his Ladye soone of this
         but as a thinge most vaine
         she weighd itt light & said I wis
         wee must to church \cer/[exp ag]taine

[81]   And serve the Lord[151] this *present* day
         the knight now[152] made him bowne
         And by the miln house laye the way
         that leads into[153] the towne.

[Folio 16v]   **The murthur of Ealand & Beau-mont &c**

[82]   The drought had made the water small
         the stakes appeared drye
         The knight his wife & servants all
         came downe the dame thereby

[83]   When Adam Beau-mont this beheld
         out[154] of the mill came he
         And there his bowe in hand he held[155]
         & shott at him sharpely

[84]   He hitt the knight upon the breast

---

[145] stayed] Watson *tarried*
[146] tooke] Watson *hent*
[147] though] Watson *with*
[148] Into the milne with hast came he] Watson *With haste into the miln came he,*
[149] him bound] Watson *bound him*
[150] secretly setled] Watson *fiecely fettled*
[151] the Lord] Watson *God there*
[152] now] Watson *then*
[153] leads into] Watson *leadeth to*
[154] out] Watson *forth*
[155] And there his bowe in hand he held] Watson *His bow in hand with him he held,*

wherewith[156] the shott did glide
William of Lockwood wrothe thereat
\sade/ Cosen you shoote wide

[85] Himselfe did shoote but yet[157] the knight
was nothing[158] hurt with this
wherewith[159] the knight had great delight
& said to them I wis.

[86] If that my father had beene cloathd[160]
in armor as I[161] certaine
your wicked hands escap'd he had
and had not soo beene slaine.

[87] O Ealand towne alacke said he
if thou but knewe of this
These foes of mine full fast would flee
and of their purpose mis[162]

[88] William of Lockwood was affrayd[163]
the towne shold rise indeed
He shott the knight quite through the head
& slewe him there with speed.

[89] His sone & heire wounded there was[164]
but yett not dead withall[165]
Into the house conveyed he was[166]
he[167] dyed in Ealand hall

[Folio 17r] **The fight and murder of Ealand Beau-mont &c**

[90] A full sister forsooth had he
and[168] a halfe brother also
The full sister his heire must me[169]
the halfe brother not soe.

---

[156] wherewith] Watson *whereat*
[157] but yet] Watson *and hit*
[158] was nothing] Watson *Who nought was*
[159] wherewith] Watson *Whereat*
[160] cloathd] Watson *clad*
[161] in armor as I] Watson *With such armour*
[162] Watson has a stanza here: *By stealth to work needs must they go, |For it had been too much, |The town knowing, the lord to slo |For them, and twenty such,*
[163] affrayd] Watson *adread*
[164] wounded there was] Watson *was wounded there,*
[165] withall] Watson *at all*
[166] was] Watson *were*
[167] he] Watson *and*
[168] ommitted by Watson
[169] Hopkinson copied *m* instead of *b* here.

'The Death of Sir John Ealand of Ealand and his sonne in olde rymthe'

[91]   The full sister his heire she was
       and Savile wedde the same
       Thus Lord of Ealand Savile was
       and since in Saviles name.

[92]   Loe here the end of all mischeife
       from Ealand, Ealands name
       dispatcht itt was unto their greife[170]
       well worthye of the same.

[93]   what tyme these men such frayes did feed[171]
       deeds have I heard & read[172]
       That Ealand came to Saviles name
       in Edwards dayes the third

[94]   But as for Beau-mont & the rest
       they were undone utterly
       thus simple vertue is the best
       & cheife felicitye.

[95]   By whittell lane end they tooke their flight
       & soo the old earth yate
       Then tooke the wood as well they might
       & spied a privye gate.

[96]   Themselves conveying craftilye
       Through[173] Aneley woods that way
       The towne of Ealand manfully
       pursued them that daye

[97]   They Lords servants they had cried[174]
       through the towne[175] with might & maine
       up Gentlemen[176] & make your bowne
       this daye your Lord is slaine

[Folio 17v]   **The murthur of Ealand & Beau-mont &c**

[98]   Whitell, Savile,[177] & Remington
       and Bunnyr, with others more[178]

---

[170] unto their greife] Watson *to their great grief,*
[171] feed] Watson *frame*
[172] deed have I heard & read] Watson *Deeds have I read, and heard*
[173] through] Watson *to*
[174] They Lords servants they had cried] Watson *The lord's servants throughout the town,*
[175] through the towne] Watson *Had cry'd*
[176] gentlemen] Watson *gentle yeomen*
[177] Savile] Watson *Smith*
[178] and Bumyr, with others more] Watson *Bury with many mo;*

	Att Brimmas bowers[179] they made them bound
	their Lords enemies to sloe.
[99]	And to be short the people rose
	throughout the towne about
	There furiously following[180] their foes
	with hue & crye, & shoute.
[100]	All sorts of menn showes their good will
	some bowes & arrowes[181] did beare
	some brought forth clubbs & rusty bills
	which had seene noe sune seven[182] yeres
[101]	To church when[183] as the parish came
	they ioyned with the towne
	Like hardy menn to stand all thinges[184]
	to fight now were they bound.
[102]	Beau-mont & Quarmby sawe all this
	and Lockwood where they stood
	who setled them to fight[185] I wis
	and shott as they were wood.
[103]	Till all their shaftes were[186] spent
	of force then must they flee
	dispatcht they had[187] all their intent
	and lost noe victorye
[104]	The stoutest[188] men of them that was
	was Quarmbye that is true
	ffor he wold never turne his face
	till Ealand menn him slewe.
[105]	Lockwood he bare him on backe
	and hyd him in Aneley wood
	to whom his purse he did betake
	of gold & silver good,

[Folio 18r] **The murthur of Ealand & Beau-mont &c**

---

[179] Att Brimmas bowers] Watson *As brim as boars*
[180] There furiously following] Watson *Then fiercely following on*
[181] arrowes] Watson *shafts*
[182] seven] Watson *that*
[183] when] Watson *now*
[184] thinges] Watson *sam,*
[185] who setled them to fight] Watson *They settled them to fence*
[186] were spent] Watson *were gone and spent*
[187] dispatcht they had] Watson *They had dispatch'd*
[188] stoutest] Watson *hardiest*

'The Death of Sir John Ealand of Ealand and his sonne in olde rymthe'

[106] Take here this gold to yow said he[189]
and to my cosens all[190] here
And in your mirth remember me
and when yow[191] make good cheere.

[107] If that my foes shold this possesse
itt were a greife to me
my friends wellfare is my riches
and cheife felicitye.

[108] Giue place with speed & fare yow well
Christ sheild yow from mischeife
If that itt otherwise befall
itt wold be my great greife

[109] Their foes soe furiously followed on
itt was now biding there
Lockwood with speed he went anon
unto his freinds where they were

[110] with haste then towards Shoters field[192]
they held their ready waye
Adam of Beaumont the way he held
to Crosland hall that day

[111] When Ealand men retorned home
through Aneley wood that waye
There found they Quarmby layd alone
Scarce dead as some menn saye.

[112] And then they slewe him out of hand
dispatchd him of his paine
The late death of their foresaid Lords
inforced them certaine.

[113] Learne Savile here I yow beseech
that in prosperitie
yow be not prous, but mild & meeke
and dwell in charitie.

[Folio 18v] **The murthur of Ealand & Beau-mont &c**

[114] ffor by such meanes, your elders came
to knightly dignitie
where Ealand then forsooke the same
& came to miserie

---

[189] Take here this gold he yow said he] Watson *Here take you this to said he,*
[190] all] omitted in Watson
[191] and when yow] Watson *When you do*
[192] Shoters field] Watson *Huddersfield.* Possibly a reference to the place known as Shooters Nab above Marsden.

[115]   marke here the breach of charitye
        how wretchedly itt ends
        marke here the huge[193] felicitye

        on charitye depends.

[116]   A speech itt is to ev*ery* wight
        please God who may &[194] can
        Itt winnes alwayes with great delight
        the heart of every man.

[117]   Where charitye withdrawes the heart
        from sorrowe & sighes deepe
        right heavy makes itt many a heart
        & many an eye to weepe

[118]   yow Gentlemenn love one another
        love well the yeomanrye
        And[195] every christian man his brother
        & dwell in charitye

[119]   Then shall it come to pass truly
        that all menn yow shall love
        Then after death shall yow onely
        be in heaven with God above.

[120]   To whom always of every wight
        throughout all yeares & dayes
        In heaven & earth both day & night
        be honor, laud, & prayse.

---

[193] The huge] Watson *how much*
[194] &] Watson *or*
[195] And] Watson *Count*

REVIEWS

Catherine A. M. Clarke, *Writing Power in Anglo-Saxon England: Texts, Hierarchies, Economies*. Anglo-Saxon Studies 17. Cambridge: Brewer, 2012. 206 pp. ISBN 9781843843191.

This book is a nuanced exploration of power and its various representations in late Anglo-Saxon texts. Catherine Clarke combines textual analysis, theoretical frameworks and historical and cultural contexts to great effect, presenting a series of case studies in impressive depth of detail. A particularly notable characteristic of these studies is how Clarke plays with genre, refusing to adhere to traditional generic categorisations, recognising the power these have to affect our expectations and analyses. Genre and language are compared and contrasted, and they present multi-level relationships which intertwine, interact and sometimes contradict.

Clarke presents structures of power in late Anglo-Saxon texts in two ways. First is the vertical hierarchy of power and authority, both secular and spiritual, which is often represented by patrons and their dependents. Alongside this, interacting and intertwining with it, is the horizontal axis of interdependent relationships of friendship and reciprocity. None of these power relationships is straightforward; they are often fluid and multifaceted, filled with ambivalences and contradictions. Individuals are shown to live within a strict hierarchy but also in interconnected relationships of mutual obligation and reciprocity. As Clarke concludes, 'identities and relationships do not have to be reduced to one single model or meaning, but can be suspended as dual, multivalent or ambiguous' (p. 172).

The case studies focus on interactions between author, reader and patron, as well as relationships within the texts themselves. In them, textual production and reception are brought to the fore. This means that the literary analysis is always grounded in the external practicalities and contexts of Anglo-Saxon England. However, it should be noted that Clarke is not attempting to extend these representations of power to the reality of Anglo-Saxon England, maintaining a distinction between textuality and history. The case studies, while detailed and impressive, still only show a snapshot of patronage and power in Anglo-Saxon England and the book leaves a sense that this is only the tip of the iceberg. Regardless, this work is impressive in its scope, its detail and its open-minded approach to the material.

The first chapter of this book focuses on the Guthlac poems of the Exeter Book and their expression of relationships of rank and hierarchy on the one hand, and personal relationships of kinship and friendship on the other. In this chapter, Clarke also explores the Anglo-Saxon aesthetic of interlace (the similar elements of Guth*lac* and *-lace* are unrelated, although Clarke connects them as a 'striking visual pun', p. 13, n. 7) and its potential for use as a metaphor for the intricacies of the Anglo-Saxon representation of power and relationships.

The relationships in the Guthlac poems, which fall within a spiritual hierarchy, are often expressed through spatial metaphors, where closeness and distance express status and rank. However, alongside these vertical hierarchies are relationships between patron and follower which are dependent on reciprocity and mutual obligation. These create an 'inter-connected, inter-dependent knotwork of reciprocity and symmetry' (p. 42) of individuals from all levels of the power hierarchy. In this way, Clarke persuasively draws together the hierarchies and relationships — both spiritual and secular — of the poems with the visual metaphor of interlace. However, despite the discussion being grounded in the manuscript contexts of the poems and making use of connections to other texts, this connection comes rather late in the chapter, as does the impact of this connection on understanding the poems' audiences (past or present).

The second chapter is devoted to the expression of reckoning and reciprocity in epitaphs in the *Anglo-Saxon Chronicle*, texts which have a 'complicated generic status' (p. 44). This chapter showcases one of the most interesting themes of this book: its engagement with genre. In it, Clarke reassesses two passages relating to Edgar as epitaphs rather than as the traditional eulogy, panegyric or laudatory verse, with the hope that this new framework will enable a new analysis. This discussion is grounded in a discussion of epigraphic tradition across the Middle Ages. The purpose of epigraphy is to memorialise the subject and to open up their life for reflection and judgement by the reader. By treating these texts as epitaphs, the reader is brought into an active power-relationship with the subject rather than remaining a passive recipient of the texts. This reassessment highlights the problem with applying modern expectations of genre to Anglo-Saxon texts, but in doing so, merely applies a new genre. While the exercise is worthwhile in exploring new aspects of the texts, and showcases some interesting power relationships, these findings are still shaped by the lens of genre.

Chapter 3 addresses absent or remote patronage in the contexts of the shifting power structures of the Benedictine Reform. Clarke focuses on prose hagiography (the *Vita Sancti Oswaldi* — describing the relationship between the distant Oswald and his community — and the two earliest *Vitae* of Dunstan) and panegyric verse (the poetry of Abbo of Fleury). Through them, she explores the textual strategies used in late Anglo-Saxon England to express the power or 'presence' of a patron in both his physical and spiritual absence (p. 90), and his relationship with his dependents. The use of these different genres in this chapter leads to a comparison of the different strategies and agendas used for each, which Clarke finds are genre-specific: the verse acrostics of Abbo express the relationship between absent patron and dependent using metaphorical and literal gift-giving (the poetry is, in itself, a gift), while the prose hagiographies use epistolary conventions and emotive spiritual narratives to express remote patronage. The effect of each of these genres is to present patronage as a practice not dependent on physical location or material presence, but rather an 'ideological system', grounded in the needs of the tenth century (p. 111).

Chapter 4 is also concerned with patronage, but this time in the relationship between patron and author. Clarke's focus here is on gender and its place in the expression of power hierarchies in literary production. To do this, the chapter explores the interplay between female patrons or protagonists and male authors and the different expressions of that relationship in three texts: Cynewulf's *Elene*, the *Encomium Emmae Reginae*, and the *Vita Ædwardi Regis*. These texts offer a strong basis for comparison as they cover Old English and Anglo-Latin and multiple genres, while falling within the same context. Tantalisingly, Clarke mentions the possibility of a comparative reading of the two extant versions of the *Encomium*, which could have added an extra dimension to the discussion of that text's representation of patronage and power, but the case study does not suffer from its absence. The portrayals of the female patron in each of these texts are complex, and perform a multitude of functions. The overriding conclusion, though, is that gender is not inherently linked with power and agency; textual gendered personae share complicated and shifting relationships which are not fixed within the hierarchy of patron and author, but adapt to reflect the complexity of the relationships themselves.

The final chapter again plays with our perceptions of genre, this time by performing a refreshing literary analysis on the charter texts of the *Libellus Æthelwoldi Episcopi*, in which different representations of power interact in two textual genres. This prosimetrical text presents patronage in the period of the Benedictine Reform through the needs of Bishop Hervey in the twelfth century and demonstrates the enduring relevance of Anglo-Saxon patronage. The *Libellus* shows Æthelwold within local networks of power with his community and with the laity. He is enmeshed in relationships of exchange, gift-giving and obligation, as each community is dependent on the other. The prosimetrical text is simultaneously panegyric and practical. It explores the asymmetric relationship between the ecclesiastic and lay communities, in which the laity is presented as opportunistic and the monastic community, represented by Æthelwold, is fair and just. Similarly, in the prose text, Æthelwold is pragmatic and politically capable, whereas in the verse he is saintly and idealised, described with hagiographic language that elevates him above the earthly concerns of the petty laity and their land-holdings. These representations of Æthelwold create for Hervey a 'legitimising' model for his own actions in the twelfth century, asserting his rights in the newly created bishopric of Ely (p. 170). This chapter successfully explores different models for expressing patronage, both practical and spiritual, using different genres.

KATE WILES UNIVERSITY OF LEEDS

Donald Scragg, *A Conspectus of Scribal Hands Writing English, 960–1100*. Publications of the Manchester Centre for Anglo-Saxon Studies 11. Cambridge: Brewer, 2012. xxii + 94 pp. ISBN 9781843842866.

Donald Scragg's *A Conspectus of Scribal Hands Writing English, 960–1100* is a welcome and valuable addition to the reference resources for the study of English scribal and manuscript culture in the later Anglo-Saxon period. The scope is limited to the narrow band of the 'long eleventh century', and the work seeks to identify and enumerate the contribution of scribes working in that period across our surviving manuscripts. In addition to the table of scribes itself, a number of other resources are included that expand the usefulness of the *Conspectus*, including five full-page, black-and-white images of scribal hands; an index of names mentioned in or otherwise attributed to the various manuscripts, cross-referenced by hand number; an index of places where the scribes are thought to have been active; and a map of the locations mentioned in the *Conspectus*, as well as a subject index based on the summary of the contents supplied by the respective scribes. The project rests on the back of a significant quantitiy of palaeographic research into the manuscripts; references to the secondary literature are condensed down to the absolute minimum form required. As such, the *Conspectus* identifies the various scribal hands writing in English in the long eleventh century and gives locations in the manuscripts where each can be found. The details of and arguments for identifying each hand are, of course, ommitted, making this work the tip of an immense iceberg that each researcher can draw on as guide before delving into the depths of the manuscripts and scribes of their own interest.

The main focus of the *Conspectus* is the enumeration of the scribal hands. Where the same scribe appears in multiple manuscripts, all examples are listed together under the hand number, usually (but not always) on the scribe's first appearance in the *Conspectus*. Manuscripts are listed alphanumerically in the *Conspectus*, first by repository and then by shelf-mark. A diamond mark is given for the hand number when a manuscript which has already been covered is reached, along with a note to refer to the entry in the *Conspectus*. In this way a user working with a specific manuscript which is not the first instance of a given a scribe can easily find the other works to which he or she contributed. Scragg notes in the introduction (p. xiv) that where there are conflicting opinions in the scholarship as to whether or not two items in a given manuscript are by the same scribe, the corresponding pieces are identified with a lower-case letter immediately following the main number for the scribal hand, e.g. '78a'. In a small number of instances, the numbering for a scribal hand is followed by '.5', such as for scribal hand '60.5'. While no explanation is given for this practice by Scragg in the introduction, it can be assumed that these sub-divisions represent scribal hands which were identified later in the compilation process and were then inserted into the *Conspectus* subsequent to the main numbering having been established.

Manuscripts and scribes are cross-referenced to their relevant entries in the other major reference works relating to the mansucripts, as appropriate: Helmut Gnuess's *Handlist of Anglo-Saxon Manuscripts*, Neil Ker's *Catalogue of Manuscripts Containing Anglo-Saxon*, Peter Sawyer's *Anglo-Saxon Charters: An Annotated List and Bibliography*, and David Pelteret's *Catalogue of English Post-Conquest Vernacular Documents*. In many instances, Scragg also includes cross references to published images of the manuscripts, although in light of the ever-changing digital environment he errs on the side of caution and only includes reference to facsimiles in hard copy, most notably the relevant volumes from the Early English Manuscripts in Facsimile series and the Anglo-Saxon Manuscripts in Microfiche Facsimile (ASMFF), as well as making reference to specific books in which images of a whole manuscript are reproduced. One minor problem is that reference to the microfiche facsimile of Cambridge, Corpus Christi College MS 383 (ASMFF 11) is omitted; but with the publication of much better quality images via the Parker on the Web and Early English Law projects, this is hardly an issue. The omission of direct reference to digitial images is justified in the introduction on the basis of the ever-changing nature of the internet and, also relating to printed images of indiviudal folios, the unfeasibile scope of identifying every single image of a given hand.

In all, there are few problems that can be identified in the *Conspectus*, once the deliberate limitations and scope of the project are taken into account; responses to problems arising during the research seem to have been clearly thought through. Most issues that occur on perusal of the *Conspectus* are addressed in the introduction, and while a bibliography would have been an appreciated supplement to the resource it provides, Scragg duly notes that such an endeavour would have extended the size of the project beyond its scope and that the forthcoming bilbiography to accompany Gnuess's *Handlist* will fulfil this need. Again, the scope and intentions of the *Conspectus* are made explicit, and Scragg clearly envisions its function in relation to the bodyof resources for the study of later Anglo-Saxon texts, manuscripts and scribes.

Overall, it is a valuable resource that will be of immense use to those working in the field. It is a project that one would like to see extended to the manuscripts containing English produced and used in other centuries of the Anglo-Saxon period. Obviously the scope of such a project would be immense, and the relationship of the numbering within this conspectus to the larger whole would require some reassessment. The potential for using the *Conspectus* in researching the scribes and English manuscript culture of the long eleventh century is enticing, and future studies of individual scribes will both draw on and refine the details that this useful work contains.

THOMAS GOBBITT AUSTRIAN ACADEMY OF SCIENCES

Peter S. Baker, *Honour, Exchange and Violence in 'Beowulf'*. Anglo-Saxon Studies 20. Cambridge: Brewer, 2013. x + 279 pp. ISBN: 9781843843467.

Peter Baker's study of violence as a social and economic construct in Anglo-Saxon England accomplishes the rare feat of being deceptively simple to read yet highly complex and eclectic in its approaches and solutions to long-lasting puzzles in *Beowulf* scholarship. Its main merit consists in making explicit a socio-economic system (and its component structures) which would have been obvious to the 'textual communities' from which the poem arose, and are therefore encoded implicitly in the text, but which otherwise remain invisible to us.[1] We might think that we know how a heroic society lives and breathes, but Baker successfully proves that we do not and that presentist biases always block the view of even consummate scholars. This lack of familiarity with the intimate life of a heroic society (albeit an ideal one, which lives only in heroic poems) makes us strangers to the meaning of many gestures which we often interpret on the basis of speculative nineteenth-century approaches uncritically perpetuated to this day. Baker astutely uses what is at heart an anthropological framework to gain access to the culture implied by *Beowulf* and makes explicit the workings of the heroic system in which honour, violence, and treasure are commensurable forms of capital.

His monograph is not merely the study of violence in Old English literature, but a successful attempt to understand the ways in which violence shapes a society and its economy. Although the idea of a socio-economic system organized around treasure and honour as signs of one's worthiness in an ideal heroic society like the one portrayed in *Beowulf* is not new, Baker's study is the first to present a coherent system which explains many phenomena otherwise poorly understood so far.

In his introduction (pp. 1–34), Baker firmly sets his work in the wake of previous scholarship on violence (Guy Halsall most recently among others), the economy of gifts (Marcel Mauss), and Anglo-Saxon studies (too many to list). While it is clear that Baker's knowledge of his eclectic range of secondary sources is thorough, his innovations come to light only slowly and modestly in the following chapters. Baker's main contention is that violence is a social practice, and every violent act is a social transaction (and hence subject to regulation and part of a system which we do not see but to which the authors, disseminators, listeners/readers of early medieval heroic poems would have been intimately accustomed).

---

[1] For the notion of 'textual communities', see Brian Stock, *The Implications of Literacy: Written Language and Models of Interpretation in the Eleventh and Twelfth Centuries* (Princeton: Princeton University Press, 1983), pp. 1–10 and 30–87.

Thus, to win honour is not only to perform violent acts by which to win treasure and renown, but to perform them according to the rules.

In his second chapter (pp. 35–76), Baker explains the rules. They make up a system which he calls the 'Economy of Honour'. This chapter has a strong Maussian flavour (updated to fit the needs of an Anglo-Saxonist), but beyond this it is a brilliant application of the theory of gift-based economy (built on reciprocity — a gift is never free) to the context of *Beowulf* to throw light on the relationships in a heroic society (especially those between lord and warriors). Violence is a means of procuring honour and booty and, in a heroic society, it is an economic force, even a form of capital (as is honour). In the world of *Beowulf*, to be rich is to be happy and have honour (a concept which Baker rightly considers more useful than 'glory'). Wealth is not measured in treasure, but also in honour and deeds of violence. Violence itself is understood to be the means of gaining or repaying wealth, hence *weorð* as transferable value (between people, but also from objects to people and vice-versa). This explains why violence enables this transfer of value: when someone is killed, their possessions and honour go to the victor. Baker is wisely careful to use poetic sources with caution, not as unproblematic reflections of the society in which they are composed, but as ideal refractions of it and as reflections of an imagined glorious (though tragic) past.

In his third chapter (pp. 77–102), Baker continues his Mauss-inspired *tour de force* by illuminating a well-known dilemma among *Beowulf* scholars: why does Unferth lend Beowulf his sword after he had previously done his best to berate him? When his Economy of Honour theory is applied, it becomes clear that Beowulf's coming devalues the honour of the Danish warriors (since he is willing to attempt something no one else dares to). Unferth, as their representative, tries to devalue Beowulf's inflationist honour by proving that he is not an honourable man in the first place (hence his pointing to the hero's troubled youth). After Beowulf defeats Grendel, when he goes against the monster's mother, Unferth 'wants a piece of the action' (p. 95), he wants to be part of the hero's honour-accruing actions by lending him his sword (which, had it been used, would have been the instrument of the violent act through which glory had been gained, thus making its original owner a partaker in the honour). However, Unferth fails to gain honour because the hero doesn't use Hrunting at all.

In chapters four (pp. 103–38) and five (pp. 138–66), Baker makes the very insightful connection between the Economy of Honour and the role of women in a heroic society. He challenges the usual interpretation of women as peace-weavers (queens exchanged in marriage between hostile nations to make peace) and proposes an alternative explanation of the word *freoðuwebbe*, instantiating this in chapter five in alternative readings of three of the queens featuring in *Beowulf*. His main contention is that women should not be seen as passive tokens of peace, but as agents with power who can use it for the better (Wealhtheow) or for the worse (Thryth).

Baker begins by deconstructing the prevalent understanding of women as peace-weavers in heroic texts as a paradigm rooted in a Victorian understanding of the woman as the angel of the house (or mead hall, in this context), then proceeding to demonstrate through a detailed semantic and etymological study that the word *freoðuwebbe* never appears in contexts having to do with marriage or peace-making, and that sources have little to say about women's role in peacemaking in any case. The prevalent interpretation of the phrase is harmful, Baker explains, because it has lead to a simplistic, all-pervasive understanding of gender roles in Anglo-Saxon England ('men made war, women peace — a clean division of labour!', p. 126). This vision remains popular because it answers the cultural expectations and the desires of many readers. But Baker argues instead that the semantic areas of *sibb/frið* are situated at the intersection of early medieval ideas concerning divine authority and good rulership, which promote harmony and good feeling (peace as absence of violent hostility). Thus *freoðuwebbe* is tied to the queen's ideal image as promoter of both material and spiritual welfare of the polity (an ideal image, not an actual role).

Baker reminds us that the Germanic ideal of making peace does not necessarily mean removing disturbing elements and letting things settle down, but rather introducing a greater power among the disputants which would be capable of enforcing peace. For peace is maintained by threat and violence, and is a state of temporary quiet (accomplished through military victory) rather than the absence of war. In fact, Baker invites us to drop the assumption that peacemaking is central to Anglo-Saxon understandings of womanhood. Thus Thryth and Wealhtheow were not included in the poem as examples of a bad versus a good queen, but as different aspects of queenship – queens wielded power, which could mean shedding blood/use of violence (pp. 144–55). In the case of Freawaru (pp. 155–66), Baker convincingly argues against the idea that princesses were given in marriage to settle disputes. In a heroic society, marriage was understood more as a gift (functioning in the Economy of Honour, just like other gifts in the early medieval economy dominated more by gift than by trade), than as commodity exchange. The queen's condition (though subordinate) was far above that of slave and was not accompanied by the loss of subjectivity. Like any gift in such a society, a queen given in marriage both acquires and confers honour, but more importantly, imposes obligation and defines the relationship between the recipient and the giver.

In his sixth chapter (pp. 167–99), Baker explains the perils of peacemaking in a thought-provoking reading of the Finn episode (performed by Hrothgar's *scop* during the celebration in Heorot after Grendel's defeat) as the story of a failed attempt to settle a dispute. In a heroic society, violence was seen (unlike today) as a reasonable — though not ideal — way to settle disputes. A dispute was a means of organizing and maintaining the smooth functioning of a society (nowadays, in similar fashion, though in less obvious ways, the violence of confrontations is ritualized and thus sublimated in elections, court proceedings where two sides confront each other, and so forth). In Anglo-Saxon England, the very idea of success included the expectation of dispute and violence, which were however always governed by well-defined rules and customs. Hence, to be a bad person was not to be violent, but to be violent in ways which did not follow the rules legislating violence.

In his seventh and last chapter (pp. 200–39), Baker interprets Beowulf's death as his 'last triumph', and not as a failure. The presentist bias we bring to the text again blurs our vision – the point of view from which the hero's death looks like a defeat is a modern one, but if the problem is set in the terms of the Economy of Honour, Beowulf's death does not look like a defeat. Baker invites us to ask not 'who is still alive?' but rather 'who has the treasure?' – this is what matters in the end. Thus he cuts the Gordian knot of the heavily disputed meaning of Beowulf's death and its aftermath. Beowulf secures the peace by making war, so fighting the dragon is not a bad decision stemming from some tragic flaw, but that which the hero simply has to do (his *heahgesceap*). Still, Baker acknowledges that *Beowulf*'s author is too great a poet to permit his audience entirely to lose sight of the costs of the heroic values that he celebrates (which is obvious in Wiglaf's lament — here the hero's death does not quite emerge as a triumph).

Although he is exhaustive in the issues he approaches, it would have been interesting to see Baker tackling institutionalized/legislated violence — Anglo-Saxon legislation that allowed for trial by ordeal (Laws of Ine) or that did not ban private vengeance but rather sought to mitigate it (by sublimating it into *wergeld*), or that clarified how vengeance could be pursued (Edmund II's blood-feud laws). However, in the short afterword (pp. 140–42), Baker lets his readers in on the original intention of his study, which was to propose a semiotics of conflict in *Beowulf*. He observes that violence is structured like a language, and any exchange of blows or a feud functions like a dialogue. This would have been a fascinating read and also a highly-needed study. Despite the author's modest demur about his ability to write it, I think it would be only fitting for Peter Baker to complete his ambitious plan. Judging by the complex approaches, the innovative solutions, and the overall high quality of his scholarship in this monograph, he has all the resources to accomplish it.

    CATALIN TARANU   UNIVERSITY OF LEEDS

Castration and Culture in the Middle Ages, ed. by Larissa Tracy. Medieval Cultures 32. Cambridge: Brewer, 2013. xiii + 351 pp. ISBN 978-1-84384-351-1.

This collection of essays brings together a range of researchers interested in the theme of castration from the late Roman to the Early Modern period. This volume is notable among similar compilations for the effectiveness with which the articles create a coherent whole, starting with the brilliant introduction by Larissa Tracy. Over the past twenty years, medieval sexuality and medieval masculinity have received much attention, but 'very little has been done specifically on *medieval* castration' (p. 3) and this excellent collection of essays provides a detailed and stimulating analysis on the subject. Students and scholars will find Tracy's introduction and footnotes a helpful overview on historical, interpretative and bibliographical matters. Moreover, the introduction lays out the primary theoretical arguments that link this collection of essays.

    The volume is divided into fourteen chapters, each containing an article treating a facet of the question, and is organized in chronological order, beginning with Reusch's article on the archaeology of castration, and proceeding, through various medieval texts and sources, to bodily mutilation in Shakespeare's works. It appears quite evident that the book could be divided into three sections, the first containing the eight chapters that deal with late Antiquity and the early Middle Ages, the second (chapters 9–13) more focused on the high and later Middle Ages, then concluding with chapter 14 on the early modern period. This incisive collection is mostly successful in achieving its aim and the only flaw is that the first chapter seems disconnected from the whole. Although the theme is obviously the same, Reusch's article ('Raised Voices: The Archaeology of Castration', pp. 29–47) is the only text that does not analyse a written source and, unfortunately, as the author openly states, her work is limited by the scarcity of historical sources describing how and where castrated people were buried. Nonetheless, Reusch provides useful information to better understand the living condition of some more successful eunuchs.

    Shaun Tougher's essay ('The Aesthetics of Castration: The Beauty of Roman Eunuchs', pp. 48–72) brilliantly explores some major works written by Roman and Byzantine historians in which the question of the aesthetics of castration is raised. After highlighting the difference between the Galli, the self-castrated religious devotees of a Mother Goddess, and the beautiful and desirable castrated slave boys who lived in the Roman Empire, Tougher provides an excellent analysis of the role of eunuchs during the Roman Empire and their relationship with the emperors. He demonstrates convincingly how these attractive, youthful eunuchs became the archetypical 'pretty boys' and how they were perceived by contemporaries.

Jack Collins, through his interest in Jewish tradition and Christian religion, stresses the points of divergence between the two cultures ('Appropriation and Development of Castration as Symbol and Practice in Early Christianity', pp. 73–86). The starting point of Collins' analysis is Matthew 19:11–12 and how these words, pronounced by Jesus, reversed the Jewish perspective on eunuchs and influenced the idea of celibacy, sexual (in)continence and castration in the early Christian communities. Collins' brilliant analysis also includes excerpts of texts written by the first Christian theologians, such as Clement of Alexandria, Tertullian, and Eusebius, among others. I appreciated the fact that Collins included in his article all the original texts (in Hebrew and Greek) with their translation.

Larissa Tracy's article (' "Al defouleden is holie bodi": Castration, the Sexualization of Torture, and Anxieties of Identity in the *South English Legendary*', pp. 87–107) provides an interesting and detailed analysis of the absence of castration as a form of torture in the thirteenth-century *South English Legendary*. She explains not only why castration is not a component of martyrdom but also how this contributes to reinforce an English notion of national identity. Her analysis also highlights the question of gendered identity, paying special attention to the construction and deconstruction of gender identity in hagiography. The only weakness of this article is the absence of a translation into modern English of the selected Middle English excerpts. Moreover, its placement between Collins' and Bremmer's articles is somewhat odd: as I mentioned, the order of the articles is chronological, so placing Tracy's study between two papers on early medieval subjects breaks the logical sequence of the papers.

In the next article ('The Children He Never Had; The Husband She Never Served: Castration and Genital Mutilation in Medieval Frisian Law', pp. 108–30), Rolf H. Bremmer Jr. provides an in-depth overview on genital mutilation in early medieval laws. Although the title refers to Frisian law, the paper deals with a wider range of examples drawn from different legal texts and compares them to Frisian material, focusing on castration as a punitive measure, along with the compensation specified in the Frisian registers for genital mutilation. It must be said that this essay is one of the most engaging reads I have had on the subject, as the descriptions offer a vivid picture of the subject.

Jay Paul Gates ('The *Fulmannod* Society: Social Valuing of the (Male) Legal Subject', pp. 131–48) states that his study of Anglo-Saxon laws 'attempts to fill [the] gap by drawing the lay, male, sexed body and work in Anglo-Saxon England into dialogue in order to consider how Anglo-Saxons understood the function and value of the sexed male body' (p. 135). Although Gates provides a thorough analysis of the law codes of Æthelberht and Alfred concerning injury tariffs, his attempt to define the man's value through Anglo-Saxon riddles is far from persuasive. Nevertheless, I found that Gates' article offers a clear and comprehensive comparison between Æthelberht's and Alfred's law codes and how they reflect the social function of the individual.

The next article (Charlene M. Eska's ' "Imbrued un their owne bloud": Castration in Early Welsh and Irish Sources', pp. 149–73) can be read as a logical continuation of Gates' paper, as Eska reviews the medieval Welsh and Irish laws that, like their Anglo-Saxon equivalents, are based on a system of compensation. By examining the Welsh and Irish law codes and annals, Eska explains that the influence of the Norman Conquest could have increased the practice of castration in these territories, although many annalistic sources possibly recorded this procedure as 'blinding' or 'mutilating', due to the sensitive nature of the matter.

Mary A. Valante's essay ('Castrating Monks: Vikings, Slave Trade, and the Value of Eunuchs', pp. 174–87) could be seen as an extension of Tougher's article, since Valante analyses the role of Vikings in the European and North-African slave trade of eunuchs. Given the increasing demand for eunuchs in Byzantine and Arab territories, Vikings raids played a key role in the economics of the slave trade and Valante effectively shows one of the functions of the traffic of monastic slaves.

The following five chapters focus on text analysis, with Anthony Adams' essay (' "He took a stone away": Castration and Cruelty in the Old Norse *Sturlunga Saga*', pp. 188–209) acting as a transition between the two sections. Adams explores excerpts of *Sturlunga saga* that mention castration and compares them to other sagas as well as to Norwegian and Swedish laws. His result is a persuasive study of Norse masculinity and Old Norse society in general, highlighting how masculinity was the feature through which people (men *and* women) and their honour were judged.

The four subsequent essays deal with French vernacular texts ('The Castrating of the Shrew: The Performance of Masculinity and Masculine Identity in *La dame escolliee*' by Mary E. Leech, pp. 210–28; 'Eunuchs of the Grail' by Jed Chandler, pp. 229–54; 'Insinuating Indeterminate Gender: A Castration Motif in Guillaume de Lorris's *Romans de la Rose*' by Ellen Lorraine Friedrich, pp. 255–79; 'Culture Loves a Void: Eunuchry in *De Vetula* and Jean le Fèvres's *La Vieille*', pp. 280–94). Leech provides a fascinating discussion of *La dame escolliee*, in which the dominating figure of the mother-in-law is punished by the symbolic transformation of her female body into a male one, subverting not only gender conventions but also the concept of masculinity. In this fabliau, a woman is symbolically castrated because she was emulating the behaviour of a man (and her husband is a failure in his role as a male) and Leech offers a particularly interesting analysis of the diegetic role of this female castration.

In 'Eunuchs of the Grail', Jed Chandler brilliantly discusses the role of Perceval and his symbolic castration in the Arthurian romances linked to the Grail (Chrétien de Troyes' *Perceval le Conte du Graal*, *Perlesvaus*, the *Queste del Saint Graal*, and the *Vulgate Lancelot*). The author's consistent close reading of the mentioned texts not only provides an in-depth analysis of the character of Perceval and of his metaphorical castration, but also examines in detail the figure of the Grail virgin/Grail beast and its sexual ambiguity, which transcends gender and associates auto-castration with virginal purity. The following chapter is dedicated to Friedrich's essay on the castration motif in Guillaume de Lorris' *Le Roman de la Rose*. The starting point of Friedrich's analysis is an unusual piece of marginalia (a self-castrating beaver) at the bottom of the opening page of Guillaume de Lorris' text in British Library MS Stowe 947. This original study asserts that this image, which recalls castration, placed below the miniature of Oiseuse, an ambiguous figure, suggests non-normative, masculine same-sex sexual desire.

The last article dealing with French vernacular literature, perfectly linked with the previous chapter, is by Robert L. A. Clark and analyses the passages on eunuchry found in the Pseudo-Ovidian Latin poem *De Vetula* and in Jean Le Fèvre's *La Vieille*. Although it would have been interesting to examine both texts equally, this study is not a comparison, even if sometimes the two texts are juxtaposed, but rather a full analysis of eunuchry in *De Vetula*. Finally, the last essay, written by Karin Selberg and Lena Wånggren ('The Dismemerment of Will: Early Modern Fear of Castration', pp. 295–313) is an interesting and somehow different study on physical mutilation in Shakespeare's plays, which follows the Freudian concept of castration applied to literature.

The select bibliography at the end of the volume is satisfactory, especially when combined with footnotes (rich and detailed in almost all papers). While the contents of this book are naturally uneven, the volume nonetheless offers several outstanding essays of significant interest and importance, and specialists will profit from reading it.

PAOLA SCARPINI   UNIVERSITY OF YORK

Traditions and Innovations in the Study of Medieval English Literature: The Influence of Derek Brewer, ed. by Charlotte Brewer and Barry Windeatt. Cambridge: Brewer, 2013. ix + 317 pp. ISBN 9781843843542.

Today's diverse and intricate approaches to Middle English literature can seem overwhelming, especially to those first reading a text or genre. Although introductory works exist, they rarely explore particular methodologies and their influence in full. *Traditions and Innovations* indirectly fills this gap by engaging with the studies of one of the field's most prominent scholars over the past sixty years or so.

Despite its appearance, this volume is not a *Festschrift*. It instead seeks 'to illustrate the importance of Brewer's ideas and influence for Medieval English scholarship both of his time and subsequently' (p. 17). Although Brewer's key role in publishing many works on medieval studies is discussed occasionally (such as by the introduction, pp. 6–7, and Barry Windeatt, pp. 262–78 at 277), the volume focuses on his works and how they affected (and affect) later scholarship. His methodology is explained as reading in the proper context of medieval culture and society, and without modern presuppositions. This approach is followed by the contributors throughout their chapters.

The contributors, who knew Brewer well, provide many anecdotes from his life while discussing his influence on their work and the field as a whole. The writing paints an intimate portrait and is sometimes tinged with colour and candour, such as Pearsall's repeated quotations from Brewer's creative writing and comparison of his life with Chaucer's (pp. 18–33). Interestingly, Brewer's experiences are presented as context for better understanding his own works and ideologies. This is in a fashion similar to Brewer's own reading of medieval literature. Pearsall's survey of the development of Brewer's theoretical approaches during his career is particularly interesting, as it suggests how some events might have inspired intellectual stances and professional growth.

The topics covered are closely related to Brewer's interests. Many of the chapters touch on Chaucer (Derek Pearsall and Alastair Minnis), and others discuss various aspects of *Troilus and Criseyde* in particular (Mary Carruthers, A. C. Spearing, and Jacqueline Tasioulas). There are also particularly interesting chapters on Malory and the Arthurian cycles (Elizabeth Archibald), class and the French of England (Christopher Cannon), and friendship in romance (Corinne Saunders). Other chapters on varied aspects of Middle English narratives (by Helen Cooper, Jill Mann, James Simpson, Windeatt, and R. F. Yeager) and the nuances of language and manuscripts (Charlotte Brewer and A. S. G. Edwards) round out the collection.

Brewer's influence is not explicitly argued or explored, but is instead shown through the chapters that engage with his work. They reiterate his arguments in old debates, reapply his methods in new studies, or continue earlier collaborations, in 'a sequence of conversations with, and developments from, aspects of Brewer's work' (p. 16). They are predominantly literary in their approach, as the title of the volume might suggest, with little consideration of other fields. Each of the fifteen chapters engages with texts and important methodological considerations. However, some of the debates covered are dated and rarely discussed today. They are sometimes conservative and omit discussion of scholarship that has not developed directly from Brewer's works.

Some chapters seem out of place in the volume, given its objectives. For example, Charlotte Brewer's chapter on Middle English word meaning and dictionaries (pp. 215–38) provides only a few passing references to Derek Brewer's thoughts on the subject. She does not show how these areas were influenced by, or are a continuation of his work, but rather implies how they validate his opinions on the topic. This chapter is also considerably longer than the others, at twenty-three pages (or forty-six, with its appendix), while the nearest in length is only eighteen pages and most are less than fifteen. While this chapter is interesting, it seems odd for it to occupy so much space and not directly contribute to the volume's stated objectives.

The focus on literary studies limits the volume's applicability in other areas of medieval studies. For example, Minnis (pp. 34–47) argues that Brewer's position on chivalry was correct and his opponents (such as Terry Jones, who argues that Chaucer was a pacifist and presented chivalry as a mere façade) are wrong for reading texts anachronistically and twisting them to suit their own attitudes.[1] He claims Brewer disproved such arguments by showing that chivalry was a sincerely held ideal, and makes no compromises in the process. For example, he does not mention that others find that some scholarly criticisms of chivalry helpfully underline its cultural tensions.[2] Minnis focuses entirely on 'literary' chivalry and omits the works of cultural historians, such as Jean Flori, Richard Kaeuper, Maurice Keen, and Malcolm Vale. This is troubling, as these scholars all made significant contributions to the field, such as Keen's two key articles on the debate of Chaucer's scepticism of chivalry.[3] This might seem reasonable, given the volume's literary focus. However, comparing literary with historical sources provides invaluable insight into such layered cultural texts, and should not be dismissed.[4]

A few key areas might have further illuminated Brewer's prominence in the field. While plenty of attention is given to Brewer's influence on others, little is paid to how he was influenced by other scholarship. Besides a few brief mentions of Freud's ideas (pp. 166, 190, 191), only social and cultural influences are noted, such as Saunders' suggestion that Brewer's notion of friendship was perhaps affected by his own experiences in war (pp. 128–43). It also would have been helpful to consider how more recent and innovative scholarship draws upon Brewer's work.

Despite its occasionally unfulfilled objectives, this volume presents a fascinating insight into the life, work, and influence of Derek Brewer. It traverses many themes and texts in the rich field of Middle English studies. Its chapters serve as useful studies, starting points, and

---

[1] Terry Jones, *Chaucer's Knight: The Portrait of a Medieval Mercenary*, 2nd edn (London: Methuen, 1994). The first edition was published in 1980.

[2] Although they reject Jones' argument that Chaucer's Knight was a mercenary modeled on John Hawkwood. Maurice Keen, 'Chaucer and Chivalry Revisited', in *Armies, Chivalry and Warfare in Medieval Britain and France: Proceedings of the 1995 Harlaxton Symposium*, ed. by Matthew Strickland (Stamford: Paul Watkins, 1998), pp. 1–12.

[3] Maurice Keen, 'Chaucer's Knight, the English Aristocracy and the Crusade', in *English Court Culture in the Later Middle Ages. Papers from the Colston Research Society Symposium, Bristol University, 1981*, ed. by V. J. Scattergood and J. W. Sherborne (London: Duckworth, 1983), pp. 45–61; Keen, 'Chaucer and Chivalry Revisited'.

[4] See for example Richard Kaeuper, 'Literature as Essential Evidence for Understanding Chivalry', *Journal of Medieval Military History*, 5 (2007), 1–15.

summaries of scholarship. It can warn of pitfalls and inform diverse methodologies. Overall, this volume proves a significant collection of works inspired by Brewer and serves as testament to his continuing influence today.

TREVOR RUSSELL SMITH   UNIVERSITY OF LEEDS

The Culture of Inquisition in Medieval England, ed. by Mary C. Flannery and Katie L. Walter. Westfield Medieval Studies 4. Cambridge: Brewer, 2013. 202 pp. ISBN: 9781843843368.

The editors of this welcome volume aim to shed light on the impact of the practice of inquisition in the literature and culture of late medieval England. Moving beyond the traditional research focusing on the legal aspect of inquisition with regard to heresy, the contributions in this volume provide the reader with case-studies investigating the literary and cultural perspective.

Indeed, inquisition has mostly been studied from a historical angle, and the geographical focus has traditionally been the French *Midi* and the Iberian kingdoms of Castile and Aragon. The focus on 'the Inquisition' as an institution rather than a legal practice, on ecclesiastical prosecution and persecution of the Waldensian and Albigensian heretical movements in the early thirteenth century and on the Spanish Inquisition from the late fifteenth century onwards has not only monopolised the interpretation of the medieval concept of *inquisitio*, but also diverted attention away from both the fourteenth and fifteenth centuries and from north-west Europe.

In the last two decades the function of inquisition in late medieval England has been the subject of a growing scholarly interest. Recent publications like Ian Forrest's seminal *The Detection of Heresy in Late Medieval England* have contributed to the appreciation of the wider role of *inquisitio* in England's ecclesiastical courts in the later Middle Ages.[1] Moreover, with a focus on the later Middle Ages, this collection of essays sits conveniently alongside David Loewenstein and John Marshall's *Heresy, Literature and Politics in Early Modern English Culture*.[2]

Aside from contributing to this scholarship orientated on the British Isles, the volume under consideration furthermore belongs within a context of recent directions in the study of medieval inquisition. It has been convincingly shown that *inquisition* was not merely the ecclesiastical institutionalisation of the prosecution of heresy, but rather part of a longer process influencing the existing religious, social, and cultural structures. Although the editors may appear rather ambitious by stating that this collection 'redefines the nature of inquisition's role within both medieval law and culture', the essays are most certainly valuable case-studies that contribute further to the investigation of the broader impact of inquisition on the different aspects of medieval society.

The articles gathered partly originated at a session on 'Inquisition and Confession' at the 2008 Kalamazoo International Congress on Medieval Studies, and at two workshops, 'Inquisition and Confession' and 'Imagining Inquisition in Medieval England', held at Queen Mary, University of London in 2009 and 2010. The editors must be applauded for their selection of highly complementary articles which represent some of the most recent developments in the

---

[1] Respectively, *The Haskins Society Journal*, 1 (1995), 197–87 and Oxford: Clarendon, 2005.
[2] Cambridge: Cambridge University Press, 2006.

field. In the introduction, 'Imagining Inquisition', the editors, Mary C. Flannery and Katie L. Walter, provide a brief overview of the recent historiography on the topic and provide brief outlines of the collected essays.

In the first article, 'Inquisition, Public Fame and Confession: General Rules and English Practice', Henry A. Kelly sets the tone and analyses the institution and development of inquisitorial procedures in canon law. After emphasising that 'inquisition' does not only refer to 'heresy inquisition' and that Pope Innocent III's inquisitorial procedure was designed for crimes in general, Kelly outlines the medieval Church's view on private sin as opposed to public crime (*publica fama*) as it should be understood from the decree *Qualiter et quando* of the Fourth Lateran Council (1215). The author goes on to discuss the application of *inquisitio* to heresy cases, the status of coerced confessions of non-public crimes, and how inquisitors dealt with the seal of confession. Kelly's investigation of inquisitorial practices in the English ecclesiastical courts, both the processes referred to as *inquisitiones* and the processes referred to as actions of 'correction' in the vernacular, shows how the practice of *inquisitio* prevailed over other practices like *accusatio* and *denunciatio* in the ecclesiastical courts. Although on the continent there was an erosion in the established inquisitorial procedures from the thirteenth century onwards, England appears to have observed the due processes. While offenders, and especially heretics, certainly feared being summoned and 'corrected', most parishioners too would be concerned about a visitation of the parish. Yet, despite the individual freedom the system left to the judge, especially concerning the rights of the summoned suspects, the paranoia about abuses in prosecuting heretics would only take root from the second quarter of the sixteenth century onwards.

In the second essay, 'The Imperatives of *Denunciatio*: Disclosing Others' Sins to Disciplinary Authorities', Edwin Craun further explores the notions of private sin versus public crime. Focusing on the pastoral tradition, Craun argues convincingly that despite the decline in the use of *denunciatio* in practice, the concept of charitable admonition remained at the core of canon law theory alongside inquisition. Referring to Guillaume Durand's *Speculum judiciale*, which outlines the three steps to dealing with sin within Christian communities (private admonition by a disciplinary inferior, admonition before witnesses, and denunciation to a disciplinary superior), the author draws attention to the third step. Drawing on the thesis he developed in his book *Ethics and Power in Medieval English Reformist Writing*, Craun points out how the Dominican friars and Augustinian canons were responsible for bringing the practice of fraternal admonition and correction from the cloister into the entire Western Church.[3] Analysing the *summae* of master confessors, Craun shows how canonists and confessors alike thought that private admonition should be bypassed when it is more likely that the sin will be corrected by public disciplinary action. Confessors were, however, aware of and concerned with the danger a sinner posed to the temporal welfare of the innocent and when the sin becomes known and threatens to infect others. Craun concludes that both pastoral writers and canonists saw the process of denunciation as a way to protect the innocent and move offenders to repentance.

Ian Forrest, in 'English Provincial Constitutions and Inquisition into Lollardy', then builds upon recent research into the English anti-heresy law that emerged between 1382 and 1428 and investigates the relationship between the response to lollardy and wider cultural developments in canon law. In particular, Forrest looks at provincial legislation and argues

[3] Cambridge Studies in Medieval Literature, 76 (Cambridge: Cambridge University Press, 2010).

that a large number of the collections of provincial constitutions (*libri synodales*) were already copied and updated in the 1410s, before Bishop Lyndwood's *Provinciale*. Forrest goes on to point out that during this time the English reaction against heresy triggered a combination of the professionalisation of ecclesiastical justice, the prolific careers of the archbishops of Canterbury Arundel and Chichele, and the influence of the papal legates. The author concludes that from the late fourteenth century inquisition prompted an intellectual creativity among English churchmen and a renewed interest in provincial canon law, resulting in a large number of *libri synodales* in the early fifteenth century. Forrest sees Lyndwood's *Provinciale*'s attainment of actual legal authority as the explanation for the discontinuation of these collections of provincial constitutions in the fifteenth and sixteenth centuries.

In the fourth contribution to the volume, 'The Contest over the Public Imagination of Inquisition, 1380–1430', Diane Vincent moves the investigation from the churchmen to the laity and to vernacular texts, and discusses how late medieval English public discourse evolved alongside procedural knowledge about heresy inquisition. Vincent sees the discovery of the consequences inquisitorial questioning had for people suspected of heresy as a crucial moment in the shaping of the public imagination of inquisition. The author uses the public debate surrounding the trials of lollard John Oldcastle as a case-study to show the extent to which both Archbishop Arundel's vernacular publication of the *Processus* (the recorded process against Oldcastle), alongside the putative bills in *The Examinacion of the Honorable Knight Syr Jhon Oldcastell Lorde Cobham* spread in London by Oldcastle's supporters, were successful in influencing public opinion. Considering also the Middle English chronicles of the fifteenth century and Thomas Hoccleve's poetry, Vincent succeeds in showing the influence of Oldcastle's process on the public opinion of inquisitorial question and answer. Vincent concludes that for both the bishops and the accused, influencing the public image of inquisitional processes was far more important than the conviction or escape of one heretic.

In the fifth chapter, '"Vttirli Onknowe"? Modes of Inquiry and the Dynamics of Interiority in Vernacular Literature', the volume's editors Flannery and Walter continue the focus on vernacular texts and point out that medieval *inquisitio* must be seen in its broader context as but one form of inquiry available to ecclesiastical courts, entangled with other mechanisms such as auricular confession, the process of public crime (*publica fama*), and excommunication. Through three vernacular texts, *Dives and Pauper*, *Jacob's Well*, and Lydgate's *Fall of Princes*, the authors investigate how different modes of inquiry relate to the dynamics of interiority. Considering the separation of canon law into the external judicial forum and the internal or penitential forum in the twelfth and thirteenth centuries, Flannery and Walter argue that in order to understand the role of the penitential forum in influencing late-medieval English notions of interiority and the production of knowledge, the concerns of the judicial forum also must be taken into account. The texts considered in the chapter show an awareness of the difficulty in accessing an individual's interiority and attest to the criticism of the mechanisms through which this knowledge was obtained by the ecclesiastical courts.

In the sixth article, Jenny Lee's 'From Defacement to Restoration: Inquisition, Confession and Thomas Usk's *Appeal* and *Testament of Love*', Lee discusses Usk's *Appeal* in a legal context, and his allegorical *Testament* from a literary perspective. Lee points out how the detailed recording of admissions of guilt in the practice of inquisitorial confession did not guarantee the same cathartic effacement of sins as sacramental confession offered to the sinner. Thomas Usk's writings represent a defendant's concern for the huge paper trail of one's sins produced by the inquisitorial system in the ecclesiastical courts. Both the *Appeal* and

Testament, Lee argues, illustrate Usk's self-fashioning and show the sinner's reaction against the defacement inflicted upon him by the inquisitional process. His *Appeal*, the self-identifying confession of his sins and the expression of penitence, ensured that the reader could connect his name to his sins and judge him. The *Testament* was intended to supercede the *Appeal*, and not only shows Usk's concern over how he would be remembered in history (*fama*), but was also meant to act as a counter-response to the documentary practices of the English courts.

James Wade's essay, 'Confession, Inquisition and Exemplarity in *The Erle of Toulous* and Other Middle English Romances', delves deeper into the cultural representation of inquisition in vernacular textual traditions and focuses on romance in particular. Looking specifically at the late fourteenth-century tail-rhyme romance *The Erle of Toulous*, Wade investigates how the reader can access and better understand the inquisitional culture of England through romance. He points out that concerns of interiority, public *fama*, and, in particular, the regulation of sexual relations are to be found in romance, and popular literature generally, just as in the legal discourses. After analysing the text of *The Erle* and identifying the protagonists as 'model characters' for the development of the inquisitional theme, Wade argues for two types of romance: confessional romance and exemplary romance. In the former's instance, Wade remarks that the confessional instances in the stories were often not orthodox and gives the examples of *Guy of Warwick* and *Sir Gawain and the Green Knight*. In *The Erle*, as Wade argues convincingly, one recognises the rhetorical device of the exemplum in the combination of comment and action, and the text belongs to the type of exemplary romance. Wade ends by linking the heroine Beulybon (*belle et bon*) to the frontispiece of Bodleian, Ms Ashmole 45 and argues that Beulybon would have served as an ideal example for the woman depicted receiving the book.

In the next contribution, 'Heresy Inquisition and Authorship, 1400-1560', Genelle Gertz explores defendants' self-authored statements of belief. At the end of a heresy trial, the defendant would show his or her rejection of the heresy he or she was accused of by means of an abjuration, a written agreement with the orthodox belief. Although this text would be written in the first-person voice and signed by the accused, it was in fact entirely drafted by the ecclesiastical court and represented the confession the prosecutors were looking for. Especially by the mid-sixteenth century, defendants would often write their own confessions of faith as a response to or reaction against the abjuration, despite being fully aware that these texts could be used by the court as evidence for a conviction. Gertz shows that the courts' pressure upon defendants to sign abjurations caused a counter reaction of written and oral confessions of faith, even by people who would normally not be inclined to write. By authoring their own confession, these defendants justified their refusal to abjure. Gertz emphasises the importance of these self-authored confessions for later protestants like John Foxe who used these texts for his *Book of Martyrs*.

Ruth Ahnert's essay, 'Imitating Inquisition: Dialectical Bias in Protestant Prison Writings', revisits the idea that the inquisitorial process was inconsistent with modern concepts of a fair trial. In particular, she points out that recent scholarship has exposed misconceptions in previous work: that the accused were arrested only on the basis of suspicion, that they were presumed guilty until proven innocent, and that trials were secret. Ahnert develops this to argue that heresy trials in the first half of the sixteenth century conformed to an ideal model of dialogue in which the defendant and the prosecutor had an equal opportunity to argue their case. However, as both the court and the accused were well aware that, in order to convince the reader, their records and confessions of faith had to look like an equal exchange of arguments, the result was a strongly biased polemic from both sides. Furthermore, Ahnert shows how Protestant defendants would appropriate inquisitorial discourse, enabling them to oppose the prosecutors and provide a true confession of faith. She argues that scholars must therefore carefully consider and oppose the dialogues produced both through *inquisitio* and in the Protestant trial narratives to identify the prejudices, acknowledge the argumentative strategy, and reconstruct the true dialogue of the trial.

The last piece in the volume is a response essay in which Emily Steiner first briefly reflects on the volume's achievement in showing how the innovation of *inquisitio* in medieval canon law both implicated and influenced literature. She urges a re-evaluation of the medieval-modern conundrum by pointing out how the relationship between legal innovations and late-medieval literature has been redefined and how the reciprocal influence represents a turning point between medieval and modern. Steiner draws the volume to a close by using Chaucer's writings as an example to demonstrate how inquisition provides an unexplored window to allow for critical interpretations of medieval English texts.

The volume aims to move away from a historical approach to inquisition and the editors set out to investigate the role played by inquisition in medieval English culture. It must be noted, however, that these essays deal for the most part with the influence of inquisitional legal procedures on vernacular textual production and the public sphere, and are but a partial representation of all contemporary cultural manifestations. Agreeing with the concluding words of the introduction, a greater awareness of inquisition's place in medieval English culture is desirable and is certainly encouraged by this collection of excellent scholarship.

JAN VANDEBURIE   UNIVERSITY OF KENT

Also published by *Leeds Studies in English* is the occasional series:

LEEDS TEXTS AND MONOGRAPHS

(ISSN 0075-8574)

Recent volumes include:

Approaches to the Metres of Alliterative Verse, edited by Judith Jefferson and Ad Putter (2009), iii + 311 pp.

The Heege Manuscript: a facsimile of NLS MS Advocates 19.3.1, introduced by Phillipa Hardman (2000), 60 + 432pp.

The Old English Life of St Nicholas with the Old English Life of St Giles, edited by E. M. Treharne (1997) viii + 218pp.

Concepts of National Identity in the Middle Ages, edited by Simon Forde, Lesley Johnson and Alan V. Murray (1995) viii + 213pp.

A Study and Edition of Selected Middle English Sermons, by V. M. O'Mara (1994) xi + 245pp.

Notes on 'Beowulf', by P. J. Cosijn, introduced, translated and annotated by Rolf H. Bremmer Jr, Jan van den Berg and David F. Johnson (1991) xxxvi + 120pp.

Úr Dölum til Dala: Guðbrandur Vigfússon Centenary Essays, edited by Rory McTurk and Andrew Wawn (1989) x + 327pp.

Staging the Chester Cycle, edited by David Mills (1985) vii + 123pp.

The Gawain Country: Essays on the Topography of Middle English Poetry, by R. W. V. Elliot (1984) 165pp.

For full details of this series, and to purchase volumes, or past numbers of *Leeds Studies in English*, please go to <http://www.leeds.ac.uk/lse>.

www.ingramcontent.com/pod-product-compliance
Lightning Source LLC
Chambersburg PA
CBHW080939300426
44115CB00017B/2879